Interdisciplinary *Yearbook of* Business Ethics

Volume 1, 2006

Laszlo Zsolnai (ed.)

PETER LANG
Oxford • Bern • Berlin • Bruxelles • Frankfurt am Main • New York • Wien

Bibliographic information published by Die Deutsche Bibliothek
Die Deutsche Bibliothek lists this publication in the Deutsche Nationalbibliografie; detailed bibliographic data is available on the Internet at ‹http://dnb.ddb.de›.

British Library and Library of Congress Cataloguing-in-Publication Data:
A catalogue record for this book is available from *The British Library*, Great Britain, and from *The Library of Congress*, USA

Cover design: Judit Kovacs, Createch Ltd., Hungary

ISSN 1661-5999
ISBN 3-03910-750-X
US-ISBN 0-8204-8010-X

Interdisciplinary Yearbook of Business Ethics

The yearbook aims to present and summarize new perspectives and cutting-edge results in business ethics and related fields.

The yearbook reports on innovative practices and policy reforms and provides a forum for discussion about theories that break new ground. The 'Opinions' section gathers critical reflections on topical issues of business and society. The 'Debate' section presents comments by a range of scholars and practitioners on provocative new ideas in ethics.

The yearbook aims to form a value-community of scholars, practitioners and policy-makers engaged in genuine ethics in business, environmental management, and public policy.

The *Interdisciplinary Yearbook of Business Ethics* is a product of the Business Ethics Center of Corvinus University of Budapest, Hungary. Its website address is http://ethics bkae.hu.

International Advisory Board

All correspondence should be sent to

LASZLO ZSOLNAI
Professor and Director

Business Ethics Center
Corvinus University of Budapest

P.O. Box 489
H–1828 Budapest 5
Hungary

Phone/Fax: (+36 1) 482 5844
Email: laszlo_zsolnai@interware.hu

Contents

The Interdisciplinary Yearbook of Business Ethics, 2006 3

Acknowledgements 14

Part 1 New Perspectives and Findings

James G. March
The Myth of Rationality 17

Stefano Zamagni
Ethical Anchoring of Corporate Social Responsibility 31

Werner Ulrich
Critical Pragmatism: A New Approach to Professional and Business Ethics 53

Gian Vittorio Caprara and Cristina Capanna
Moral Disengagement in the Exercise of Civic-ness 87

Laszlo Zsolnai
Ethical Decision Making 99

Part 2 Innovative Practices and Policy Reforms

David Boyle
Authenticity 121

Robert Earhart
The Maturation of Sustainable Investment 129

Zsolt Boda and Emese Gulyas
The Ethical Consumerism Movement 141

Frank Dixon
Gross National Happiness – Improving Unsustainable
Western Economic Systems 155

Part 3 Opinions: Ecological Sustainability of Business

John M. Gowdy
Sustainable Business Requires a Social Support System 173

Ananda Das Gupta
Sustainability and Business from an Indian Perspective 177

Richard B. Norgaard
Corporate Sustainability: Impossible Alone, Participation Essential, Leadership Needed 181

Diana Schumacher
The Principles of Sustainability 187

Karl-Henrik Robert
Social, Ecological, and Economic Sustainability – Risks, Challenges and Strategies 193

Part 4 Debate: The Ethics Management Paradox

Luk Bouckaert
The Ethics Management Paradox 199

Henk van Luijk
Facing the Ethics Management Paradox 202

Ronald Berenbeim
Finding Space to Discuss Ethics 205

G.J. Rossouw
A Response to Bouckaert's Ethics Management Paradox 208

Robert Allinson
The Paradox of Business 211

Luk Bouckaert
When More Ethics Create Less Ethics – Some Further Clarifications on the Ethics Management Paradox 215

Contributors to The Ethics Management Paradox Debate 219

The Interdisciplinary Yearbook of Business Ethics, 2006

It is my pleasure to introduce the first volume of the *Interdisciplinary Yearbook of Business Ethics*. The yearbook is a product of 21 scholars and practitioners from Europe, America, Asia and Africa. Contributors represent a diversity of fields including organizational science, economics, systems theory, personality psychology, business ethics, finance, management, philosophy, political science, sociology, and ecology. All the papers stand for a more human and ethical approach to economics and business.

In his paper "The Myth of Rationality," American organizational scientist *James G. March* of Stanford University shows that the case against the myth of rationality is reasonably strong. Rationality has problems as a description of human behavior, as a prescription for human behavior, and as a characterization of the human spirit. March argues that the real excitement lies not in inventing complicated arguments that fit human existence into the myth of rationality but in exploring alternative visions.

He explores four alternative visions. He begins with a vision of human existence organized around *identities* rather than instrumental choices. In this vision duties and obligations are more central than preferences and interests. The key processes are to discover and create conceptions of self and match them to situations. Second, he explores a vision of human existence organized around the *search* for *meaning*. In this perspective, the focus shifts from action to interpretation. We consider the ways in which the symbols of life are organized to shape the telling of accounts. Third is a vision of human existence enriched by *ambiguity*, contradiction, inconsistency, ambivalence, and irrelevance. Fourth is a vision of human existence defined as *path dependent*, as traversing a history characterized by local positive feedback, multiple equilibria, and irreversibilities.

Considering human beings (and organizations) as identity-seeking, interpreting, ambiguous and path-dependent entities has great significance to business ethics, as it badly needs a more realistic concept of man.

In his paper "Ethical Anchoring of Corporate Social Responsibility," Italian economist *Stefano Zamagni* of the University of Bologna deals with two questions: How robust are the critiques against corporate social responsibility (CSR)? and Which ethical anchoring can offer more solid support for CSR? Zamagni shows that the mother of all criticism of CSR, *Milton Friedman*'s, is untenable. Friedman advocates that the only social responsibility of business is to increase its profit. Zamagni convincingly argues that in suggesting that the only social responsibility a firm has is to increase profits, Friedman and other like-minded scholars must presuppose conditions under which firms don't get more profits.

Zamagni examines alternative ethical theories for anchoring CSR. He favors the *ethic of virtues* because it resolves the opposition between self-interest and interest for others. The solution to moral motivation of managers is not that of setting constraints or providing incentives for acting against their self-interest, but to offer them a more complete understanding of their own well-being. Only when ethics becomes part of the objective-function of the agents does moral motivation cease to be a problem. Since institutions influence economic performance, the task is to intervene in the institutional setup of society to encourage disseminating civic virtues. If the market can compensate for the civil culture of the firm, in the long run the dispositional and the motivational structure of the economic agents will adapt as a result.

In his paper "Critical Pragmatism: A New Approach to Professional and Business Ethics," systems theorist and philosopher *Werner Ulrich* (University of Fribourg & The Open University, Milton Keynes) stresses that most approaches to professional and business ethics seek to ground ethical practice in ethical theory. But this does not work. *Ethical theory* can provide us with basic principles or general norms of ethical action; but, because there is hardly ever one right way to define an ethical problem, it cannot tell us which specific concerns and stakeholders "count" in a concrete action.

Ulrich believes that *critical pragmatism*, a pragmatist view of ethics following the philosophy of American pragmatism, might help. Rather than seeking generic theoretical criteria of moral action, we should seek practical ways of dealing critically with contexts of action. The *ethical boundary critique* – a methodology developed by him – aims at exposing the moral implications of claims posed by different interested parties. It aims to trace a claim's ethical implications within a wider context and to unfold the claim's distributive effects.

Ulrich's methodology can be used in revitalizing the moral and democratic vision of business in which people regulate their conflicts in peaceful ways, through processes of decision making and conflict settling that are argumentatively and democratically based.

The paper "Moral Disengagement in the Exercise of Civic-ness" by Italian psychologists *Gian Vittorio Caprara* and *Cristina Capanna* (University of Rome "La Sapienza") starts with the observation that a division between thought and action takes place when people break the rules or get involved in dirty business. What is most surprising in rule violation and misconduct is that people are not bothered by their conscience, do not fear any sanction and do not feel obliged to make reparations.

Caprara and Capanna are indebted to world-renowned Stanford psychologist *Albert Bandura*, who discovered the *mechanisms* of *moral disengagement*, the psychosocial maneuvers by which moral self-sanctions become disengaged, giving free way to a variety of misbehaviors without carrying any moral concern. Self-sanctions can be disengaged by reconstructing the conduct, obscuring personal causal agency, misrepresenting or disregarding the injurious consequences of one's actions, and vilifying the recipients of maltreatment by blaming and devaluating them.

Caprara and his team developed a scale to assess civic moral disengagement (CMD). Their empirical findings suggest that the more people are concerned with *self-enhancement goals*, the more they are inclined to resort to mechanisms that permit them to *disengage* from the duties and obligations of civic life and to justify transgressions when their self-interest is at stake.

This result has important consequences for economics because it can refute the naive belief of *Adam Smith* and his followers in the beneficial impact of the "Invisible Hand" of the market. If economic agents become self-concerned then it is likely that – by employing moral disengagement mechanisms – their self-exonerative maneuvers will do *harm* to *others*. In serving the common good we need agents who care about and pursue self and community interests.

In his paper "Ethical Decision Making," Hungarian business ethicist *Laszlo Zsolnai* of Corvinus University of Budapest argues that the self-centeredness of modern organizations leads to environmental destruction and human deprivation. Using *Hans Jonas'* principle of responsibility Zsolnai claims that ethical decision making should create a synthesis of *reverence* for ethical norms, *rationality* in goal achievement, and *respect* for the stakeholders. The ethical decision can be made by the maximin rule, which selects the "least worst alternative" in the multidimensional decision space of deontological, goal-achievement and stakeholder values.

In Zsolnai's view the *ethical decision maker* is characterized as having the ability to take multiple perspectives and make right balances across diverse value dimensions. Modern organizations should develop a critical sensitivity to and empathy toward human and non-human beings with which they share a common environment.

In his paper "Authenticity," British economist and writer *David Boyle* (New Economics Foundation, London) criticizes fake in business. He states that more and more people search for *authentic living*. They are turning against lies – the big corporate lie that artificial food, artificial intelligence, virtual sex, virtual teachers and bank managers are as good or as real as the real thing. Boyle observes that there is an increasing commitment to real food, real culture, real politics, real schools, real community, real medicine, real culture, real stories. This is apparent in the rise of local brands, real ale, reading groups, organic vegetables, complementary medicine, slow food, poetry recitals, unmixed music, materiality in art and unbranded vintage fashions. These are all symptoms of the same thing – a demand for human-scale, face-to-face institutions and real experience.

Humanity is the essence of authenticity, and it is why the big brands have difficulty meeting this demand. They are one-dimensional non-human approximations. Demand for authenticity has been the way companies are rowing backwards from the Coca-Cola ideal – the same everywhere – to one where every package tells a story of its own.

So what can companies do to be authentic? asks Boyle. *Principles* of *authenticity* can be put into practice: (i) Avoid glitz and rationalized delivery systems, and garner trust by telling simple stories and wandering off-message as needed. (ii) Connect with what is human – either because the brand is an expression of one personality, or because it shows the personalities of the people behind it, or because the service is genuinely personal. (iii) Have genuine roots to a specific place, or create a portal to ordinary producers or sellers in specific places. (iv) Allow customers and employees to feel better connected to their own ideals and values.

In his paper "The Maturation of Sustainable Investment," American financial expert *Robert Earhart* (Brooklyn Bridge/TBLI Group, Amsterdam) focuses on *sustainable investment* (SRI) as a specialized financial practice and shows that it is going mainstream. More assets are flowing into SRI investments. From 1995 to 2003, public equity assets under management subjected to some form of social or environmental screening grew by 240 percent. As of 2003, 11.3 percent of assets under management, $2,164 billion, were covered under some form of screening in the United States. Individual activism, corporate activism, and the increase in information technology, combined with recent scandals and the need to cater to individual investors, are drivers for the increase in sustainable investment in the corporate and financial world.

We do not know yet – argues Earhart – whether this is a lasting trend. The obstacles SRI is facing are based on how it is defined by financial institutions, how it is regulated, and how it can be presented to the consumer. *Politics* will determine how quickly or slowly sustainable investment becomes part of our economies, as governmental and regulatory policies affect the true financial cost or benefit of these investments.

In their paper "The Ethical Consumerism Movement," Hungarian political scientist *Zsolt Boda* and sociologist *Emese Gulyas* (Corvinus University of Budapest) distinguish between *ethical consumption* as a link of personal consumption with environmental, human and animal rights concerns and *ethical consumerism* as a new political movement by which people seek to consciously influence economic and social institutions. They stress that today the goals of ethical consumer movements are moving beyond the logic of single-issue movements. Boycotts are still launched against individual companies, and "specialized" NGOs exist which focus their activities on one topic. But, more and more organizations emphasize complex objectives promoting social and environmental sustainability, global justice and fairness towards society, nature and the future generations.

Boda and Gulyas argue that ethical consumerism is one among many social movements that shows today's conflicts between business and society. It should not be seen as isolated from anti-corporate protests, the alter-globalization movement, CSR initiatives and developments in ethical investment. It might significantly contribute to raising the ethicality of business, because consumers are supposed to be the most important stakeholders of firms, on which the companies' survival depends. Ethical consumerism has certainly gained considerable strength and it can be predicted that it will continue to organize itself, using new communication means and building on new sensibilities.

The paper "Gross National Happiness" by American investment analyst *Frank Dixon* (Innovest, New York) concerns improving unsustainable Western economic systems. He introduces the Gross National Happiness index (GNH) which is intended to be a more accurate measure of social well-being than Gross National Product (GNP), the primary indicator of social well-being in Western nations.

He believes that *Western economic systems* have produced great improvements in many areas including technology, medicine and the provision of essential and non-essential goods and services. But, as industrial economies continue to grow in a finite world the impact is increasingly negative. Inefficient use of resources, high levels of pollution and many social disruptions resulting from industrialization have caused human society to be grossly *unsustainable*.

Dixon argues that *GNP* is a *crude measure* that counts many social negatives as positive (for example, incarceration). It also fails to count services that enhance social well-being (for example, parents caring for children), degradation of critical assets (forests, water, air, and the like) and intangible factors, such as happiness (the ultimate goal of many people). It is no coincidence that Western economies are rapidly degrading environmental life support systems and making many people unhappy (as shown by growing obesity, anti-depressant drug use and other factors). What doesn't get measured doesn't get managed.

Dixon suggests *Gross National Happiness* as the measurement component of a plan to maximize social well-being. It would comprehensively look at all tangible and intangible aspects of society, including education, health care, housing, clothing, food and nutrition, shelter, environmental and habitat protection, parents spending time with and raising children, arts, business practices, infrastructure, legal and regulatory issues, reported levels of happiness, and so on. Once metrics and performance standards have been established, they can be assembled into a Gross National Happiness measure. Rather than rendering the state of society down to one number such as GNP, Gross National Happiness would give a suite of performance indicators. The performance of society is highly complex and needs to be expressed on many dimensions. The real development of the economy can only be based on a *total system perspective*.

The *Opinions* section of the Yearbook focuses on the *ecological sustainability of business*. We asked a distinguished panel of academics and practitioners to answer the following questions: What are the features of ecologically sustainable business? What makes a sustainable business possible? Can a company alone achieve ecological sustainability? What are the main hindrances to companies becoming sustainable? What are the effects of economic globalization in this respect?

In his response, "Sustainable Business Requires a Social Support System," American economist *John M. Gowdy* (Rensselaer Polytechnic Institute) states that a sustainable business monitors and controls its production process from "cradle to cradle." The environment should be the same at the beginning and the end. So a sustainable business means having *ecologically sustainable production processes*, recycling wastes from the production process, and minimizing the environmental impact of the final product. Sustainable businesses require a support system of pro-environmental and pro-social regulations. Achieving sustainability depends on the surrounding social and environmental regulations.

Gowdy stresses that in the US corporation laws and regulations pose a critical hindrance to sustainability. Corporations are defined as "legal persons" yet they are exempt from basic checks and balances controlling their behavior. He warns that it is important to realize that the market system is not a "natural" outcome of an "invisible hand" but is imposed by laws and regulations to protect the power structure and prevailing free market ideology.

In his response, "Sustainability and Business from an Indian Perspective," Indian management scholar *Ananda Das Gupta* (Indian Institute of Plantation Management, Bangalore) stresses that the drive for increased *productivity* is an issue in which the logic of individual decisions has a perverse collective impact on society. Raising productivity is an economic imperative. A company must raise its productivity and reduce its labor costs to increase its profitability. The economic system ignores *the poor*. Because they are insignificant consumers, the poor are excluded or forgotten. Their starvation illustrates a basic failure in present mechanisms for redistributing wealth in society.

He notes that the economic system works at the *wrong scales* in time and space. The economic system is short term, while most environmental problems are long term, and occur on a large scale. Businesses only deal with small fragments of such problems. The result is a basic mismatch when it comes to dealing with such large-scale problems as carbon-dioxide accumulation, the ozone hole, persistent organic pollutants, soil and water management, and the like. The economic system fails to come to grips with the essential issues because it tries to deal with them at the wrong scales in space and time.

Das Gupta believes that the root of the problem lies in the way in which *economic institutions* are structured. We need to explore how we can maintain the vitality of corporate structures within a framework built around ethical, moral and spiritual values that will help the system work for society as a whole.

In his response, "Corporate Sustainability: Impossible Alone, Participation Essential, Leadership Needed," American economist *Richard B. Norgaard* (University of California at Berkeley) refers to *The Millennium Ecosystem Assessment*, a study of some seven hundred scientists from around the world and another seven hundred external reviewers, completed in 2005. The findings of the study are grim. Of the twenty-four types of ecosystem services examined, the ecosystems of fifteen are being degraded or used unsustainably. The degradation has resulted in lower flows of ecosystem services. Only four ecosystem service flows, three of which provide agriculture, have increased over the past fifty years, but these increases do not appear to be sustainable.

The assessment makes a strong case that we are rapidly *diminishing* the *natural capital* on which the future of humanity depends. But Norgaard hopes that corporations that begin to explore the transition to sustained ecosystem management will be in a position to help design and insist on effective institutions and develop the new technologies we need.

In her response, "The Principles of Responsibility," British environmentalist *Diana Schumacher* stresses that the task is a worldwide change of culture by millions of businesses and the people who work in them. From being a society driven by ever-increasing "wants," the change will have to be towards a culture of conservation and ever-increasing simplicity of lifestyle.

Diana Schumacher lists seven principles to which companies should adhere. The principle of efficiency ensures that the consumption of inputs is minimized per unit of output. The principle of human scale implies that a company must be of a size such that all of its employees can recognize and relate to each other both socially and professionally. The principle of autonomy dictates that a company's authority structure is such that decision making is delegated to the lowest possible level. The principle of evaluation requires a full portfolio of available measures and standards and a system to monitor performance against set goals. The principle of complementary parts states that companies can only achieve ecological sustainability if they are fully in control of all the component parts required to complete a "whole work process." The principle of integration demands a high degree of cooperation from all employees in a company. There needs to be a common strategy aimed at encouraging teamwork throughout the company. The principle of authority states that because voluntary sustainability cannot be maintained indefinitely, all companies should be required by law to appoint a senior manager responsible for overseeing the discharge of the company's environmental obligations.

In his response, "Social, Ecological, and Economic Sustainability – Risks, Challenges and Strategies," Swedish ecologist *Karl-Henrik Robert*, the founder of The Natural Step, states that sustainability puts the highest demands on strategic leadership today. The strategic dimension of the sustainability game is about investing in "flexible platforms"; i.e., investments that are economically feasible in the short term and can serve as strategic stepping-stones to a sustainable future. Each step needs to systematically become more and more compliant with basic sustainability principles. Companies investing in sustainable strategies can see a good return. They save by avoiding increasing costs for energy, tax, insurance, waste management and material resources and they earn money through product and service innovation, competitive advantage, customer and employee loyalty and increased shareholder value.

What is needed, observes Robert, is less about new technology than changing traditional thinking. Businesses today are often delaying solutions that are close at hand. But a growing number of companies are not only proactive but also strategic, showing that this works. The whole world can *increase* its *life-quality* within the constraints set by ecological sustainability, if we only de-couple real value from physical flows.

The *Debate* section of the Yearbook is about the paper "The Ethics Management Paradox" by Belgian philosopher *Luk Bouckaert* of The Catholic University of Leuven. In his paper Bouckaert states that the *EU document* of CSR policies is written under the veil of a rational and technocratic conception of ethics. Also, he explains that this rational conception of CSR is unable to overcome through its own logic the problems of *opportunism* in business and politics.

Bouckaert argues that by reducing ethics to a functional and instrumental management concept we lose something vital. We are crowding out genuine moral feelings and genuine moral commitment, substituting them for rational and technocratic management tools. This substitution fails.

In his view the *ethics management paradox* is the following. By creating new regulations to temper opportunistic behavior in and among organizations, we might temper the symptoms but often reinforce the underlying roots of opportunism. We introduce economic incentives like benefits, such as premiums or tax relief for those who respect the new regulations, but by doing this, we substitute moral feelings for economic calculations. Preaching moral concepts such as trust, responsibility or democracy on the basis of calculative self-interest or as conditions of systemic functionality opens the door for suspicion and distrust because calculations and systemic conditions can easily be manipulated. When the fox preaches, guard your geese.

Bouckaert warns that the more economic democracy can be sustained by a rational and economic discourse, the more it risks crowding out the spiritual and moral commitment, which is a necessary condition for sustaining genuine entrepreneurship and stakeholding. Therefore we must put forward not only the question of how to make business ethics operational, but also the question of how to make it *genuinely ethical.*

In his reflection "Facing the Ethics Management Paradox," Dutch business ethicist *Henk van Luijk* from Amsterdam states that the remedy Bouckaert proposes is dubious. It sounds like an *all-too-purist view*, as if moral motives are only of value as long as they are pure and uncontaminated. Pure motives are an exception. The normal state of affairs is a mix of motives, the moral value of which is determined by the extent to which some form of moral inspiration is clearly recognizable as part of the mixture.

Van Luijk argues that ethics in business is a too serious matter to make it depend on the morality and spirituality of individuals. It is not mainly on the personal level that we should expect a gain, but on the *social* and *institutional level.* Personal moral and spiritual excellence is something we can hope for, but we can hardly influence it. When it comes to active interventions in the domain of business, it is the conditions that we should tackle, the institutional configurations that define the behavioral alternatives. Only at that level can sustainable improvements be furthered.

In his reflection "Finding Space to Discuss Ethics," American lawyer and business ethicist *Ronald Berenbeim* (The Conference Board, New York) suggests that the sustainability concept is a good first step in alerting decision makers to the potential ethical considerations of a business choice. Most business ethics problems confront the practitioner with a choice of whether to exploit market failures such as monopolies or information asymmetries. An ethical decision in this context entails the *exercise* of *moral restraint.*

He warns that the ethicist accepts the possibility of a stark choice between business success and doing the right thing. What remains to be discussed is how to make that choice. At the outset, ethics problem solving demands rigorous insistence on factual accuracy. The reliability of data is not just critical in its own right. Decisions must often be based on limited information. It is all the more important that the facts used be true. Often the decision maker will need more information about the company to weigh and determine the data's relevance and importance. Berenbeim believes that commercial practice is a *project* of *reason*, not faith. "Spiritual and moral commitment" for business professionals is the outcome, not the departure point, of an ethical dilemma.

In his "Response to Bouckaert's Ethics Management Paradox," South-African business ethicist *G.J. Rossouw* (University of Pretoria) states that actions that are beneficial to one and that promote one's own well-being are not excluded from the domain of ethical behavior. A moral motive, in the non-self-interested and non-expedient sense that Bouckaert seems to endorse is *not required* for actions to be considered moral.

Rossouw asserts that although an overemphasis on self-interest as the basis for moral behavior is problematic, a lack of emphasis on self-interest in ethics is equally problematic. In his own definition of business ethics, which is developed around the "self," the "good" and the "other," the imperative of finding a proper *balance* between what is good for oneself and what is good for others is stressed. Ethical behavior is not non-self-interested or altruistic behavior. It is about not only considering what is good for oneself, but balancing that with what is good for others.

And he adds that a lack of recognition of the role that self-interest plays in business, and in business ethics, will result in imposing *unrealistic moral demands* on business. It will treat business as a pseudo-public institution, which is supposed to serve the public interest, while neglecting its obligation to create value for shareowners and employees and to insure its own sustainability.

In his response "The Paradox of Business," American philosopher *Robert Allinson* (Soka University of America & The Chinese University of Hong Kong) states that the problem presented in Bouckaert's paper is due to a more general cause, which is the conception of business based on calculative self-interest. In his view the problem is not so much an "ethics management paradox" as a "business paradox." He thinks that the *business paradox* is the understanding of business as a wealth-producing enterprise for owners that simultaneously creates value for stakeholders.

For Allinson the solution is to develop a new definition of business that focuses on creating *social value* as the motivation and mainstay of business enterprise. Profit must be perceived as a side effect, not as the main goal of business enterprise. We need a cooperative model. If when setting up a business one considers what social value one can create, an ethical motivation will be built into the business from the outset. It is possible that such motivations will produce profits for their owners. There is no built-in contradiction between creating social value and creating profit. As long as creating social value is the motivation for business, the business paradox can be resolved.

In his reply, "When More Ethics Create Less Ethics – Some Further Clarifications on the Ethics Management Paradox," *Luk Bouckaert* does not accept that the problem behind the ethics management paradox is the conflict between self-interested versus ethical/altruistic behavior. He argues that although instrumental reasoning often refers to self-interested goals and ethical motivation as caring for the other, this is not the core meaning of the ethics management paradox. The relevant distinction is the one between *intrinsic* versus *instrumental motivations.* The ethical assumption behind the paradox is that genuine ethical behavior must have its origin in an inner-directed, non-instrumental inspiration and orientation (be it an altruistic or self-oriented one).

Bouckaert adds that the paradox does not imply that ethical behavior must be purely inner directed. That would be an unrealistic and unproductive assumption. The claim is more restrictive: genuine ethical behavior gives intrinsic motivation *priority* over instrumental motivation. A consequence is the need for a more spiritual approach to business ethics. A *spiritual approach* to business ethics has two objectives: to sustain consistent and inspiring moral commitment in business practice and to radicalize the basic concepts of business life.

Bouckaert favors *stakeholder democracy*, which means to organize human cooperation to create value for all the stakeholders and with all the stakeholders. The final aim is not an external goal but an internalized goal that is defined by all stakeholders and to the benefit of all stakeholders. Radicalizing stakeholder theory into economic democracy is an example of showing how a spiritual approach to business ethics can have far-reaching consequences.

It is our hope that the papers presented in the *Interdisciplinary Yearbook of Business Ethics*, 2006 will provide good food for thought and inspiration for action for those who are engaged in the never ending "business" of ethics.

Laszlo Zsolnai
Editor-in-Chief

Acknowledgements

For producing the *Interdisciplinary Yearbook of Business Ethics*, 2006 we received financial support from *Antenna Hungaria Co.*, the *MOL Corporation* and the *Faculty of Business Administration* of the *Corvinus University of Budapest*. We are also grateful to our language editor, *Doug Shokes*, who corrected the English of the papers, and to our graphic designer, *Judit Kovacs*, who developed the visual format of the yearbook. Special thanks goes to my father, *Professor Jozsef Zsolnai*, who suggested that the Business Ethics Center of Corvinus University of Budapest should produce an international journal of its own.

Budapest, January 2006

Laszlo Zsolnai

PART 1

New Perspectives and Findings

James G. March
Stanford University

The Myth of Rationality*

Social science seeks to tell stories and construct theories about human history and human behavior. The stories and theories we display are built on foundations of widely shared themes and constructs. These deeply held foundations can be called "myths." By calling the idea of rationality a myth, I do not mean to imply that it is either necessarily false or necessarily unfortunate. It is simply a recurring, legitimate theme for the theories and stories that we construct. Because they provide a structure for interpreting experience and taking action, myths allow human life to be portrayed as taking place within a comprehensible story, rather than an incomprehensible reality.

* This essay is based on a talk given at the Laszlo Rajk College, Corvinus University of Budapest, April 2005. It draws from a piece previously published (in Danish): James G. March, "Myten om rationalitet", pp.11–27 in James G. March *Fornuft og Forandring*. Copenhagen: Samfundslitteratur, 1995.

The stories found in business cases and newspapers, business and national plans, histories of human institutions, and the theories of organizations, economics, and social science reflect a shared consciousness of a few central myths. Among these myths, none is more important in modern Western life than the myth of rationality. By the myth of rationality I mean the idea that the human spirit finds definitive expression through taking and justifying action in terms of expectations of its future consequences for prior values. Rationality embodies and elaborates a critical part of human traditions as reflected in our recorded histories and philosophies throughout the world. It is the basis for most contemporary prescriptions for human behavior, and for most contemporary descriptions of that behavior. It is a fundamental element of modern faith.

1. The Myth of Rationality

The word "rational" has a number of interrelated meanings when applied to human action. Some of these meanings define rationality in terms of the outcomes of action. A "rational" action, from this perspective, is an action that leads to outcomes that turn out to be desired. Within this kind of meaning, rationality is intelligent by definition. It is not a basis for action but its outcome. The meanings with which I will be concerned are somewhat different. They focus on the process by which action is taken. They define rationality as a class of procedures for taking action. These meanings make the intelligence of rational action not a definitional necessity but a theoretical or empirical question. And one of the issues is whether procedural rationality is either a necessary or a sufficient condition for intelligent action.

In a rational process of action, we imagine the following: (1) that there is a set of alternatives; (2) that those alternatives are associated with their expected future consequences; (3) that those consequences are evaluated in terms of a set of preferences; and (4) that the alternative selected is characterized by a set of expected consequences that are the best possible as evaluated by the preferences. In the pure version of this conception of rationality, we assume that all alternatives are known, that all consequences of each alternative are known (at least up to a probability distribution), that the consequences can be ordered in a way that is consistent, and that the alternative with the highest expected value is taken. Few students of action accept such a pure form of the idea, recognizing various limits of rationality as a practical matter.

The myth of rationality is the idea that this process of choice is more likely than alternative processes to yield intelligent behavior and that, as a result, rational procedures for choice can be used to characterize actual human behavior. The central presumption of the myth is the presumption that rational processes are intelligent, or equivalently lead to high likelihood of survival. The argument is not a definitional one but an assertion about the outcomes that follow from procedural rationality.

The myth of rationality tells us that human beings should follow rational procedures in order to maximize achievement of their own values. And it conjectures that we can expect humans to follow the precepts of rationality and that if they do not behave that way, they will be eliminated by the processes of evolutionary competition. Thus, rationality is simultaneously a prescription for human behavior and a speculation that in a competitive world, the processes of competition will – given enough time – drive all behavior to be what is prescribed by rationality.

This idea of rationality pervades modern Western ideology. It is embedded deeply in our customs and language. For example, it dictates a stylized response to the question: "Why did you do that?" Normally, if we wish to claim full standing as a human being, the response to such a question is in the form: "I did it because I expected it would have positive consequences in terms of my preferences." If we wish to plead that we were momentarily (or perhaps for a longer time) not a full individual, our answer might be in the form: "I did it because I was drunk; or wasn't thinking; or any of a number of proclamations of human inadequacy."

The myth of rationality also dictates a stylized interpretation of the behavior of others. If we ask "Why did she do that?" the conventional answer is in the form: "She did it because she thought it would serve her interests." The litany is familiar: Why did a legislator vote for a particular bill? Because she believed the consequences for her (or the country) of voting for that bill were better than the consequences of not doing so. Why did an engineer work for a particular employer? Because he believed the consequences of working for that employer were better for him than the consequences of other alternatives available to him.

These stylized stories are almost as true of social science as they are of journalism or ordinary discourse. The concept of rationality has taken over substantial parts of the Western versions of economics, political science, psychology, sociology, etc. Economists can claim a certain priority, of course (if we ignore the precedence of people like Aristotle and Machiavelli in political science, von Clausewitz in military strategy, and Ibn Khaldun in history), and all of contemporary economic theory is told in terms of rationality. Indeed, the conventions of contemporary economics define a satisfactory explanation as one that rationalizes an observation. Nothing more. Nothing less. Or as Kenneth Arrow wrote in 1974: "[A]n economist by training thinks of himself as the guardian of rationality, an ascriber of rationality to others, and the prescriber of rationality to the social world" (Arrow 1974, 16).

Political science has a much stronger institutional tradition than economics and has been somewhat slower to accept fully the dogma of rationality, but a description of studies of politics as analyses of interests, their articulation, and their pursuit is certainly consistent with modern literature. And the best formalized, contemporary theoretical position in political science is rational choice political science, a schema that seeks to discover rational explanations for political behavior and institutions.

Psychology has its own versions of expected value theory in the form of valences and expectancies, and certainly can claim some strong counter traditions in the forms of things like behavioral versions of learning and conceptions of social balance or consistency. But much of psychology, including Freudian psychology and contemporary behavioral decision theory, are dedicated less to alternative myths of the foundations of proper and actual behavior than they are to exploring some limitations in human execution of rationality Freud tended to glorify the instrument of rationality – the ego – and Tversky, Kahneman, Ross, Nisbet, and others have tended to see deviations from rationality as failures of human intelligence.

Finally, although sociology is traditionally associated with an emphasis on norms and roles as descriptors of the process of human action, it has long flirted with rationality as an explanatory mechanism for interpreting the comparative statics of social structures and behaviors. Functionalism – the imputation of function to observed form and of survival to function – is both a trait and an issue of sociology. More recently, rational theories of deviance, social structure, formal organizations, marriage, the family, and conflict have become commonplace in sociology.

The generality of acceptance of the myth of rationality invites an obvious question: Why, of all the possible ideas in the Western world, has the myth of rationality survived and thrived so well? As with all matters of faith, asking such a question is likely to seem sacrilegious, for it suggests that the myth is to be understood as something other than self-evident truth. In that sense, it requires us to be both of Western culture and not of Western culture at the same time – to accept the faith, yet accept that this faith can be an object of comprehension as well as belief.

The sacrilegiousness of the question is somewhat ameliorated if we treat the question as an invitation to rationalize the myth, as we are very likely to do given that we exist in this world and this social science. Then we are led to consider the ways in which the myth of rationality justifies and supports other ideas and interpretations of experiences that we have. Max Weber's analysis of capitalism and Protestantism is the model of this kind of explanation. The presumption is that ideas serve institutions (and vice versa). Rationality is explained by its contribution to the social order.

The formulation is certainly a sensible one, but it simply moves the questions to a new one: Why of all the possible combination of beliefs and social orders that might be observed, do we observe this particular combination? The answer probably lies in some understanding of the processes by which beliefs and institutions originate, spread, and decline. For the most part, theories of such processes emphasize strong homogenizing forces that lead to widespread sharing of beliefs (i.e., to myths). One set of ideas comes to dominate other sets of ideas largely because support breeds support. Any one new set of ideas is very likely to be extinguished before it can secure enough support to challenge the received doctrine. Every once in a great while, support for a new doctrine is sustained long enough to secure enough support to challenge an old one. And occasionally that challenge is successful, after which the process begins again.

What is (relatively) certain is that beliefs will become shared; but exactly which beliefs will come to dominate, among the many that might, is a much less obvious thing. Within this interpretation, the mythic quality of rationality is not due primarily to any specific properties of rationality but to the (possibly chance-like) event that the inexorable social processes for generating myths happened to become tied to rationality.

All of this, of course, carefully avoids suggesting that perhaps the success of ideas of rationality has something to do with their accuracy, correctness, or truth-value. One of the theories of ideas, particularly within science, is the theory of scientific progress, the idea that over time, and with some errors along the way, good ideas supplant poor ideas, or at least better ideas supplant poorer ones. It is a comforting thought, but any reasonably careful examination of processes of competition and survival in path-dependent systems of co-evolution, however, will suggest why the simple survival of ideas is not a persuasive argument in favor of their superiority.

2. Critiques of the Myth

Although the myth of rationality is well established in contemporary life and social science, it has not entirely escaped criticism. Two standard criticisms are made of the dogma and of its preeminence. The first is that the myth of rationality is an inaccurate characterization of human behavior, both at the individual and at the organizational levels. The argument has descriptive, prescriptive, and spiritual components.

With respect to rationality as a description of human behavior, the critics point to the many indications that human beings are, at best, only very approximate users of rational decision procedures. They do not seem to have the capabilities required by the myth. Neither human capabilities nor human instincts seem to lead to consistent preferences or to information processing that follows the canons of rationality. Those limitations have been extensively catalogued in studies of college students, statisticians, business executives, and political leaders. Consciousness of the constraints has led much of modern microeconomic theory to become a theory of limited rationality, seeking to understand the limitations as stemming from a higher order rationality, but students of individual and organizational decision making persistently present evidence of additional significant inabilities of human subjects to pursue the canons of rationality.

Moreover, even when they are not conspicuously constrained by capabilities, human beings do not reliably follow procedures of rationality. It appears to be true that human behavior can often be better described in terms of other kinds of logics. For example, there is the logic of imitation by which an action is taken because it conforms to the actions of others. There is a logic of experience by which an action is taken because it has been reinforced in the past. There is a logic of appropriateness by which an action is taken because it is appropriate to an identity in a situation. There is a logic of faith by which an action is taken because of confidence in the superior wisdom of prophets or experts. Each of these has some serious claim to being a better descriptive characterization of human behavior than is calculated rationality.

For many observers who accept the proposition that the myth of rationality does poorly in describing human behavior, it nevertheless remains a more-or-less self-evident proposition that rationality is the appropriate model of intelligent behavior. It is commonly assumed that following, or attempting to follow, rational procedures will, on average, lead to more desirable outcomes than other alternative procedures. However, such a link between rationality as a process and superior intelligence as an outcome is, in fact, uncertain both theoretically and empirically. Theoretical proofs of the intelligence of rationality depend on doubtful assumptions about the precision of knowledge of alternatives and their consequences and about the stability of preferences. Each of the alternative logics of action sketched above has contending theoretical claims to superior intelligence. It is not hard to construct an argument for the superior intelligence of processes of imitation, appropriateness, or faith under some, easily realized, circumstances. It is often more sensible to follow traditional rules of behavior, or to imitate the behavior of others, than it is to try to calculate behavior on one's own.

Similarly, the empirical evidence that trying to pursue rational procedures leads to intelligence is, at best, mixed. The issue is not whether, in principle, rationality is a good idea. It is, rather, whether when we instruct individuals that rationality is the best procedure and they implement it in whatever way they do, we actually achieve better results than if we instructed them differently. For example, among all those situations in which a calculated answer is possible and optimal, in which of them is it better to tell someone to make the calculations rather than follow a suboptimal rule? Among all those situations in which strategic planning – if done properly – can be shown to be a good idea, in which of them is it a good idea to implement a procedure to develop a strategic plan?

Camus argued that many more atrocities to human spirit had been produced by rationality than by more traditional processes of choice. Similar stories are told by modern social science. The general empirical evidence seems to be that it is much easier to persuade individuals and organizations to adopt rational procedures in principle and to justify action in terms of rationality than it is to teach them to follow the procedures appropriately. And even when the procedures are followed appropriately, they often seem to lead to disaster.

Finally, rationality in its modern form is problematic as a spiritual basis for the glorification of the human species. It provides a limited vision of human uniqueness. Part of the limitation is the consequence of the transformations of the meaning of rationality over time. There has been a gradual shift in meaning from a conception of rationality and reason as imagined by Aristotle and Aquinas (in which a substantial component of the idea of reason was the interactive, social, reasoning construction of valid objectives and values; that is, discursive rationality in modern terms) to the subjectivism of utilitarian rational philosophy in Bentham and Mill, and finally to the transformation of individual value to ideas of relatively narrow self-interest. To judge the magnitude of the change, one might observe that we have managed to retain the terminology of rationality while transforming ordinary greed from a conspicuous vice to a conspicuous virtue.

There has always been a strong counter vision of human uniqueness, one that sees the pursuit of consequence as demeaning to human spirit, or at least as an inferior characterization of that spirit. From this perspective, action that can be justified by its consequences may be useful, but it is hardly distinctively human. In such a spirit, Kierkegaard argues that any religion that can be justified by its good consequences is not a religion. The essence of religion is unjustifiable faith. And Quixote says: "For a knight errant to make himself crazy for a reason warrants neither credit nor thanks;

the point is to act foolishly without justification." Action that follows rationality may be important, useful, and necessary; but it is merely economics. Within the vision of Kierkegaard and Quixote, action becomes truly human precisely when it is not justified by its instrumentality.

The second standard criticism of the myth of rationality is that although the dogma contains real elements of fundamental truth, there is great social, intellectual, and moral danger in the dominance of any one set of ideas. Adaptive life requires a balance between the exploitation of known things and the exploration of the unknown. Maintaining this balance is a central issue in theories of rational choice, in theories of limited rationality, in theories of learning, and in theories of variation and selection. In theories of choice, it is known as the two-armed-bandit problem. In theories of learning and selection, it is known as the optimal-experimentation, or variation, problem.

Although it is easy to see that there are tradeoffs between exploration and exploitation, it is extraordinarily difficult to determine the optimal mix. We know it is not at the extreme points that you can suffer from too much exploration or from too little. The difficulties in identifying the optimal mix of exploration and exploitation stem partly from the difficulty we have in anticipating highly uncertain realities. They stem partly from the indeterminacy of optimality when outcomes are distributed over time, when what is good in the short run may not be good in the longer run. And they stem partly from the indeterminacy in optimality in a nested system of interacting actors, where what is good for one part of the system is not necessarily good for another part.

Even without knowing the precise balance, we know that there are some special features of adaptive processes that are important to the present argument. The returns to exploitation are systematically more certain, nearer in time, and closer in space than are the returns to exploration. On average, experiments with new ideas are experiments with error. If they yield results, it will be in some indefinite future. And (for the most part) the rewards will tend to be realized by others rather than by those who do the experimenting. These factors combine to make adaptive processes self-destructive in the sense that they tend to drive out exploration.

The process is an unending one in the history of ideas, and the situation today with respect to the myth of rationality is not much different from earlier periods when other ideas about the nature of the world and of morality were dominant. Retrospectively, we can easily see that earlier periods of intellectual stability contained the seeds of their own self-destruction in their tendency to label new ideas as wrong, foolish, or excessively risky. Social science is in a similar period of stability, en route to stagnation.

Notice that the argument is not that deviant ideas are, on average, better than the dominant ones. By any reasonable measure, new ideas are likely (on average) to be inferior to established ideas. The problem is that adaptation requires variability – even at the short run cost of a reduction in average quality. It is a problem well known to students of optimal socialization and learning rates in a society.

These considerations – first, that the myth of rationality may be fundamentally wrong as a basis for guiding or predicting or humanizing behavior and second, that in any event it has become too dominant a belief – lead, in some quarters, to considerable alarm about the dominance of this religion. To the alarmists, at least, modern social science has become as doctrinaire as Catholic thought before the reformation, astronomical thought before Copernicus, and Marxist thought before 1980. From such a perspective, the myth of rationality is, in important ways, wrong and dangerously hegemonic.

3. The Myth of Rationality as a Problem

The case against the myth of rationality is, I think, reasonably strong. Rationality has problems as a description of behavior, as a prescription for behavior, and as a characterization of the human spirit. And even if those problems were not as significant as they are, the overwhelming dominance of rationality poses problems to an adaptive intelligence.

However, I think both the critics of rationality and its champions share a common tendency to overlook one of the powerful human mechanisms by which human beings maintain diversity in the face of thought police. It is called hypocrisy, or in this context, rationalization – the ability to conceal deviant ideas under a veneer of legitimacy, to pay lip service to orthodoxy while corrupting it. The process is well known to all great systems of thought. In a Marxist society, Marx becomes a gloss over every event and thought that we have. In a Freudian society, Freud becomes a gloss. Similarly, we populate a society that requires rationalization as justification of action, and social science insists on rationalization as explanation of action. Rationalization has become an exercise in cleverness. Modern economics, for example, contains a number of deviant ideas covered with a veneer of rationality to make them acceptable to the intellectual establishment.

The case can be illustrated by the modern history of theories of decision-making in individuals and organizations. In the beginning, we had a theory of choice that presumed action depended upon two improbably precise guesses: a precise guess about the future consequences of current action and a precise guess about future sentiments with respect to those consequences. This conception was challenged by the observation of limitations to individual and organizational capabilities for processing information about alternatives and their consequences. In turn, this led to theories of bounded rationality and the interpretation of organizational forms and information structures as solutions to the problems of dealing with limited cognitive and informational capabilities, with the costs of information.

Ideas of simple rationality were subsequently challenged by observations that environments are not exogenous but consist of other rational actors, thus action is properly strategic. This led to theories of strategic action, as prototypically represented by game theory. In more recent years, the ideas have been challenged by observations that preferences are neither consistent, stable, nor exogenous. This has led to attempts to develop rational theories of preferences.

At the same time, the idea of rationality has been challenged by observations that rather little human behavior involves calculation of the sort anticipated but is better described as rule following or imitation, that most of the variation in a game situation depends not on the strategies but on the rules. This has led to considerable interest in rational theories of imitation, rules, and norms, including theories that see rules as equilibrium solutions to metagames. This history of rationalization of anomalies has sustained the myth of rationality through the elaboration of a fairly Keplerian structure. Because there are various costs to gathering information and interpreting it, decision makers follow rules; because there are costs to developing one's own rules, decision makers copy the rules of others; because there are costs to changing rules, rules are mostly stable – in short, because there are costs to acting rationally, it is rational not to do so.

Much of the pursuit of rationality in modern social science theories of human action can be seen as an elaborate game in which every deviation from the myth is concealed behind a rhetoric of conformity. Modern students of rational choice models are deeply reformist, but they conceal their heresies within a flexible mythology. So, in the end, we are left with a myth that is powerful and important, but largely devoid of content. By making the meanings of self-interest and strategic dominance flexible, the defenders of rationality have achieved an extraordinary level of intellectual plasticity and freedom. We all know the catechism. We accept it, and repeat it, but it no longer has any significant bite, either theoretical or ethical.

We now have a classic division of labor between the philosophers of rationality and the observers of social institutions. As each new observation raises issues about the myth of rationality, the philosophers fold it into the faith by finding new ways of imagining costs at some level or over some time period. Like dishonest lawyers, they are full of imagination and without shame. Much of the intellectual energy of social science goes into this effort to discover rationality in action, institutions, norms, forms, practices, and behavior. One version of the "new institutionalism," for example, is an effort to rationalize rules, norms, and institutions. The intellectual sophists of rationality protect us all from being exposed as heretics. It is a necessary and valued craft that has attracted and profited from some of the best and the brightest of our trade.

For a variety of reasons, bright people are attracted to the job of transforming heresies into dogma. As long as the church was responsible for reconciling ordinary life with the rhetoric of virtue, smart people were recruited to theology. Now, when the game is basically to make everything rational, smart people are recruited to the job. And the rest of us profit from the clarifications they provide, the insights that such clarifications stimulate, and the legitimacy they provide for those of us who observe behavior that seems inconsistent with rationality.

In any stable intellectual world, vitality and excitement (as well as ignorance and stupidity) are concentrated outside the establishment, in the catacombs of deviance. Social science is such a world now. Much of the real excitement lies not in inventing complicated arguments that fit human existence into a myth of rationality but in exploring alternative visions of the human experience and the human spirit. Among these visions, I would list four that are far from novel, and which can indeed claim to have histories at least as long as the vision of rationality and to have modern voices of eloquence:

First, a vision of human existence as organized around identities rather than instrumental choices, a vision in which concepts of duties and obligations are more central than concepts of preferences and interests. In a world of identity, the human estate is manifested through answering the question, What does a person such as I do in a situation such as this? The key processes are those that discover and create conceptions of self and match them to situations in a way that gives coherence and comprehension to existence. The logic is one of appropriateness and the major uncertainties are uncertainties in the definitions of situation and self.

Second, a vision of human existence as being organized by the search for meaning, for an interpretation and construction of life. Theories of rational action assume that action is understood in terms of choice and choice is understood in terms of its outcomes. Thus, they assume that humans enter the processes of life in order to affect the outcomes of those processes, and that the point of life is choice. Alternatively, we can highlight the way in which life and institutions are organized around the development of meaning. In this perspective, the focus shifts from action to interpretation. We consider the ways in which the symbols of life are organized to shape the telling of accounts. We examine the ways in which preferences are molded within social institutions. We see action less as a consequence of the social construction of meaning than as an instrument of that construction.

Third, a vision of human existence as enriched by ambiguity, contradiction, inconsistency, ambivalence, and irrelevance. The metaphors of rationality and choice are metaphors of clarity, consistency, and consequence. But much of human experience, including some of the noblest and most productive, is not devoted to resolving ambiguity but to creating and exploring it. For many years, I used to ask three questions of my colleagues, students, and friends on a Friday afternoon over wine: Why are there more great women than great men in the world? Why do good communication theorists make poor conversationalists? And why is it better to be seduced by a poet than an economist? The answer to all three lies in the evocative use of ambiguity to discover new meanings, new identities, and new relevancies.

Fourth, a vision of human existence as path dependent, as traversing a history characterized by local positive feedback, multiple equilibria, and irreversibilities. As we come to understand interactive, developmental processes better, we keep discovering histories that are not easily described as necessary. Small differences at one point in time are amplified by local positive feedback and network externalities into large, irreversible differences. As a result, observed historical paths are a mixture of almost inexorable movement that is, at unpredictable times, deflected from one path to another. Those deflections sometimes are produced by massive interventions, but sometimes, at critical moments, by barely perceptible actions or events. As a result, the forms, practices, and institutions that characterize a society at any one time are not uniquely explicable in terms of the conditions facing that society.

These visions seem to me to be of some possible significance to the future of social science. Some of the best theoretical work in modern social science is in the elaboration of the implications of the axioms of rationality; but it seems to me that, in the continual struggle to find a reasonable balance between exploiting the ideas we know well and exploring the ones we might come to know better, social science is in danger of becoming a bit too orthodox.

Deviant ideas are, on average, bad ones. And the people who deal in deviant ideas are, on average, neither as smart nor as well-trained as those who deal in established ones. As a result, in the near neighborhood of where we are, neither our experiences nor our incentives propel us away from received doctrine, particularly since predicting which specific deviant sect is likely to survive and thrive in the market for ideas is notoriously difficult. Nevertheless, it seems to me that we have gone too far in inventing rationalizations of behavior. A social science that commits as many scarce intellectual resources as we do to elaborating and protecting a sacred myth of rationality, and as few resources as we do to nurturing alternative perspectives on the nature and glory of human existence, is probably making a mistake.

James G. March

James G. March is professor emeritus at Stanford University, where he has been on the faculty since 1970. Before that, he was on the faculty of the University of California, Irvine, and the Carnegie Institute of Technology. He received his B.A. degree from the University of Wisconsin and his M.A. and Ph.D. from Yale University. He has received honorary doctorates from several European and North American universities.

He has been a member of the National Science Board (1969–1974) and the National Council on Educational Research (1975–1978), as well as a member or chair of a number of committees for the National Research Council of the National Academy of Sciences and the Social Science Research Council. From 1984 to 1994 he was a member, and from 1991 to 1993, chair, of the Board of Trustees of the Russell Sage Foundation. He has also been a member of the Board of Directors of Sun Hydraulics Corporation (1989–1992 and 1996–2000), the Scandinavian Consortium for Organizational Research (1988–1999), and Wally Industries (1996–2001). From 1994 to 2001 he was a member of the Board of the Citigroup Behavioral Sciences Research Council (chair, 1994 to 2000).

He received the Wilbur Cross Medal from Yale University in 1968, the Academy of Management Award for Scholarly Contributions to Management in 1984, the Walter J. Gores Award for Excellence in Teaching from Stanford University in 1995, the John Gaus Award from the American Political Science Association in 1997, the Distinguished Scholar Award from the Academy of Management in 1999, the Viipuri Award from the Viipuri Society in 2004, the Aaron Wildavsky Award from the Public Policy Society in 2004, and the Herbert Simon Award from Laszlo Rajk College (Budapest) in 2005. In 1995 he was made a knight first class in the Royal Norwegian (Olav V) Order of Merit, and in 1999 he was made a commander of the Order of the Lion of Finland.

He is best known professionally for his writings on decision making and organizations, including *Organizations*, *A Behavioral Theory of the Firm*, *Leadership and Ambiguity*, *Ambiguity and Choice in Organizations*, *Decisions and Organizations*, *Rediscovering Institutions*, *The Pursuit of Organizational Intelligence*, *Democratic Governance*, *A Primer on Decision Making*, and *The Dynamics of Rules*.

Stefano Zamagni
Department of Economics
University of Bologna

The Ethical Anchoring of Corporate Social Responsibility*

In this essay two specific questions are dealt with: one, How robust are the critiques against corporate social responsibility (CSR)? and the other, Which ethical anchoring is capable of offering more solid support for CSR? I will not deal with the history of CSR, a rather recent history all told that usually begins with the pioneering contribution of Bowen in 1953, which contains an early definition of CSR (Chirielieson 2004); nor will I comment on the reasons for which, with the development of globalization beginning at the end of the 1970s, the problematic nature of CSR has exploded onto the scene (Zamagni 2003). Nor will I confront, finally, the contents of corporate social responsibility, what is understood by CSR and the ways of implementing it at the level of firm praxis (Sacconi 2004).

* A somewhat different version of this essay was published, in Italian. (Zamagni 2005).

I would like to observe that, notwithstanding the plethora of studies and debates that have taken place over the course of the last quarter century, there still exists no commonly accepted definition of CSR. We are still in the phase of the "privatization" of the definitions, which is at the origin of many interpretative problems and grave miscomprehensions that cause quite often bitter and useless polemics. The fact is that a definition makes sense only if it becomes the common property of a scientific community, since the nature of a definition in a particular field of knowledge is that of a public good. Indeed, the idea of a private definition is an oxymoron.

1. On the Robustness of the Critique of CSR

1.1 The "Pars Construens" of the Critique

It should not be surprising if, among experts in the economic disciplines, but not only, the *fin de non recevoir* still dominates regarding the themes of CSR – it is a fact that the theoretical economic literature, for example, is all but mute about the causal reasons and effects of CSR – and the critiques of the very idea of CSR, not to mention its actual application, are frequent. After more than a century of pronouncements on the thesis of axiological neutrality of economic science, i.e., of the affirmation according to which there exists a sphere of social relations taking place in the market that don't need to be subjected to any external ethical judgment, what I have just suggested comes as no surprise. Is it not perhaps true that economic behavior, that of the firm in particular, is in and of itself oriented toward the good, inasmuch as the firm produces value? It follows that economic behavior is different from every other type of human behavior because it eludes morality without being contrary to it. As we will see later, it was the impressive development of the market economy itself and of its most important institution, the firm, that sent into crisis that consoling image that has allowed, for a long time, the economist to work "undisturbed" by ethical concerns. But it is a fact that such a realization has not yet become common within the profession despite the mass of events and facts that should indicate an overdue change in course.

Before moving on to the examination of the criticisms of CSR and to their confutations it is, however, opportune, not to mention intellectually honest, to recognize the elements of truth contained in those criticisms. I will indicate three. In a recent essay, Beltratti (2003) discusses the case of socially responsible investing – essentially, ethical finance – under the hypothesis that voluntarily renouncing investment in certain stocks results in lower returns. The problem studied in the paper is that of deciding under which conditions such an investment is capable of changing the equilibrium of the system. The relevance of the problem is that rational agents will accept socially responsible behavior only if, through operating this way, they believe they will be able to modify the final equilibrium of the system through the induced effects of their behavior on prices in the stock market and on the curve of equity yields. Let us not forget that the familiar hypothesis of rational behavior implies that one aims to maximize the objective for which one acts, regardless of whether or not profit or one of its variants is involved. Well, Beltratti demonstrates that there is a critical threshold for the level of socially responsible investments, below which the particular objective pursued is not reached. What is the meaning of this result? It suggests that if the number of firms adhering to the CSR project does not reach the critical mass, at the end of the day, what wins in the market is the combination of acquisitive behavior and instrumental rationality on the part of economic agents.

A second element of truth that emerges from the criticisms is that CSR can sometimes serve as a screen that allows unscrupulous firms to eliminate their rivals or to reduce their competitive force. In brief, the argument is as follows: Let's assume that on the market there operate two types of firms, those that are opportunistic and those intrinsically motivated by CSR. Let's assume in addition that the critical consumers, which are today increasing in number everywhere, are willing to reward the latter type of firm and sanction (through boycotts and condemnation campaigns) the former. In situations of this type, it is possible that opportunistic firms decide to behave initially in a manner that is even "more ethical" than the others with the aim of marginalizing them on the market so that they can eventually return to their old behavior. Such eventualities will be all the more probable as more public institutions – such as governments or public agencies – intervene in the process of CSR by offering incentives and various forms of economic advantages to firms that agree to conform to the guidelines determined by the public institution. In this case, the heterogenesis of the ends would be assured: CSR would become an instrument for crowding out or pushing aside the virtuous firms and increasing the monopolistic rent of the opportunistic firms.

Finally, the critics of CSR are right when they observe that socially responsible behaviors can conceal a dangerous tradeoff; namely, the tradeoff between moral commitment and social commitment. As we know, the specific logic of CSR is to combine – in the sense of the *ars combinatoria* – the logic of pure business (which says that the only thing that counts for the firm is the economic result as measured by its profit) and the logic of pure philanthropy (which suggests the firm must commit a part of its profits to socially important uses). It is typical of CSR to reject the celebrated dichotomy of J.S. Mill between the laws of production of wealth and the laws of distribution of wealth. A firm is not socially responsible if it ignores human rights and moral integrity while producing wealth and then becomes compassionately generous in the moment of the distribution of the wealth. The noted historical cases of A. Carnegie and J.D. Rockefeller of the USA at the end of the 19th century are eloquent examples of what it means, in practice, to accept Mill's dichotomy (Zunz 2002). Well, the danger that I hinted at above is that with the social commitment – i.e., corporate philanthropy, falsely confused with CSR – cynical managers can cover up the absence of moral scruples. And because the capacity for philanthropic donations is correlated to the size of the firm, large pressure groups are able, more easily than the smaller groups, to "buy" the good reputation that is considered necessary to them and thereafter change the strategy when the competitive scenario becomes particularly severe. For example, Enron's *2000 Report on Social Responsibility* reads: "We want to work to promote reciprocal respect with the communities and stakeholders that are touched by our activities. We treat others as we would like to be treated." Everybody knows, today, how the celebrated "golden rule" was applied by Enron!

1.2 Milton Friedman's Position

Let me return to the main argument. What do we find deep down inside the mother of all criticisms of CSR? We find the vivid affirmation by Friedman that foretells in CSR a grave threat to the capitalist system: "Few tendencies can threaten the foundations of our free society like the acceptance by top managers of a social responsibility that goes beyond making as much money as possible for their shareholders" (Friedman 1962, 133). This thesis was further advanced in a famous *New York Times* article of September 1970, with the evocative title "The only responsibility that corporations have is to increase profits," in which one reads: "[T]he shortsighted vision is even exemplified in the speeches of businessmen on social responsibility… here, as happens with price and wage controls, businessmen seem to reveal a *suicidal impulse.* The real social responsibility of the firm is to obtain the highest profits – obviously in an open, correct and competitive market, producing wealth and work for all in the most efficient way possible" [1] (Italics added).

1 The synthesis of Friedman's thinking on the theme discussed here can be found in Friedman (1993).

More recently, and moving in the same direction, Steinberg writes in an influential volume, "The aim of the firm is not to promote the public good.... If the *nature* of the goods or services or the *mode* in which they are produced has priority over the long-term maximization of value for the shareholder, then the activity in question *is no longer a business activity*" (italics added); and a few pages later: "Just as you have prostitution when you have sex for money, instead of for love, a company prostitutes itself when it pursues love or social responsibility instead of money" (Steinberg 2000, 36 and 42).

We must admit that this thesis is not without a certain intellectual appeal, but it is much less solid than it seems. The central point of the thesis is this: The market is the place in which the coordination of economic activity happens through voluntary cooperation. This is due to the fact that "both parties to an economic transaction benefit from it, provided the transaction is bilaterally voluntary and informed" (Friedman 1962, 13). It follows then that when two (or more) parties, in the absence of cheating and coercion, give life to an economic transaction, those parties also agree to the consequences that derive from that transaction. It can be noted that herein lies the ethical justification of consequentialism. The notion of consent founded on free choice is well expressed by Posner (1981) when he writes, "It is my contention that a person who buys a lottery ticket and then loses has 'consented' to the loss so long as there is no question of fraud or duress" (Quoted in Peter 2004, 94). Therefore, outside of these cases, choosing means giving one's consent, and giving consent means to legitimize. As Peter argues (2004), the market does not therefore need to ask for certificates of legitimacy since the market is capable of self-legitimizing behavior. This is not the case, for example, with the state that – as Peter (2004) observes – needs the approval of the citizens via democratic elections in order to be able to use coercion, which is the way it achieves its objectives.

We are now at the point of arrival of the reasoning: Because the firm is the most important institution of the market, the self-legitimacy of the latter is automatically extended to the self-legitimacy of the former. This is why the only social responsibility of the firm is to create wealth and increase profits while respecting the rules of the game. Also – the critics of CSR add – because of objective cognitive limits, the firm is unable to gauge the real interests of its various classes of stakeholders. Citing A. Smith (incorrectly because out of context) who, in *The Wealth of Nations,* had written: "I have never seen that much good has been done by those who declare to do business for the public good" (Book IV, cap.2), these critics conclude that the only wise thing to do is to let each business – which knows best its own interests – maximize profit. It will be up to the shareholders, to whom the profits go, to decide freely whether to destine part or all of them to socially useful ends. The more the firm remains a profit machine, the more the common good is served.

1.3 The Aporetic Character of the Critique of CSR

What doesn't fit in this apparently persuasive argument? First of all, it is not necessarily true that freedom of choice postulates consent. I agree with Peter (2004) that this would be the case if the choice were not constrained, as is typically the case in economics. The subject who voluntarily (i.e., with no coercion) offers his organs for sale to reduce his suffering due to poverty and hunger certainly would not consent to the consequences that would stem from this act. Free choice has a legitimizing force only if the set of the alternatives among which the agent has to choose is also under the agent's control or, at least, is part of the agent's choice problem. If the menu of choice is given – as is the case in reality – that condition is certainly not satisfied. In other words, for the prospect of uncoerced choice to find consensus one requires that everyone agree to the constraints on which each person acts.

As is well known, the centrality of the category of consent is typical of the contractualist school of thought from Hobbes through Rawls. The idea is that if I have signed a contract with you – let's say a labor contract – to do something that I no longer want to do, you can always respond by saying, "You were in agreement – now you are obligated." That is to say consent is the foundation of obligation, not simply a procedure to implement or regulate it. However, Rawls (1971) majestically argues that in order for the consent obligation to exist it is necessary that constraints under which the parties to the social contract make their free choice be accepted by both. In other words, that which is requested is a justification – legitimacy is not enough – for the constraints, a justification that is agreed upon by all who take part in the social contract. Only if we can show that the subjects have given their consent (or would have a reason for giving their consent) for a certain institutional setup can we argue that the agreement is just and therefore obligatory. Now, it is not difficult to understand why this condition is never met in practice in our market economies. Indeed, the freedom of choice describes the absence of any coercion. It has to do with the *possibility* of choice, which says nothing about the *capability* of choice. This is the message stemming from the work of Sen (1988) when he reminds us that the *use* of freedom is essential to its definition. In arguing that freedom consists in the ability to realize self-determined ends, Sen (1999) incorporates a substantive claim into his analysis of freedom: An agent's freedom is directly linked to what opportunity he/she has to realize his/her ends. It follows that the opportunity set an individual is presented with is as important to evaluating its freedom as it is its autonomy in decision making.

More can be said on the issue at stake. The syllogism on which Friedman's thesis rests – that the market is self-legitimizing and the firm is the main pillar of the market; *ergo*, the firm is also self-legitimizing – takes for granted something which is in reality not so, that the organizational principle of the market is the same as that for the firm. This is not the case, because while the market postulates horizontal and symmetrical relationships among all who take part in it – if it were not like this, the contract could not be its principal instrument – the internal organization of the firm is founded, today as yesterday, on the principle of hierarchy, so much so that command is the firm's main instrument. This is a point that R. Coase had already clearly illustrated in his celebrated essay *The Nature of the Firm*, in 1937, when he argued that the firm and the market are alternative institutions, a point that has been recently reiterated by Zingales: "Governance is synonymous with the exercise of authority, management and control. These words sound strange, however, when they are used in the context of a free market economy. Why do we need any form of authority? Is it not, by chance, true that the market is responsible for the efficient allocation of all the resources without the intervention of authority?" (Zingales 1989, 497) I therefore conclude that the most insidious weapon that the critics of CSR have at their disposal is truly blunted.

Now I'll pass to the second aporia present in the reasoning that I am examining. Even if we leave aside the first aporia, the anti-CSR thesis would make sense, would even have a bit of weight, *if* the markets, both of inputs and outputs, were perfectly competitive; *if* income distribution were equitable, at least in the minimal sense of allowing everybody to participate in the market game; *if* the preferences of the economic agents went unchanged with respect to the carrying out of economic activity. Well, the same economic textbooks teach us that these are very demanding conditions, none of which is ever satisfied in a real economy. In particular, it is well known that preferences do indeed change endogenously. When this is the case, the individual is sometimes forced by rationality to follow a course of action which, by the agent's own standards, is inefficient, i.e. reduces his or her well-being. As shown by Yaari (1977), if in an exchange process an agent, even if endowed with perfect information and perfect foresight, is in a position where behaving inefficiently is the only rational thing to do, then the exchange process contains an ethical fault. Arrow's paper (1973), by providing a very effective account of the reasons the three conditions above are never met, contains (perhaps) the first economic justification for enterprise ethical codes. It would be proper, at this stage, to shed some light on the paradox that the anti-CSR line of thought brings us to.

An antique idea of economic science, one that has touched almost all schools of thought except, for example, the Austrian school, is that the economy exists in a space separate from both the political space and the space of civil society. This idea is revealed in the conviction that while economic variables (prices, quantities, income, asset values, etc.) can fluctuate from one period to another and can be impacted by events in the fields of politics and social relations, in the long run, such variables tend to approach their standard of reference, determined by market fundamentals, as one would say in the current jargon. There are different theories that explain how these standards are determined, but the conviction is that prices and market magnitudes cannot go too far, or indefinitely, from their specific attractor, whatever it may be.

Clearly, only a conception of the economic system as a field of human interaction separate from the rest of society can give meaning to propositions of this kind. In the same moment we speak of *market fundamentals*, we affirm that the market possesses its own dynamic, which is not disturbed by the other social dynamics. If it were not this way, how could we even speak of market "fundamentals"? Today we know that this is not the case, but this is not my point. Rather, my point regards the above-mentioned paradox. The anti-CSR thesis presupposes, for its own validity, the existence of both perfectly competitive markets (first condition) and market fundamentals (third condition). But if this were the case, in a long-run competitive equilibrium, profits would be zero, as Leon Walras demonstrated as early as 1874 with his theory of general economic equilibrium. This is to say that in order to be right in suggesting that the only social responsibility a firm has is to increase profits, Friedman and other like-minded scholars must presuppose conditions under which firms don't attain any more profits!

Finally, I come to a third aporia inherent in the argument of the CSR critics. These authors all agree on one point, which is that the pursuit of profit by the firm must happen with full respect for the rules of the economic game, and in particular of the legal norms in vigor. If we think long enough about it, it becomes obvious that this is just circular reasoning. It is clear, in fact, that *if* the rules of the economic game were complete; *if* the processes of lawmaking were able to follow, quickly enough, the evolution of the economic happenings in phases of accelerated social dynamics such as the one we are living in; *if* all this were assured, then it would be true that it would make no sense to talk about CSR. But the necessity of CSR is born by the fact that these circumstances are never met, as everyone knows. It is exactly because the contracts are basically incomplete and because markets don't always exist that agency problems and problems stemming from abuse of authority on the part of those who possesses the residual rights of control emerge in reality (Sacconi 2003).

To put it another way, it is of course true that allowing the firm, which definitively knows its own good better than anyone else, to pursue it freely and then leave it up to the market to direct individual interests toward the common good, would be an intelligent strategy. But this would be true only if the economic game were played inside *civil* and *just* institutions, as the tradition of the civil economy, long before A. Smith, had understood and explained (Bruni and Zamagni 2004). It is when civil and just institutions don't yet exist, or are incomplete and imperfect, that the pursuit of the common good requires something more and different from the mere pursuit of interest. In a well-known passage, Smith writes of the "obvious and simple system of natural liberty "where each one" is left perfectly free to pursue his own interest in his own way," and to interact with others by bringing "both his industry and capital into competition with those of any other man." However, Smith puts a double constraint on his account. The first, which is usually overlooked, is the requirement that the individual is free to pursue his own interest "as long as he does not violate the laws of justice." The second is a constraint of social benefit: although each one "intends only his own gain… he is… led by an invisible hand to promote an end which was no part of his intention…. By pursuing his own interest he frequently promotes that of the society more effectually than when he really intends to promote it." Thus Smith places the self-interested behavior within the double constraints of justice and social benefit. This is why the truly socially responsible firm cooperates to define a civil ethic that favors the emergence of forms of organizational condensation from which civil and just institutions can emerge. Acting in respect of *given* rules is not enough, if those rules need to be changed.

2. The Ethical Anchoring of CSR

That the concept of responsibility finds, today, many difficulties in being accepted, let alone applied, is all told understandable. On one hand, globalization is increasing, in unprecedented ways, the distance between action and the ultimate consequences of action. One thinks about the impact of processes of mergers and acquisitions on the phenomenon of "short-termism": Firms fearing takeovers tend to pay scarce attention to all that does not have a return in the short run – including social responsibility. On the other hand, the new technologies that connote the third industrial revolution tend to reduce the sense of responsibility insofar as they tend to increase the number and typology of the unpredictable consequences of the actions. The notion of responsibility is strictly connected to that of accountability. Responsible are those who know how to manage situations, adequately evaluating their risks and results. But the current technological changes render this exercise ever more difficult, if not impossible. As Baumann writes, "[T]oday, the organization in its own is a tool for canceling responsibility" (Baumann 1992, 225). Therefore, it shouldn't be surprising if there are still many doubts, first of all cultural, with regard to CSR on the part of both academics and business people.

In what follows, I will critically examine the four ethical theories that – often unknown even to many of their users – hold up the various positions on CSR present in the current debate.

2.1 The Ethics of Intentions

Why should the firm ever act in a *socially* responsible way, if no canon of economic rationality exists that justifies that behavior? Is it not perhaps sufficient to have a personal ethics based on the principle of intentionality that reduces ethical questions to interpersonal relations? According to the ethics of intentions – upon which many critics of CSR base their arguments – an action is defined as good when it conforms to two rules: the proximate rule (conscience) and the remote rule (the law). The person who, harmonizing conscience and the law, behaves accordingly, commits a morally good act. It is the intentions, and not the consequences, of action that must come under the definition of ethical behavior. That is like saying the ends justify the consequences. This is where the famous expression, that sums this up nicely, comes from: *good business is good ethics*. The firm that turns a lot of profit is also highly responsible because by creating wealth, it allows well-intentioned people to pursue their goals. There is no better illustration of this way of thinking than that professed by Andrew Carnegie, the great American philanthropic capitalist whose methods of doing business were anything but civil. In his *The Gospel of Wealth* of 1889 one reads, "Wealth concentrated in the hands of one man alone is the result of the labor of an entire community and must go back to that community in one way or another. The rich person is the custodian of a fortune and that must be at the disposal of the common good and his career *must be divided into two parts*: acquisition and distribution" (Quoted in Picard 1999, 26; italics added).

What is the principal limit of such an ethical theory? That it doesn't give enough weight to the induced and indirect effects of individual actions. If my activity guided by good intentions, generates negative externalities that fall on other subjects, the act that was subjectively just becomes objectively, that is, ideopraxically, unjust. Deciding to entrust my savings to a financial institution so that it maximizes my rate of return is a just act according to the criteria of the proximate and remote rule. But if that institution invests my savings in any one of the many illicit ways, the act in question is objectively censurable. This means that the anticipation of the effects of an action is an integral part of ethical behavior. More generally, the fact that the firm operates today within a system in which it is the globalized market that constrains, more than ever before, the economic agents is not a sufficient reason for freeing them from their social obligations. Also, one can't want that the market is, at the same time, the place of maximum entrepreneurial freedom and such a constraining place that it renders firms socially irresponsible. Thinking in this way would bring us to a pragmatic contradiction.

2.2 The "Good Ethics Is Good Business" Thesis

An ethical theory that seeks to remediate some of the deficiencies just highlighted is that of *enlightened self-interest*. Because of the tight interconnection between external environment and the firm, if it wants to compete successfully in the long term in the market, it must take into consideration the needs of the context in which it operates, and in particular those of its stakeholders. Just as that version of utilitarianism known as social utilitarianism suggests, *good ethics is good business*. This is the same as saying ethics pays in one way or another. Cochran explains the difficulties of development in the western United States in the second half of the 19th century: "[T]he low level of business ethics among many American entrepreneurs was a grave impediment both to economic efficiency and raising capital" (Cohran 1964, 96). The famous economic historian Rostow (1961) pushes himself so far as to claim that the root cause of the Great Depression was a lack of ethical behavior on behalf of the economic leadership.

The ethical theory in question represents certainly a step forward but too short of a step to be interesting. Reducing social responsibility to just another constraint to the strategic management of the firm, the enlightened self-interest approach inverts the natural order of things. Instead of being a presupposition or a guideline for economic action, ethics becomes in fact a consequence of economic success. ccording to this theory, ethical behavior is visualized as a superior good in the sense that the demand for such a good grows at a larger rate than income and vice-versa. (The demand income-elasticity is larger than one). The more people become rich, the more the need, or the demand, for ethical behavior grows, and vice-versa. Consider now the case of a firm that competes on the global markets and intends to put CSR procedures into practice. If its rivals, through illicit behavior (for example the use of child labor) are able to lower production costs and therefore the selling price, there will be a reduction in income for the firm in question. The latter will then lower the demand for ethical behavior until this is brought in line with average behavior. In a situation of this type the strategy that Shleifer (2004) suggests adopting is to accelerate, as quickly as possible, the process of income growth, through an intensification of the levels of competition and without too many moral scruples (better to use child labor, for example, than to see people die of hunger). The increase in the disposition to "pay" for higher ethical levels would come as a consequence.

But if ethics is simply a byproduct of economic growth – Marx would have said a superstructure of the economic structure – what sense would there be in talking about CSR? And why speak ever of ethical behavior as an ulterior constraint under which to maximize long-run profits if ethics is a consequence of economic results? As it can be understood, the above line of reasoning is opposite to the great Socratic message according to which virtue is not born out of riches; on the contrary, from virtue itself is derived all the riches and all the other good things to men.

2.3 *The Ethics of Responsibility*

The moral theory currently more in vogue in studies of CSR is the ethics of responsibility as interpreted by the well-known stakeholder model. We can consider Max Weber the father of such a theory who, in his celebrated essay *Politics as a Profession,* indicates the ethics that must characterize "he who wants to place his hands on the gears of history" (Weber 1969, 101). He adds, a few pages later, that responsibility is the "willingness to respond to the *foreseeable* consequences of one's actions" (109). To the Weberian formulation of the ethics of responsibility Jonas (1990) has added an important qualification. Basing his idea on a "heuristic of fear," Jonas does not consider it sufficient to stop only at the foreseeable consequences; one must go further and take into account the *possible* consequences of actions. The appropriate imperative for the new type of human action is, for Jonas, "to act in such a way that the effects of your action are compatible with the continuation of an authentically human life." From the Kantian imperative "you can, because you must" we pass to "you must, because you can."

It is not difficult to understand the meaning of Jonas' qualification. Limiting oneself only to the control of the foreseeable effects of one's actions is too little in economic contexts in which the *proprium* of the entrepreneurial function is to continuously generate unforeseeable effects. On the other hand, is there not perhaps in this – as Schumpeter acutely anticipated – the basic difference between entrepreneur and *rentier* or bureaucrat? Think, in addition, about the possibility, which is enormously greater today with respect to the past, of so-called rational errors made by the firm. As experience suggests, the cost of such errors too often exceeds the monetary value of the capital conferred by shareholders. In cases like this, the calculation of the foreseeable consequences does not constitute a solid anchoring for the notion of responsibility. (Think about the corporate scandals of Enron and Parmalat, among the many others).

Well, it is on such a foundation that stakeholder theory affirmed itself, beginning in the 1960s. In the words of its most representative exponents, Evan and Freeman: "We believe that the legal, economic and moral challenges to the current theory of the firm require a revision in an essentially Kantian perspective. This means that each group of stakeholders has the right not to be treated as a means oriented toward some end, but must participate in the determination of the future direction of the firm" (Evan and Freeman 1988, 101). It follows that the objective of the firm is not the maximization, under constraints, of profit, as is the case in the shareholder theory. The latter defends the position according to which the shareholders, being ultimately responsible for the destiny of the firm, have the right to a special and different consideration with respect to other classes of stakeholders. Rather, "the authentic objective of the firm… is that of operating as a vehicle for *coordinating* the interests of the stakeholders" (Evan and Freeman 1988, 104, italics added).

The primary task of management is therefore to operate for the realization of a balancing of different interests: "Management is the bearer of a financial relationship that links it closely to the stakeholders as much as to the firm as an abstract entity. Management is asked to act in the interest of the stakeholders as if it was an agent of theirs and must act in the interest of the business to guarantee its survival, safeguarding in the long-term the shares of each group" (Evan and Freeman 1988, 104). Finally, in a very recent essay, Freeman, after having reaffirmed that "the firm is a *nexus of relationships* among groups that have an interest in its activities" adds: "The firm has to do with the world in which clients, families, employees, investors (shareholders, bondholders, banks), local community and managers interact and create value. To understand the firm one must understand how these relationships function" (Freeman 2004, 1). From this follows the conclusion that the central objective of stakeholder theory is that of studying how to make the interests of the various stakeholders move in the same direction. "The creation of value and not the conflict of value is the metaphor of reference" (Freeman 2004, 1).

But how to achieve the compatibilization of the interests of all those who, inasmuch as they are bearers of specific investments (finance capital; human capital; trust; social capital; etc.), cooperate within the firm for the creation of value? In other words, how to respond to the objections of many, and in particular of M. Jensen and K. Goodpaster,[2] according to whom a multi-stakeholder model of governance would leave the managers confused, without the so-called bottom line that can be utilized to evaluate their performance?

As Sacconi (2004) indicates, the response is the social contract among all the stakeholders as a *normative* device for defining the contents of CSR. The Rawlsian contractualist version of stakeholder theory, as opposed to the original Kantian version, is capable of supplying a criterion for judgment, not only of the legitimacy of the firm as an institution, but also of its strategic management. Asking the interested subjects if they would give their consent to being part of a firm in a state of nature in which they were guided only by enlightened self-interest – and not also by conventions and traditions – Rawlsian contractualism allows for the identification of a bargaining equilibrium. The fundamental property of such an equilibrium is that each stakeholder would accept it in order to cooperate voluntarily, given that it would be the expression of an impartial procedure in which the moral equality of all the participants would be assured. The normative force of contractualism is, therefore, in linking justice (or equity) to consensus without renouncing the rational calculus. In formal terms, instead of maximizing the profit function, the firm maximizes the function that represents the solution to the negotiation game among all the stakeholders. Sacconi (2003) demonstrates how, under reasonable conditions, such a solution exists, in general.

Is everything okay, then, regarding the possibility of using CSR as a model of enlarged governance of the firm? Not quite, because once the fiduciary obligations of the firm regarding its stakeholders are identified, there still remains the problem of

2 The "paradox of the stakeholder" of Goodpaster goes like this: On the one hand, the manager is paid by the shareholders so that he looks out for their best interests (that is to maximize profit); on the other hand, the manager must act so as to balance the interests of all. (Goodpaster 1998).

their practical application. Where is the guarantee that the obligations decided upon in the social contract will be effectively met? Let's assume that, following the deliberative process that brought the stakeholders to agree to the social contract, the firm decides to give itself an ethical code, or something similar. What ensures that the self-imposition of some canon of behavior fixed in the ethical code is, in reality, respected? The answer the literature is able to give is based on the mechanism of reputation: The firm that self-inflicts the sanctions called for by the ethical code following defective behavior will see its reputational capital grow in the eyes of all of its stakeholders and this will improve its economic performance, for obvious reasons.

As Sacconi has observed (2004), things would happen this way if it weren't for the fact that the reputational mechanism suffers from grave cognitive fragility. It requires a perfect awareness by stakeholders, and in particular consumers and civil society, in order for them to be able to determine that what was supposed to have been done, was done. On the other hand, one can't forget that the ethical horizon of contractualism is always that of axiological individualism, according to which the normative foundation is the impartial agreement of rational individuals. In other words, in the contractualist view, rational individuals realize that it is in their interest – whatever that may be – to agree on common norms of behavior to avoid phenomena such as free-riding, shirking, the many difficulties of coordination. This is tantamount to saying that the ethical code is visualized as a *rational constraint* that the firm imposes on itself. It is nonetheless always a constraint. And therefore if, given the contextual conditions, there is a chance of transgressing the norms without penalty, i.e., without tarnishing the firm's reputation, this will occur.

2.4 The Ethics of Virtues

It is at this point that the fourth ethical theory to which I referred at the beginning of the section comes into play. This is the ethic of virtues, as Adam Smith, on the heels of the line of thought inaugurated by the civil humanists in the 15th century, elaborated in his fundamental work *The Theory Moral Sentiments* (1759). The institutional structure of society – says Smith – must favor the dissemination among citizens of the civic virtues. If economic agents don't already embody in their structure of preferences those values that they are supposed to respect, there isn't much to be done. For the ethic of virtues, in fact, the enforceability of the norms depends, in the first place, on the moral constitution of individuals; that is, of their internal motivational structure, long before any system of exogenous enforcement. It is because there are stakeholders with ethical preferences – who value the fact that the firm practices equity and works for the dignity of people *independently* of the material advantage that can be derived – that the ethical code can be respected *also*, even in the absence of the mechanism of reputation. And that there are subjects endowed with ethical preferences is, today, a fact documented by research.[3]

Consider, to give just one example, the relationship between a company and its employees. As is well known, this relationship can assume the forms of "social exchange" or "market exchange." In the former case, nonmaterial elements such as loyalty, honesty, and attachment to the mission enter into play. These elements cannot be negotiated, since they are non-verifiable. In the latter case, everything passes through the definition of "optimal" incentive schemes. Now, everyone realizes that there is a great difference, as far as the company performance is concerned, between the two types of relationships. But it is evident that the worker will enter into a "social exchange" instead of a "market exchange" only if the firm appears to him or her a moral subject that believes in and puts into practice the principle of reciprocity.

The point worth highlighting is that the key to the ethic of virtues is its capacity to resolve the opposition between self interest and interest for others, between egoism and altruism, by moving beyond it. It is this opposition, child of the individualistic tradition of thought, that prevents us from grasping that which constitutes our own well-being. The virtuous life is the best not only for others – like the various economic theories of altruism would have it – but also for us. This is the real significance of the notion of common good, which can never be reduced to a mere sum-total of individual well-beings. Instead, the common good is the good of being in common. That is, it is the good of being inserted into a structure of common action, which is exactly what the firm represents.

Viola (2004) suggests that common is the action that, in order to be carried out, requires both the *intentional* coming together of many subjects (and of which all the participants are aware) and of inter-subjective relationships that lead to a certain unification of efforts. More precisely, there are three elements that distinguish a common action. The first is that it cannot be concluded without all those who take part being conscious of what they are doing. The mere coming together or meeting of many individuals is not enough. The second element is that each participant in the common action must retain title, and therefore responsibility, for that which he does. It is exactly

3 For a review see Fehr and Fischbacher (2002) and the essays in Sacco and Zamagni (2002).

this element that differentiates common action from collective action. In the latter, the individual's identity disappears and with it the personal responsibility for the action. The third element is the unification of the efforts on the part of the participants in the common action for the achievement of the same objective. The interaction among many subjects in a given context is not yet common activity if they follow diverse or conflicting objectives. Therefore, the firm, inasmuch as it possesses all three of these elements, represents a common action.

Diverse are the types of common action in relation to the object of commonness. The commonness, in fact, can realize itself around the means or around the ends of the action itself. When the commonness is extended to the end of the action – as happens in the firm – the final result of the action has the nature of a true joint product. This means that it is *de facto* impossible to determine the specific contribution of each stakeholder. This was attempted more than a century ago by the neoclassical theory of distribution of income with the principle of marginal productivity of factors; but with rather scarce success as we know, nowadays (Screpanti and Zamagni 2005). Note that, while in the contract – which is another example of common action – the commonness is limited to the means (each party accepts that the other will pursue his/her own ends, even if the ends are not the same), while in the firm the end is realized through common action. This is why in the firm, cooperation – and not coordination – is the principal form that inter-subjectivity assumes. The contracts have to be coordinated, but the stakeholders in a firm must cooperate if they want to achieve an optimal result. The question then arises, How is one to positively resolve a problem of cooperation? Bratman (1999) gives a convincing response when he outlines the following three conditions. In the first place, each participant in the common action assumes that the intentions of others are relevant, and therefore worthy of respect, and knows that this is reciprocal. This is the condition of "mutual responsiveness." It is not enough that the members intend to do the same activity; they must want to do it together. In the second place, each person commits to a joint activity – even if for different reasons – and knows that the others also intend to do the same. This means "commitment to the joint activity," in which it is *de facto* impossible to quantify the specific contribution of each person to the joint product. Finally, each person commits to helping others in their efforts so that the final result will be the best possible "commitment to mutual support." Reciprocal aid must manifest itself while the joint activity is being carried out, not *a latere*, nor at the end of the activity. Such a commitment should not be confused with self-interest, nor with disinterested altruism. There is a connection of interests; by providing help to others one pursues one's own interests.

Now we can appreciate the specific value that the ethic of virtues offers us, which is to liberate us from the obsessive Platonic idea of Good, an idea that says there is an *a priori* good from which an ethic is extracted to be used as a guide to our actions. Aristotle – the initiator of the ethic of virtues – in total disagreement with Plato, indicates instead that the good is something that happens, that is realized through activities. As Lutz (2003) puts it, the most serious problem with the various theories of business ethics stemming from the individualistic tradition of thought is that they are not capable of offering a reason for "being ethical." If it's not good for us to behave ethically, why do what is recommended by ethics? On the other hand, if it *is* good for us to "be ethical," then why would it be necessary to offer managers incentives for doing that which is in their own interest to do? The solution to the problem of moral motivation of managers is not that of setting constraints (or providing incentives)[4] for acting against their self-interest, but to offer them a more complete understanding of their own well-being. Only when ethics becomes part of the objective-function of the agents does moral motivation cease to be a problem, because we are authentically motivated to do that which we believe is best for ourselves.

This is why cultivating civic virtues is the undeniable task not only from the point of view of citizenship – something known for a long time – but also from the point of view of CSR. Since institutions, contrary to what the theorists of market fundamentals think, influence economic performance also in the long term, the task is to intervene in the institutional setup of society in order to encourage – and not penalize, as happens stupidly today – the largest possible dissemination of civic virtues through education and actual deeds. The results will then follow, notwithstanding what the skeptic thinks. For the skeptic the managers, under pressure from the movement of ideas that have come about around CSR, will attempt to imitate or mimic behavior inspired by the ethic of virtues, while continuing to not really believe. This way – the skeptic reasons – market competition will select in accordance with those stated values proven to be most profitable. Today we know, both theoretically and empirically, that things do not proceed this way. The "cynical" manager who, without believing it, behaves like a "virtuous" manager will sooner or later begin to perceive himself/herself as *homo reciprocans* – just as the theory of self-attribution teaches (Schlicht 2002) – and stop behaving in a merely opportunistic way. Therefore, if the market is capable of "recompensating" in a coherent way what I call the civil culture of the firm,

4 One observes that an incentive, like a constraint, is always the expression of a relationship of power. That which changes is only the form with which the power is expressed.

in the long run both the dispositional and the motivational structure of the economic agents – managers included – will adapt as a consequence. This is not an insignificant advantage of the approach, of moral evolution according to which the affirmation of the values of CSR ultimately depend on the process through which these values are edified as virtues.

References

Arrow, K., 1973. "Social responsibility and economic efficiency." *Public Policy*, Vol. 21, 303–318.

Baumann, Z., 1992. *Modernità e Olocausto.* Il Mulino, Bologna.

Beltratti, A., 2003. "Socially responsible investment in general equilibrium." Fond. E. Matteri WP, Milano.

Bratman, M., 1999. "Shared cooperative activity." In: *Faces of Intention.* Cambirdge University Press, Cambridge.

Bruni, L. and Zamagni, S., 2004. *Economia Civile.* Il Mulino, Bologna.

Buchanan, J. and Tullock, G., 1962. *The Calculus of Consent.* University of Michigan Press, Ann Arbor.

Chirieleinson, C., 2004. "L'evoluzione del concetto di corporate social responsibility." In: G. Rusconi and M. Dorigatti (eds), *La responsabilità sociale di impresa.* F. Angeli, Milano.

Cochran, T.C., 1964. *The Inner Revolution.* Harper & Row, New York.

Evan, W. and Freeman, R.E., 1988. *Ethical Theory and Business.* Prentice Hall, Englewood Cliffs.

Fehr, E. and Fischbacher, V., 2002. "Why social prefernces matter. The impact of non-selfish motives on competition, cooperation and incentives." *The Economic Journal*, Vol. 112.

Friedman, M., 1962. *Capitalism and Freedom.* University of Chicago Press, Chicago.

Friedman, M., 1993. "The social responsibility of business is to increase its profits." In: G.D. Chrissides and J.H. Keler (eds), *An Introduction to Business Ethics.* Chapman, London.

Goodpaster, K., 1998. "Business ethics and stakeholder analysis." In: K. Goodpaster and L. Nash (eds) *Corporations, Persons and Morality*. Free Press, New York.

Jonas, H., 1990. *Il principio responsabilità*. Einaudi, Torino.

Lutz, D., 2003. "Beyond business ethics." *Oikonomia*, Vol. 2.

Peter, F., 2004. "Choice, consent and the legitimacy of market transactions." *Economics and Philosophy*, Vol. 20, 1–18.

Picard, J.F., 1999. *La Foundation Rochefeller et la Recherche Midicale*. PUF, Paris.

Posner, R., 1981. *The Economics of Justice*. Harvard University Press, Cambridge (MA).

Rostow, E.V., 1961. "To whom and for what ends is corporate management responsible?" In: E.S. Mason (ed.) *The Corporation in Modern Society*. Harvard University Press, Cambridge (MA).

Sacci, P. and Zamagni, S. (eds), 2002. *Complessità relazionale e comportamento economico*. Il Mulino, Bologna.

Sacconi, L., 2003. "L'autoregolazione dell'economia via norme etiche." *Etica e Economia*, 1–2.

Sacconi, L., 2004. "Responsabilità sociale come governance allargata d'impresa." In: G. Rusconi and M. Dorigatti (eds) *La responsabilità sociale dell'impresa*. F. Angeli, Milano.

Schlicht, E., 2002. "Social evolution, corporate culture and exploitation." IZA DP GS1, Nov.

Sen, A., 1988. "Freedom of choice: concept and content." *European Economic Review*, Vol. 32, 280–299.

Sen, A., 1999. *Development as Freedom*. Random House,New York.

Schleifer, A., 2004. "Does competition destroy ethical behaviour?" NBER, WP10269, Genn.

Screpanti, E. and Zamagni, S., 2005. *An Outline of the History of Economic Thought*. Oxford University Press, Oxford.

Steinberg, E., 2000. *Just Business Ethics in Action*. Oxford University Press, Oxford.

Viola, F., 2004. "Il modello della cooperazione." University Di Palermo. (Mimeo).

Weber, M., 1969. *Il lavoro intellettuale come professione*. A. Giolitti (ed.). Einaudi, Torino.

Yaari, M., 1977. "Endogenous changes of tastes." *Erkenntnis*, Vol. 11.

Zamagni, S., 2003. "L'impresa socialmente responsabile nell'epoca della globalizzazione." *Notizie di Politeia*, Vol. 72.

Zamagni, S., 2005. "La critica delle critiche alla CSR e il suo ancoraggio etico." In: L. Sacconi (ed.) *Guida Critica alla Responsabilità Sociale e al Governo d'impresa*, Bancaria Editrice, Roma.

Zingales, L., 1998. "Corporate Governance." In: *New Palgrave Dictionary of Economics and Law*. MacMillan, London.

Zuns, O., 2002. *Perché il secolo americano?* Il Mulino, Bologna.

Stefano Zamagni

Stefano Zamagni was born on January 4, 1943, in the city of Rimini, Italy. He graduated from the Catholic University in Milan in 1966. He did post-graduate studies at the University of Oxford (1969–73) under the supervision of John Hicks and Peter Hammond.

In 1966 he became an assistant lecturer at the Catholic University, a post he held until 1969. Later, from 1973 to 1979, he was a professor at the University of Parma. Since 1979, he has been a professor at the University of Bologna. Additional career-related activities in which Professor Zamagni has been involved include serving as a visiting professor at the University of Bocconi (Milan) since 1985, and as an adjunct professor at Johns Hopkins University (Bologna Center) since 1983. He has been director of the Department of Economics at the University of Bologna since 1982 and acted as chairman from 1985 to 1993. Moreover, he was dean of the Faculty of Economics from 1993 to 1996 and a visiting professor at the State Victoria Bank of Deakin University in Australia.

Professor Zamagni is the author of several books, including *Microeconomic Theory* and *Civil Economy* and *Paradoxes of Growth*, both published in 1997. In addition, he has co-authored *History of Economic Thought*, OUP, 1995 and 2005; *Living in the Global Society*, 1997; *Non-Profit As Civil Economy*, 1998; *Economics; An European Text*, 2002; *Multiculturalism and Identity*, 2002;

Relational Complexity and Economic Behaviour, 2002; *The Italian Non-profit at the Crossroad*, 2002; *Civil Economy*, 2004; and *A Civil Economic Theory of Cooperative Firm*, 2005.

He was named the McDonnel Distinguished Scholar in Helsinki in 1992 and a Paul Harris Fellow by Rotary International in 1995. He was the recipient of the St. Vincent Economics Prize from Aosta Valley Regional Goverment in 1989, the Capri Economics Prize from the Association of the Development of Social Sciences in 1996, the Golden Sigismondo Prize from the Municipality of Rimini in 1997, and the Gold Medal of the International Center Pio Manzu in 1998. He has also been named an honorary citizen of the City of Rosario (Argentina).

Professor Zamagni was a member of the Executive Committee of International Economy Association (1989–1999) and the Steering Committee of Pontifical Academy of Social Sciences. He is a fellow of the Academy of Sciences of Milan, the Academy of Sciences of Bologna and the Academy of Sciences of Modena. He is also a fellow of the New York Academy of Sciences, New York. He is president of ICMC (an NGO based in Geneva dealing with migrant and refugee issues) and member of the Executive Committee of FIVOL (The Italian Foundation for Volunteer Activities). He also values active civic participation.

Werner Ulrich
University of Fribourg and The Open University, Milton Keynes

Critical Pragmatism: A New Approach to Professional and Business Ethics

Major contemporary conceptions of ethics such as discourse ethics and neo-contractarian ethics are not grounded in a sufficiently pragmatic notion of practice. They suffer from serious problems of application and thus can hardly be said to respond to the needs of professionals and decision makers. A main reason lies in the tendency of these approaches to focus more on the requirements of ethical universalization than on those of doing justice to particular contexts of action – at the expense of practicality and relevance to practitioners. If this diagnosis is not entirely mistaken, a major methodological challenge for professional and business ethics consists in finding a new balance between ethical universalism and ethical contextualism. A reformulation of the pragmatic maxim (the methodological core principle of American pragmatism) in terms of systematic boundary critique (the methodological core principle of the author's work on critical systems thinking and reflective professional practice) may provide a framework to this end, *critical pragmatism.*

1. Introduction: The Unsolved Problem of Grounding Ethical Practice

Pragmatism unstiffens all our theories.

William James
(James 1907, 21)

Most approaches to professional and business ethics, different as they are, share a basic assumption: They seek to ground ethical practice in ethical theory. There is nothing wrong with this idea, except that it doesn't work. Regardless of which theoretical conception of ethics we use, ethical practice requires strong judgments about the situation at hand: Why and in what way does this situation pose an ethical problem? What are the relevant circumstances and considerations? How should we weight conflicting concerns? *Whose* concerns are they, that is, who should be considered a legitimate stakeholder? Ethical theory can (ideally) provide us with basic principles or general norms of ethical action; but, because there is hardly ever a single right way to define an ethical problem, general norms cannot tell us which specific concerns and stakeholders "count" in a concrete context of action. At best, "we" – a group of involved people – can agree; but still, "our" definitions need not be the same as "yours" and "theirs." That was of course Kant's point when he invented the principle of ethical universalization (or generalization) as the highest expression of practical reason. The categorical imperative[1] should provide any agent of good will with a guideline for taking the notional step from "my" (or "our") to "their" point of view.

Theoretical developments such as Rawls' (1971) neo-contractarian approach and Apel (1973, 1976) and Habermas' (1983, 1991) language-analytical approach have shed some new light on the significance of Kant's idea;[2] however, the basic difficulty remains the same. The universalization principle is an idea that *explains,* but does

1 "Act so that you can will that the maxim of your action be made the principle of a universal law." (Kant 1788, A 54, similarly 1786, B 52).

2 It certainly can be debated to what extent these approaches meet Kant's intent; I have found Wolff (1977) and Höffe (1984) useful examinations of the question in the case of Rawls, and Wellmer (1986) in the case of Apel and Habermas. For a detailed account of my understanding of Habermas and of the way in which my work on critical heuristics departs from him, see Ulrich (1983, Ch. 2, 106–172).

not *solve,* the problem of moral action. It elucidates the moral idea by answering the question, What does moral action mean, *in principle?* That is, What kind of argument could substantiate a claim to the moral rightness of an action? The answer is something like this: An action is morally justified (or "right") when its normative content is generalizable and therefore deserves recognition by everyone. The difficulty lies in the "everyone": it includes all conceivably concerned parties, here and there, now and in future; which is to say, there is no natural limit to the group of people whose concerns we have to consider. The point is – and this makes universalization a necessary element of ethical reasoning – only thus can we be *certain* that no parties will be affected in ways that might harm their dignity. *The thrust of the moral idea is a de-contextualizing one*; it obliges us to look beyond the context of action that is of immediate concern to us. This "looking beyond" is therefore a necessary methodological principle of all ethical reasoning. But of course, the principle is recursive in nature: Whatever larger context we consider, we will again need to expand it, and so on, until we have included all conceivably concerned parties. Ethical reasoning bursts *any* particular context that we might be prepared to consider or take for granted. In this expansionist, de-centering, and ultimately de-contextualizing consequence resides the *holistic kernel* of the moral idea.

It follows that we cannot equate *ethical practice* with the moral idea in any direct, uncomplicated way. The moral idea is a standard of ethical perfection; ethical practice is a reasoned state of ethical imperfection. The power of the moral idea consists in helping us to understand why all human practice is morally imperfect, but certainly not in offering us a device for claiming the very contrary – that a particular action is moral. Let us not, therefore, mistake the principle of universalization for a *methodological device* that would allow us to justify specific norms in particular contexts of action. This is the basic illusion to which any "application" of discourse ethics (or of other forms of strict ethical universalism) risks succumbing. Methodologically speaking, the universalization principle has no justification power whatsoever!

Nor should we fall into the other extreme and blame the universalization principle for *causing* the difficulties of which it only reminds us. That would merely mean to shut our eyes to the theoretical level of insight achieved by Kant and contemporary ethical theorists, without gaining anything for handling the difficulties they help us understand. At issue is not the universalization principle as such but only the role we give it in the quest for grounding ethical practice. We tend to assign it a role that no theoretical insight into the in-principle requirements of moral action can fulfill, namely, that of a guarantor of ethical practice in concrete contexts of action. We tend to forget that the principle embodies a theoretically powerful *diagnosis* of the problem of moral action, but not its *solution.* No kind of theoretical insight can secure holistic practice, as there *is* no theoretical solution.

In spite – or perhaps because – of its theoretical sophistication, the discourse on discourse ethics and on how to "apply" it appears to have lost sight of what ethical practice is all about, namely, *dealing reasonably with conditions of necessarily imperfect rationality and morality.* From a practical rather than theoretical perspective, *it is the very tension between the un(w)holy nature of all practice and the holistic implications of the universalization principle that constitutes the problem of grounding ethical practice.* Leave out either side and you have no practical moral problem at all.

If this observation is not entirely mistaken, we may be well-advised to *look for an alternative understanding of the principle of universalization.* As a strategy for grounding ethical practice, I propose that we look for ways to *maintain the tension* between the theoretical requirement of universalization on the one hand and the practical requirement of coming to terms with conditions of imperfect rationality and morality on the other hand, rather than focusing on any one requirement. Ethical practice then is to be understood as a systematic effort to manage that tension in ways that are conducive to ethically alert practice.

Consequently, we will have to renounce the ideal of a theory-based justification of ethical practice (or of underlying norms of action). This price is easy to pay, however, once we accept that as a matter of principle, there can be no such justification at all. What we gain, on the other hand, is essential for grounding ethical practice: We can bring back into the picture the role of the *context,* from which the universalization principle had to abstract but which in practice is indispensable for understanding ethical issues and arguing moral claims. Accordingly, our notion of "grounding" ethical practice will change. Rather than seeking generic theoretical criteria of moral action, we will seek practicable ways of dealing critically with particular contexts of action. Once we accept that we cannot ultimately justify particular norms of action through ethical theory, the central issue becomes this: How can we accomplish at least a *critical solution to the problem of practical reason*, that is, make sure that we do

3 The idea of an at least critical solution to the problem of practical reason is fundamental to my work on critical heuristics of social practice, as distinguished from critical theory of society. For a detailed comparison of the differing aims and assumptions of these two programs of research, see the section titled "Conclusions: Critical Theory or Critical Heuristics?" in Ulrich (1983), 152–172.

not succumb to an illusion of sufficient justification?[3] A critical solution does not yield any positive justification of normative validity claims; instead, it helps us in dealing openly and honestly with the unavoidable *lack* of sufficient justification.

This, then, is the logic of the proposed argument: The first basic step towards a satisfactory framework for professional and business ethics consists in searching for a new methodological balance between the theoretical principle of universalization on the one hand and the practical requirement of doing justice to the context of application on the other hand. I will argue that a *pragmatist view of ethics*, following the philosophy of American pragmatism (esp. Peirce and James), has much to offer in this respect (Section 2). A second essential step consists in taking the concept of a critical solution seriously, by facing the need for a *critical turn* of a pragmatically oriented practical philosophy (Section 3). Taken together, these two steps lead to a framework for ethically alert practice that I would like to describe as *critical pragmatism*; its methodological core principle is the principle of *boundary critique*, which I will briefly introduce in the concluding section (Section 4).

2. Back to the Pragmatic Roots of Ethical Practice

To know what we think, to be masters of our own meaning, will make a solid foundation for great and weighty thought.

Charles S. Peirce
(Peirce 1878, par. 393)

If there is any philosophical tradition that may help us strike a balance between the divergent requirements of ethical universalism and ethical contextualism, it may be American *pragmatism.* As the term is prone to misinterpretation in the sense of epistemological subjectivism and ethical utilitarianism or even a denial of philosophical reflection in favor of plain commonsense and managerialism, I should immediately point out that I associate with pragmatism a much-neglected *critical kernel.* In the present section, I would like to explore this critical kernel by going back to the roots of pragmatic thinking in the works of Kant and C.S. Peirce and, in addition, drawing on the ideas of W. James and C.W. Churchman.

2.1 Kant: Practical Reason – "Pure" and "Pragmatic"

It was Immanuel Kant (1724–1804),[4] the father of Critical Philosophy, who first used the term "pragmatic" as a modern philosophical term, along with the term "practical reason." In one of the concluding sections of the *Critique of Pure Reason*, he introduced a distinction between the *pure* and the *pragmatic* employment of *practical* reason. "By 'the practical'," he explained in his inimitable terseness, "I mean everything that is possible through freedom," that is, through the exercise of our free will (Kant 1781, B 828). Practical reason is "pure" when it determines the will entirely *a priori*, so that its rules of conduct are not conditioned by any empirical contingencies. The moral employment of reason is necessarily oriented towards pure practical reason; for its task is to identify rules of action that "are prescribed to us not in an empirically conditioned but in an absolute manner ... such are the *moral* laws" (1781, B 828).

> When, however, the conditions of the exercise of our free will are empirical, reason can have no other than a regulative employment in regard to it, and can serve only to effect unity in its empirical laws.[5] ... In this field, therefore, reason can supply none but *pragmatic* laws of free action, for the attainment of those ends which are commended to us by the senses; it cannot yield us laws that are pure and determined completely a priori. [Kant 1781, B 828]

That is to say, practical reason is "pragmatic" whenever it is not pure. The task that then remains for moral reasoning is to discipline pragmatic reasoning with a view to giving "systematic unity" to our acts of free will (B 835f), so that we have "ground to hope for happiness" (B 837) – in other words, so that we may not only achieve but *deserve* happiness (B 834).

In the light of our introductory discussion, Kant's reference to the pragmatic employment of practical reason gains a new significance. As soon as we redefine the moral problem in terms of how we can ground ethical practice *under real-world conditions of imperfect rationality*, it follows that all real-world employment of practical reason is inevitably pragmatic. Morality as *pure* practical reason is a "heuristic fiction" (B 799) that cannot become a lived reality, except in conjunction with a pragmatic

4 The reader will find a detailed account of my understanding of Kant in chapters 3–5 of *Critical Heuristics*, see Ulrich (1983, 175–314).

5 Read "laws" as referring to "rules of conduct" or "rules of action."

orientation. When we act morally, we act not only as rational beings belonging to the world of thought and free will, but also as agents exercising causality in the world of empirical conditions. There is no other way we can bring the ideational moment of "pure" morality into practice. Strictly speaking (although Kant does not say it in this way) the pure employment of practical reason is merely a *limiting case of practical reason,* as is its opposite of a merely empirical orientation. *Between* these two limiting cases lies the range of ethical practice, and it is coextensive with pragmatic reason.

2.2 Peirce: The "Pragmatic Maxim"

Enter Charles S. Peirce (1839–1914),[6] the "American Kant" and – together with William James – the founder of American pragmatism. A chemist and mathematician of academic training as well as a practicing geodetic, his chief interests were in logic and semiotics, the theory of signs that he was pioneering.[7] In his 1878 essay "How to make our ideas clear," Peirce named his proposal for a method of clarifying our thinking *pragmatic*, primarily in experimental science and mathematics but also (informed by it) in everyday "opinion-settling." His concern was to develop a kind of logic – we would today call it a logic of inquiry – that would go beyond the "old trivialities" of traditional logic and would recognize that "nothing new can ever be learned by analyzing definitions" (1878, par. 392). In order to support processes of learning and opinion settling beyond a mere analysis of definitions, an adequate logic was needed to put us in touch with reality; it could not remain in the Kantian realm of "pure" thought and *a priori* principles.

Peirce saw two basic requirements for such a logic. First, it needed to understand reality as something that was ultimately independent of thought, so that it could serve as a touchstone for the meaning and validity of our ideas. Second, it needed to understand inquiry as a public, intersubjective and societal rather than individual, process; as an effort of a *community of inquirers* that was indefinite in space and time, so that the results of inquiry could be independent of individual assumptions. Thus, although what is understood to be true at any specific moment in time is a function

6 For a first brief overview of Peirce's extensive writings, see Burch (2001); for a biographical background, see Menand (2001), esp. Ch. 7. Specifically on the comparison of Peirce's early and later pragmatism, Atkin (2005) provides a helpful short account.

7 The name "semiotics" was suggested by Morris (1938).

of a particular context of knowledge that is defined by contingent historical, cultural, and socioeconomic conditions, it must also make room for the future and include anticipated or conceivable new findings of inquiry. Peirce therefore insisted on a definition of truth that bursts any contextual contingencies. Truth, he argued, is that conception of reality on which a community of inquirers will agree *in the long run*:

> The opinion which is fated to be ultimately agreed to by all who investigate, is what we mean by the truth, and the object represented in this opinion is the real. That is the way I would explain reality. [Peirce 1878, par. 407]

I find this a surprisingly modern conception of a pragmatic logic of inquiry indeed. Particularly interesting and relevant to our present purpose is not only its *discursive* character but also its implicit recognition of the *contextual* nature of all claims to truth and reality: the real is defined within an argumentative context. The argumentative element, due to its intrinsic reference to an indefinite future, points *beyond* the contingencies of any actual context; but that does not alter the fact that any conception of the real, any truth claim, is conditioned by the current context of inquiry and therefore requires careful attention to the empirical circumstances that constitute this inescapable contextual element. I find it helpful, therefore, to think of Peirce's philosophical method as an early – however insufficient – form of *hermeneutic contextualism*.[8] In order to capture an author's significance, what matters most is not so much the details of his writings but the vision that speaks to us through them. I understand Peirce's vision of inquiry to be an open (we might also say public) community of research engaged in an unending, because forever imperfect and fallible, quest for knowledge. Both empirical science and discursive efforts at reaching mutual understanding are inextricably involved in the quest, and both efforts are at all times conditioned by their inescapably contextual nature; we do not observe but (together) *make* truth. The community of inquiry – the scientific community – is always at the same time a community of interpretation, that is, a *hermeneutic community*.

This was a thoroughly new concept of inquiry then; I would dare to say it anticipated later developments in phenomenological, hermeneutic, and existential philosophy, and perhaps even in postmodern thinking, however unhappy Peirce might have become about such prospects. But this is only one side of the coin. The

8 I follow here a suggestion by Oehler (1968), 151.

other shows a totally different picture. His conception of the logic of inquiry as an "experiential method of settling opinion" (Peirce 1878, par. 406), along with the experimentalist and operational thrust of his thinking, clearly also paved the way to the logical positivism of the Vienna Circle and to contemporary fallibilist (or falsificationist) science-theory as pioneered by Popper's (1959) "critical rationalism."[9] But what at first may look like a somewhat ambivalent philosophical legacy is actually an expression of what I find particularly thought-provoking and relevant in Peirce's logic of inquiry today, namely, that it builds a bridge between "scientific" and "hermeneutic" thinking and thus can help us to overcome the persisting divide between the "two cultures" (Snow 1959) of the natural sciences and the humanities.

The essence of Peirce's method is condensed in his well-known *pragmatic maxim*:

> Consider what effects, that might conceivably have practical bearings, we conceive the object of our conception to have. Then, our conception of these effects is the whole of our conception of the object. [Peirce 1878, par. 402]

That is to say, the meaning of an idea or proposition is our concept of all its possible effects – the sum-total of the consequences we associate with it, whether in everyday life (e.g., changes in the way we experience or "see" things, of the beliefs we hold, or the kind of actions we deem reasonable and ethical) or in science (e.g, new experimental consequences). Hence, what an idea means is a function of the *difference* it makes to us as compared to other ideas. To be sure, we may not *know* what difference it will actually make, but if we don't know what difference we *expect* (or in Peirce's terms, *conceive*) it to make, we do not think or argue clearly. There can be no meaningful distinction of ideas or propositions without *anticipating* some difference in practice, as not only the truth but also "the rational meaning of every proposition lies in the future" (Peirce 1905, 173, par. 427).

Nevertheless, Peirce makes a clear distinction between constitution of meaning and validity. We may fail to anticipate all the effects in question properly. Only an intersubjective process of inquiry can, in the long run, establish the validity of such

9 I would argue, though, that Popper's conception of fallibilism does not live up to that of Peirce, for Popper reduced fallibilism (once again) to a merely deductive – rather than pragmatic – logic of inquiry. I have given a detailed account and critique of Popper as I understand him elsewhere (see Ulrich 1983, 41–105).

anticipations and related claims to knowledge and rationality. Pragmatism for Peirce is thus not equated with subjectivism and utilitarianism. Peirce's point is not subjectivism but *intellectual clarity*; the implication for our present purpose is not utilitarianism but *contextualism*.

By *contextualism* I mean a philosophical attitude that gives careful attention to the particular context of knowledge and action in which an issue arises, with a view to understanding the way this context conditions all claims to knowledge and rationality. With regard to ethics, we may distinguish contextualist from universalist approaches. While Kant is the prime proponent of ethical universalism, I consider Peirce to be a prime source for ethical contextualism, although Peirce himself (as far as I know) did not apply the pragmatic maxim to ethics. I would argue that the pragmatic maxim implies a *contextualist turn of ethics,* for two reasons: first, because the "practical bearings" of a claim pose a relevant ethical issue; and second, because they cannot be understood and evaluated properly except by considering the difference we expect them to make in real-world contexts of knowledge and action.

With a view to grounding ethical practice, I therefore associate with the pragmatic maxim a critical *methodological intent*: It might serve as a *corrective to any one-sided ethical universalism*, such as, for instance, that of discourse ethics. This is not to throw ethical universalism entirely overboard; of course not. Ethical contextualism *alone* is hardly more practical than universalism. The pragmatic maxim, if we take it seriously and don't forget about the issue of validity, has its own, similar difficulties. What does it mean to consider *all* the practical bearings that we may anticipate an idea or a claim to have? There is no natural boundary to the context that defines the "all." Pragmatism leads us back to ethical universalism, albeit in a new way. It clearly breaks through the Kantian de-contextualization of ethics in that it implies a need for considering *concrete* contexts, however remote they may be from the context of interest to us. At the same time, though, no particular context can be said to be the only conceivable or relevant one for judging a claim; hence, we cannot be content to look at any current context *only* but must equally consider alternative contexts – more precisely, all alternative contexts that conceivably may cast a different light on the claim! Not unlike the principle of universalization, then, the pragmatic maxim has strong holistic implications; but they concern the process of inquiry as a whole rather than the content of any single claim. The holistic implications of the pragmatic maxim, for me, translate into methodological pluralism rather than de-contextualization.

My conclusion is that the pragmatic maxim, properly understood, both *requires* and *enables* us to integrate ethical universalism with ethical contextualism. Rather than seeking to ground ethical practice in either perspective alone, we need to find a methodologically clear and practicable way for them to support one another.

2.3 James: The "Pragmatic Attitude"

William James (1842–1910)[10] first publicized the name "pragmatism" in 1898 (James 1989), although he (respectfully but erroneously) ascribed its first use to Peirce (1878). Pragmatism largely owes its rise and popularity to James, who saved Peirce's pragmatic maxim from 20 years of total oblivion. If I had to summarize the significance of his contribution in a phrase, I would say that he took Peirce's pragmatism out of the experimental scientist's laboratory and related it to the world of human affairs in general. For James, a man of wide-ranging interests, a physician as well as a self-trained psychologist and philosopher, it made little sense to limit the pragmatic method to the object domain of empirical science; taking it seriously meant applying it equally to everyday experience and to the inner, psychological world that conditions it. We cannot separate the meaning of our ideas, claims or actions from our inner world of who we are and how we relate to others.[11] Thus Peirce's "practical bearings" must include the difference that an idea makes to our worldviews, beliefs, and emotions; to our self-perception as much as to our interpersonal relationships. *Making sense of ordinary experience* is the subject matter in which James excels.

Due to this interest, the pragmatic maxim gained a new significance. Its role was no longer limited to that of a criterion of meaning, it now also became a criterion of truth and validity in general. Since absolute truth in an ontological sense is not available, the best way we can judge the validity of an idea is by whether it "fits," is "expedient" or "works," that is, whether it makes the kind of difference in real life we expect it to make and insofar proves "satisfactory" or demonstrates its "cash value." James liked to use such psychological and commercial phrases, and they have led many commentators to accuse him of epistemological psychologism and subjectivist ethical utilitarianism. Regarding utilitarianism, I do not think the accusation does justice to his intentions. At the heart of his conception of truth lies epistemological *instrumentalism* rather than utilitarianism:

10 For a useful and easily available first overview, see, Goodman (2003); for a biographical background, compare Menand (2001), esp. Chapters 4 and 13.

11 See James (1899) for a beautiful expression of this thought.

> 'Truth' in our ideas and beliefs means the same thing that it means in science.... [They] become true just in so far as they help us to *get into satisfactory relation with other parts of our experience*, to summarize them and get about among them by conceptual short-cuts instead of following the interminable succession of particular phenomena. Any idea upon which we can ride, so to speak; any idea that will carry us prosperously from any one part of our experience to any other part, linking things satisfactorily, working securely, simplifying, saving labor; is true for just so much, true in so far forth, true *instrumentally.* This is the 'instrumental' view of truth.... [Peirce 1907, 23; 2000, 30, italics modified]

James demonstrates the explanatory force of this instrumental view of truth (and the way he means to use it) with the example of how new truths come to be accepted. When a new observation is incompatible with old ones, yet irrefutable, we will revise our ideas about the subject just so much as is necessary to integrate the new finding into the stock of established ideas with a minimum of disturbance:

> New truth is always a go-between, a smoother-over of transitions. It marries old opinion to new fact so as ever to show a minimum of jolt, a maximum of continuity. We hold a theory true just in proportion to its success in solving this 'problem of maxima and minima'.... 'To be true' *means* only to perform this marriage-function. [James 1907, 24 and 26; 2000, 31 and 33]

The reproach of epistemological psychologism is less easy to refute. Obviously James approached epistemological questions from a psychological perspective. For example, the instrumental view of truth for him indeed meant that "when old truth grows ... by new truth's addition, it is for subjective reasons" (James 1907, 25; 2000, 32). But then, is this so wrong? Fairness demands that we recognize that James dealt with epistemological issues for which epistemology itself had, and still has, no definite solutions. James' aim was not to *reduce* these issues to psychological ones but, rather, to help us deal pragmatically with the *lack* of epistemological answers. He is the messenger who brings us the bad news; blaming the messenger for the bad news is never particularly helpful.

What I find more problematic about James' conception of truth is that he tends to claim too much for it. He presents it as if instrumental validity amounted to validity in general, including ethical and metaphysical validity. Compared to Peirce's extension of the experimental model to a discursive theory of truth in science, James' *direct* extension of the pragmatic maxim to a general theory of truth in all domains of experience looks methodologically unsophisticated. It refers decisions on validity to subjective *acts of belief* rather than to intersubjective argument. It thus fails to tell us how we can justify or criticize validity claims *rationally*, and hence represents no methodological achievement at all. The implication is that virtually any idea is capable of truth, including metaphysical claims about the existence of God, free will, determinism, and so on.

But James had a point: questions of meaning and of validity are indeed interdependent. We can meaningfully – and credibly – claim an idea's validity only within the contexts in which we previously examined its meaning. The omnipresent symptom of unexpected "side-effects" of our policies and technologies illustrates the scope of the issue. I suspect the issue is not usually the job of the experts who investigated the effects in question but rather, lacking clarity regarding relevant contexts and inadequate inference from one context to another. James got it right: the *epistemological* implication of the pragmatic maxim is that for all practical purposes, we must not separate questions of validity from questions of meaning. He may have drawn the wrong conclusions from this insight, but it certainly represents a genuinely epistemological, rather than merely psychological, employment of the pragmatic maxim.

Another interesting consequence of pragmatism as James understood it is this: For him, even more than for Peirce, it did not stand for any particular worldview or doctrine with specific results but for an open-minded *attitude* of "looking forward" to concrete consequences rather than "backwards" to first abstractions. Philosophy for James was never an authority that could provide "the" answers to the questions that move us; rather, it should guide us in working towards *our own* solutions. This is the liberating, even emancipatory aspect of James' pragmatic thinking. He summed it all up in a few eloquent paragraphs in his lecture "What pragmatism means," from which I would like to offer a short concluding extract here. Although his purpose in the lecture was primarily to demonstrate the relevance of pragmatism for settling unproductive metaphysical disputes, what he said about abstract philosophical concepts applies just as well to the principle of ethical universalization:

> If you follow the pragmatic method, you cannot look on any [philosophical abstraction] as closing your quest. You must … set it at work within the stream of your experience. It appears less as a solution, then, than as a program for more work, and more particularly as an indication of the ways in which exisiting realities may be *changed.*

> *Theories thus become instruments, not answers to enigmas, in which we can rest.* We don't lie back upon them, we move forward, and, on occasion, make nature again by their aid. Pragmatism unstiffens all our theories, limbers them up and sets each one at work....
>
> Against rationalism as a pretension and a method, pragmatism is fully armed and militant. But, at the outset, at least, it stands for no particular results. It has no dogmas, and no doctrines save its method. As the young Italian pragmatist Papini has well said, it lies in the midst of our theories, like a corridor in a hotel. Innumerable chambers open out of it. In one you may find a man writing an atheistic column; in the next someone on his knees praying for faith and strength; in a third a chemist investigating a body's properties.... But they all own the corridor, and all must pass through it if they want a practicable way of getting into or out of their respective rooms.
>
> No particular results then, so far, but only an attitude of orientation, is what the pragmatic method means. *The attitude of looking away from first things, principles, 'categories', supposed necessities; and of looking towards last things, fruits, consequences, facts.* [James 1907, par. 21f; 2000, 28f]

2.4 Churchman: "Ethics of Whole Systems," or the Heroism of Pragmatism

Our last guide to pragmatism is C. West Churchman (1913–2004),[12] research philosopher and founding father of operations research and of the "systems approach," whose student and collaborator I was in the second half of the 1970s at the University of California, Berkeley. Churchman's main philosophical teacher at the University of Pennsylvania, Edgar A. Singer, Jr. (1936; 1959), had been a student of William James.

More than anyone else I know, Churchman took to heart James' credo that in order to make sense of our experience, we must look *away* from first things and supposed necessities, and must instead look *towards* last things and ultimate consequences. For Churchman this meant that in order to understand what an *idea* means, we must ask what *ideal* it implies! Sound inquiry is at the same time experiential and ideal-

12 For a brief overview and appreciation of Churchman's work, see Ulrich (2004a); for more detailed accounts, compare Ulrich (1999) and (2004b), and for a comprehensive bibliography, Ulrich (2002).

seeking. This may be fairly obvious when we talk about professional intervention in situations of problem solving or policymaking with a view to securing improvement; but it also holds for purely empirical questions. In cost accounting, for example, to understand a company's cost of holding inventory, we need to consider what else it could reasonably do with the capital tied up in the inventory. That is, we first need to determine its ideal use of resources! The empirical question of what *is* the inventory cost is at bottom a normative question.

If, then, the inquirer is basically talking in an "ought" mode, we need to apply as much rigor to determining "ideals" as to identifying "facts." Science and ethics ultimately converge. This is where, for Churchman, the *systems idea* comes in. We cannot fully understand the normative implications of our descriptions of the real world or of our designs for improving it unless we carefully explore what they imply for the "larger system," that is, for a wider view of the issue at hand. But of course, this same observation applies to any larger system we may consider, too. We thus need to expand our perspective ever more, until it comprises the "whole" conceivably relevant system. Therein consists for Churchman the basic methodological intent and, at the same time, the basic moral intuition that he associates with systems thinking. These two aspects are inseparable in his conception of a "systems approach" (Churchman 1968, 1971, 1979).

Accordingly, Churchman's (1968, 127–134; 1971, 202–204) moral agent is bound to become a *hero* engaged in an unending quest for learning more and more about the world, so as to "*sweep in*" more and more facets of any particular problem. "Sweeping in" is the methodological core principle that Churchman adopts from his teacher E.A. Singer (1959; compare Churchman 1971, 197f, and 1982, 125f). We here encounter the "forward" looking stance of James' pragmatic attitude in a new form, combined with a strong moral imperative as well as a belief in the power of science. Churchman's preferred way of expressing this stance was through a question:

> How can we design improvement in large systems without understanding the whole system, and if the answer is that we cannot, how is it possible to understand the whole system? [Churchman 1968, 2]

In a world of ever-growing systemic interdependencies, moral action – beyond individual goodwill and mutual understanding – requires an *ethics of whole systems* (Churchman 1968, 4 and 15); for improvement is a property of the whole system.

Throughout his academic life, Churchman struggled with the difficult methodological implications this had for grounding ethical practice. Unfortunately, the "sweep-in" principle could not carry the burden. The more he sought to live up to it, the more it led him into an impasse. An ethically grounded practice of inquiry needed to be conceived in terms of a systems approach, but the ideal-type of sound and rigorous inquiry, science, had no means for accomplishing such an approach.

Churchman ultimately resorted to a *dialectical* resolution of the dilemma, through his concept of the "enemies" of the systems approach (Churchman 1979). "Enemies" are those non-systemic approaches to inquiry and practice which undermine the quest for an ethics of whole systems by elevating their own partial rationalities to the status of the only arbiter of improvement; among them, politics, religion, aesthetics, and morality (the latter insofar as it expresses itself through personal morals rather than ethical reasoning). Yet the systems approach must not commit the same error and make its own perspective the only arbiter; for otherwise it betrays its own quest for comprehensiveness. As Churchman avowed, "what's really happening in the human world is politics, or morality, or religion, or aesthetics" (Churchman 1979, 53). The systems practitioner, then, has no choice but to find ways of incorporating the enemies' viewpoints, even though they undermine his or her notion of rationality.

There is some irony in this call for the systems approach to listen to the partisans of particularism, an irony that reminds us of the work of another pragmatist thinker, Richard Rorty (1989). Whether it is the postmodern "ironic" implications of Churchman's systems thinking or rather its "heroic" holism that kept it from reaching many of those to whom it was addressed – practicing researchers, professionals, and decision makers – I do not know. I find it hardly surprising, though, that his systemic-dialectical pragmatism did not appeal to practitioners as much as it challenged his students. The "sweep-in" principle assumes such an ideal concept of rationality that it cannot provide practical guidance in dealing with real-world conditions of imperfect rationality and conflict. Nevertheless, Churchman's vision of an ethics of whole systems is hardly irrelevant. Can we give it a practical face?

3. Critical Pragmatism: The Critical Turn of Pragmatism

We cannot, by complaining about the narrow limits of reason, escape the responsibility of at least a critical solution to its questions.

Immanuel Kant
(Kant 1781, B 508)[13]

3.1 Redefining the Quest for Comprehensiveness

However indispensable the "sweep-in" principle may be from the vantage points of both epistemological and ethical theorizing – methodologically speaking, it is helpless. Not even the most comprehensive efforts of inquiry and deliberation can ensure we understand the "whole system" that is (or ought to be) relevant for securing improvement. The implication, though, is not that Singer and Churchman got it wrong with their sweep-in principle. The principle *is* theoretically relevant, for it stands for the unavoidable holistic implications of both the moral idea and the pragmatic maxim. Insofar, Churchman's attempt to understand ethical practice in terms of whole-systems inquiry and whole-systems ethics is compelling. The difficulty is, the sweep-in principle does not tell us *how* to accomplish comprehensiveness; it formulates an ideal, not a methodological device. For me, therefore, Churchman's call for a "systems approach" is a question rather than an answer: *How can we achieve ethically grounded practice despite its implication of an unbounded quest for comprehensiveness?*

Once we have reformulated Churchman's question in this way, a Copernican revolution of our understanding of the systems idea is in order. Its essential message is no longer that sound research and practice depend on comprehensive understanding and justification. Rather, it seems to me, the message is that we urgently need to develop methodologies for dealing openly and systematically with the inevitable *lack* of comprehensiveness in all our claims (Ulrich 1983, 21 and 260–62; 2001, 5 and 23f). The conclusion I draw from Churchman's quest for comprehensiveness is accordingly different from his: What matters in the first place is not how comprehensive we are

13 Since the translation of this passage in Norman Kemp Smith's usually elegant translation (the one I use) is for once rather awkward, I use my own translation here. It provided the motto for *Critical Heuristics* (Ulrich 1983).

but how openly and self-reflectively we handle the inevitable limitations of our claims. Therein consists the *critical turn* that I propose in our understanding of sound inquiry and practice. We need, then, to take another look at the pragmatic maxim. Can we reformulate it so that it incorporates the critical turn?

3.2 Reformulating the Pragmatic Maxim

In the light of the previous discussion, Peirce's formulation of the pragmatic maxim has an obvious (but rarely discussed) shortcoming. Its application clearly depends on *boundary judgments* regarding the relevant context for examining a claim's meaning and merits. Yet it does not give us any guidance as to how we should select that context. It simply assumes that the proper context includes "all" conceivable consequences; but in real-world inquiry and action, this answer begs the question. A holistic reading of the maxim risks leading us back to Kant's de-contextualization of practical reason. Since Peirce remains silent on the issue, we need to find some way of doing justice to his intentions without falling into the trap of holism. I would argue that the critical turn offers such a way out. Remember that our discussion of Peirce's work revealed not only holistic but also hermeneutic-contextualistic implications. After all, Peirce invented the pragmatic maxim in an effort to overcome the rationalistic bent of Kant's transcendental logic and to ground inquiry in concrete experience and intersubjective argumentation! Hence, it cannot be that Peirce meant for us to read the pragmatic maxim as a call to abstract holistic reasoning and de-contextualization.

How, then, can we square the circle and live up to the maxim without losing focus on concrete contexts of application? With particular regard to grounding ethical practice, how can we reconcile universalism with contextualism? My answer is: by subjecting to careful examination not only a claim's *consequences* but also, and in the first place, the *contexts* that define what consequences we will identify and how we will evaluate them. Context-critical thinking rather than the hopeless quest for comprehensiveness! That is the key to rendering the pragmatic maxim both practicable *and* critically tenable. Let us reformulate the maxim accordingly (Figure 1).

Figure 1

The pragmatic maxim, reformulated in the terms of critical pragmatism

> *"Consider what consequences a claim may conceivably have and what contexts we take to be relevant for identifying and evaluating them; likewise, consider what differences it makes if we take other contexts to be relevant. Then, our conception of all these consequences, identified and evaluated in their respective contexts, is the whole meaning that we give to the claim."*
>
> (By analogy with Peirce 1878, par. 402)

What this reformulation achieves is that it uncovers the *critical kernel of the pragmatic maxim* and thereby points the way to critical pragmatism. It acknowledges the fundamental problem of boundary judgments (Ulrich 1983), with which any application of the maxim confronts us (we will turn to it in a moment). To be sure, the pragmatic maxim does not *cause* the problem – it is of no avail simply to discard the maxim – but it obliges us to *acknowledge* the context-bound nature of any consequences we recognize. It allows us to clarify both a claim's meaning and merits to the precise extent to which we are aware of this contextual limitation and handle it self-reflectively. This is what the proposed reformulation intends; it redefines the pragmatic notion of "clear thinking" in terms of a conscious and critical employment of boundary judgments, that is, of systematic *boundary critique* (see Section 4).

3.3 Reconsidering the Relation of Context and Justification in Ethical Practice

Let us now take a closer look at the relationship of ethical contextualism and universalism, giving particular attention to the difference that critical pragmatism may make to discourse ethics. We have seen that Peirce distinguished between questions of the *constitution of meaning* and questions of the *justification of validity.* Apel (1973, 1975, 1976) and Habermas (1971, 1975) concluded from their reading of Peirce that Kant's transcendental examination of the *a priori* conditions of knowledge and morality could be reconstructed today only by dividing it into the two different problems of the *a priori of experience* (conditions of *intersubjectively* meaningful experience) on the one hand, and the *a priori of argumentation* (conditions of *intersubjective* examination of validity claims) on the other. Critical pragmatism adopts this distinction; but it does not take it so far as to attempt to solve either problem on its own. It seems to me Habermas in effect tried just this, not only with his original reliance on a theory of knowledge-constitutive interests (Habermas 1971), but equally with his later focus on discourse theory and discourse ethics (Habermas 1983, 1991). Behind this shift of interest from the a priori of experience to the a priori of argumentation was his recognition, in the "Postscript to Knowledge and Human Interest" (1975), that his earlier work, as much as it owed to Peirce, had not given sufficient attention to Peirce's separation of questions of validity from questions of meaning. Habermas took this insight to heart; so much so that the a priori of experience – and with it, the pragmatic maxim – subsequently moved out of focus and gave way to an almost exclusive focus on the a priori of argumentation.

This shift had consequences for the way discourse ethics now handles the relation of context and justification in ethical practice. Whereas for Peirce, as I understand him, his discursive conception of truth was a necessary counterpart of the pragmatic maxim – a corrective to its contextualist implications – in discourse ethics the universalization principle has become, once again, the *only* arbiter of moral justification. The pragmatic maxim can no longer be mobilized against the de-contextualizing thrust of universalization. Justification and context are separated in an irreconcilable way. Justification is everything, but nothing can be said about what it is that ought to be justified in the first place. Thus the very question that under real-world circumstances of ethical conflict is probably the most crucial and difficult to answer – how we should identify and bound a particular ethical problem – is no longer a subject of ethical discourse but at best of "ideology critique." That is why, as we noted at the outset, discourse ethics is of virtually no use in handling real-world ethical problem situations.

If universalization is taken to be everything, it risks being nothing. The more a practical discourse succeeds in approximating ideal conditions of rational discourse, the less we can expect it to justify any particular norms of action. And conversely, the more it pays attention to the constitution of meaning in particular contexts, the more it loses its justifying power. The growing attention that the literature around discourse ethics – following a suggestion first worked out in detail by Günther (1988) – now gives to the so-called problem of application amounts to a tacit recognition of the dilemma. However, the new tendency to distinguish between "justification discourses" and "application discourses" cannot solve the problem: *to the extent that discourse-ethical justification succeeds, there is nothing left to "apply."* Universalization, whether conceived monologically or discursively, simply is not a practical strategy for determining and justifying norms. Ethical practice cannot do without both its universalist *and* its contextualist poles. If we want to support ethical practice, there is no way round striking a methodological balance between these two poles.

4. Critical Pragmatism at Work: The Principle and Practice of Boundary Critique

Reason must in all its undertakings subject itself to criticism;
... its verdict is always simply the agreement of free citizens,
of whom each one must be permitted to express,
without let or hindrance, his objections or even his veto.

(Kant 1781, B 767f)

Reason always stands to gain.

(Kant 1781, B 774)

The two quotes from Kant's first *Critique* capture the tension with which any framework for ethical practice has to come to terms – the tension between the two poles we just mentioned. The issue of the constitution of meaning – What is the ethical problem at issue? – pushes us towards ethical contextualism, whereas the issue of validity – Can we justify the normative content of what we do about the problem? – pushes us towards ethical universalism; but neither of these two ethical perspectives can stand alone. Critical pragmatism holds that the task of grounding ethical practice stands or falls by its ability to integrate the two poles in such a way that each can play a *critical* role in dealing with the unavailability of a positive solution to the other. Neither can carry a heavier burden than this. But if each at least serves a critical purpose against the other's claiming too much, they may *together* support the quest for a critical, *and practicable,* solution to the problem of practical reason.

4.1 Two Critical Perspectives

The crucial task of critical pragmatism with a view to grounding ethical practice, then, is to mobilize the reformulated *pragmatic maxim* (P) for a critical handling of claims to moral justification (i.e., rightness) and, at the same time, to mobilize the *universalization principle* (U) for a critical handling of claims to proper contextualization (i.e., relevance). Because the two underlying issues of meaning constitution and validity are so closely intertwined, we can expect that the critical roles of (P) and (U) will be similarly difficult to keep apart. Their common subject is the unavoidable *selectivity* of ethical practice. Only the perspective from which they approach this subject differs. From perspective (P), selectivity manifests itself as arbitrariness of contexts; from perspective (U), as dubious universalizability of claims, that is partiality. Thus the thrust of (P) is primarily (although not always) towards pushing out the boundaries of any assumed context, while the thrust of (U) is primarily towards zooming in on the rationale behind particular problem definitions and responses.

But of course, what claims we raise depends on the contexts we consider, and vice-versa. This is why (P) gains critical force against any overstretching of (U) beyond its proper use as a merely critical principle, and vice-versa. As soon as a claim does not qualify itself by declaring its contextual limitations, we can make a compelling argument against its assertion of objective rightness, as it were, by using (P) to demonstrate that there are options for framing the issue. Conversely, when a claim does qualify itself properly but remains all too partial, we can always use (U) to demonstrate the wanting universalizability of its particular concern. The system of *checks and balances* works well in political practice to assure to each branch of government its rightful claims but nothing more; Why should it not work equally well in ethical practice, to assure to each pole of ethical reasoning its rightful critical claims but nothing more?

Hence, more important than setting the two perspectives apart analytically is bringing them together methodologically within one and the same critical approach. Both perspectives can then help us in dealing, as it were, with the "*small print*" of ethical claims – the small print in the constitution of the problem (P) as well as the small print in the justification of problem-responses (U). Neither the pragmatic maxim nor the universalization principles can do away with the small print, but at least they can serve as a kind of magnifying glass that allows us to read the small print and to correct its most obvious errors. After that, ethical *reasoning* has to defer to legitimate *practice* regulated by democratically institutionalized arrangements at all levels of society. This is the basic strategy that I propose for responding to the central question of this paper, of how we might ensure at least a critical solution to the unresolved problem of practical reason.

4.2 *Boundary Judgments, Boundary Critique*

Boundary critique is my methodological proposal for operationalizing such a critical solution. The philosophical framework that gave rise to the development of the principle of boundary critique is *critical heuristics* (also called critical systems heuristics or CSH, Ulrich 1983).[14] Since a practicable solution to the problem of practical reason is unavailable, critical heuristics focuses on developing frameworks for reflective practice – critical heuristics of social practice rather than critical theory of society![15] The basic idea, as the reader will have understood by now, consists in a critical handling of the problem of boundary judgments.

The *problem of boundary judgments* consists in the fact that there is no such thing as a single right way of bounding the contexts of meaning clarification and validity examination. Consequently, neither questions of meaning nor questions of validity can ever be decided in more than a provisional and hypothetical way; for all argumentation about the meaning and the validity of claims remains conditioned by

14 For introductory accounts, see Ulrich (1987, 1993 and, most updated and perhaps also most readable, 2000). German-speaking readers may wish to start with Ulrich (1984). Special aspects are covered in Ulrich (1988, 1996, 2001, and 2003). For the philosophical underpinnings of critical heuristics, the main source remains Ulrich (1983), of which a 1994 paperback reprint edition is still in print. Practical applications can be found in the book as well as, for example, in Carr and Levidow (2000).

15 The two approaches do not compete with each other; the one (critical theory) pursues a relevant theoretical aim and the other (critical heuristics) an equally relevant practical aim. Neither approach can supersede the other. Likewise, with a view to other methodological frameworks aiming at reflective practice, it should be clear that CSH does not intend to replace them but rather, to offer methodological support for their practice. CSH does not see itself (though this is frequently misunderstood) as a self-contained problem-solving methodology, nor does it claim that boundary critique is the only approach there is to promoting reflective practice – of course not. Its only claim is that in some form or other, the principle of boundary critique does have an indispensable role to play in any framework for reflective practice that deserves its name. (I would thus argue that Schön's [1983, 1997] well-known approach to "'reflective practice'" is not satisfactory from a CSH perspective. Due to its focus on the intuitive and emotional sides of professional mastery, it offers virtually no help in dealing with the ethical dimension of sound professional practice and appears to have no grasp of the issue of ethical boundary critique at all.)

boundary judgments, and these can at all times be challenged. The best we can achieve methodologically is to secure systematic efforts of boundary critique *before* handing them over to democratically institutionalized processes of decision making, which alone can then assure legitimacy to particular interpretations of meaning and related validity claims.

The *principle of boundary critique* (B) says, accordingly, that context-critical thinking is indispensable for understanding both the meaning and the validity of a claim, and that this can be achieved through a critical handling of boundary judgments in the dual sense of employing them both self-reflectively and critically against claims that are not so self-reflective. (B) is the methodological core idea that allows us to operationalize both (P) and (U) for critical purposes, and thus simultaneously put (P) and (U) in the service of such context-critical thinking.

The *practice of boundary critique* consists in supporting systematic processes of surfacing and unfolding a claim's selectivity with respect to the "facts" (empirical circumstances) and "values" (normative considerations) on which it relies. Which facts and values it considers and which others it leaves out is conditioned by boundary judgments that define the *reference system* of relevant facts and values. To appreciate a claim's selectivity, then, we need to understand the way in which underpinning boundary judgments condition its reference system, and how different relevant facts and values may look when we modify that reference system. To this end, critical heuristics offers (among other tools) a framework of boundary categories and questions that the interested reader will find in the literature.

A useful way to explain how boundary critique works is by means of the *eternal triangle* (Ulrich 2000, 252). Let us assume, for example, that in discussing a claim, we hear of new facts that we have thus far ignored but do find relevant for assessing the merits of the claim. These new facts then prompt us to modify our boundary judgments so that the new facts now belong to the relevant context. If for example we learn of previously unknown long-term effects of a proposed action, we may want to expand the considered time horizon. The meaning of the claim has thus changed, for we now see it in a new context (i.e., our reference system has changed). This change of reference system in turn questions our previous value judgments; we may need to adjust them, say, because the newly considered long-term effects in question are unacceptable to us. In turn, the resulting new value judgments may make the facts look different and cause us to question our boundary judgments further, and so on. Whenever we change one of the three angles, the other two will equally change. Boundary critique may thus be understood as a process of working systematically through the triangle (Figure 2).

Figure 2

Boundary critique: a process of working through the "eternal triangle" of boundary judgments, observations, and evaluations

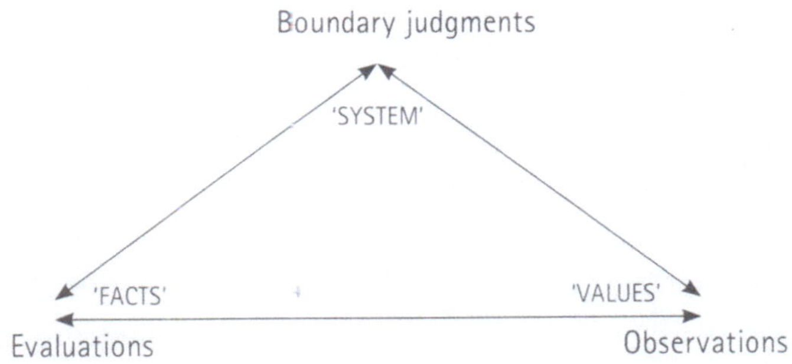

Source: Ulrich 2000, 252.

The eternal triangle equally explains why the two analytically separate issues of meaning clarification and validity examination are in practice inseparable: namely, because they both depend on our boundary judgments regarding the problem at hand. It does not matter whether it is an issue of meaning or of validity that causes us to revise our boundary judgments – in either case, we will need to review the other issue, too.

4.3 *Ethical Boundary Critique*

Ethical boundary critique aims at exposing the moral implications of claims with two particular issues in mind. First, it aims to trace a claim's ethical implications within a wider context than the one assumed by the directly interested parties; second, it aims to unfold the claim's distributive effects – the way it may affect different parties differently – within whatever context is considered. Common to both issues is the question of whether a claim (if taken as a basis for action by those involved) may impose on those not involved consequences that might not respect their dignity and intrinsic autonomy but might instrumentalize them for the purposes of others – the basic intuition that critical pragmatism, like many other approaches, associates with the moral idea.

From the viewpoint of boundary critique, both issues amount to boundary judgments regarding the "client" (beneficiaries) the claim is to serve, as distinguished from those who may be affected without being served. Both issues imply that we look beyond the context of relevant facts (consequences) and values (concerns) assumed.

This process of "looking beyond," that is, of integrating into our reference system other considerations than those held relevant in the first place, tends to have strong ethical implications. It relates claims to moral rightness or improvement to larger contexts of application, so that we must include (at least conceptually) step-by-step more stakeholders and their concerns. The meaning and validity of a claim thus change, and its ethical selectivity becomes increasingly apparent. This is not to say that it is always necessary or reasonable to defend a claim in terms of the interests of humanity in its entirety; the process is, however, useful for clarifying the ethical implications of a claim. The point is not to achieve moral universalization (an impossible feat) but to raise ethical awareness with respect to the unavoidable *lack* of universalizability.

Such awareness raising is reasonable even though it cannot, and should not, stop us entirely from acting on behalf of limited (e.g., local) concerns. In an imperfect world, perfectly rational action is nonexistent, but inaction is not an ethically defendable option either. If ethical claims are not to bypass democratically legitimate processes of decision making at all levels of society, the best we can achieve is democratically legitimate decision making *based on* ethical awareness. For that, we do not depend on the possibility of ethical universalization but only on everyone's awareness of its absence, so that the concerns of those on the "losing side" of an ethical position are given due consideration. Fortunately, the fact that universalization is not an operational principle for securing positive ethical justifications need not mean it loses its power as a *critical* principle. Ethical boundary critique makes sure it doesn't.

4.4 Emancipatory Boundary Critique

A related requirement is that those on the "losing side" must not remain entirely dependent on the readiness of those in control to disclose their boundary judgments and to submit them to critical discussion. Hence, we need to find ways to assure to everyone not only a voice but a *competent* voice, so that they can argue their concerns and, if those in control close down the discussion, can carry them into wider arenas of public discussion and decision making. This leads to another application of boundary critique, called *emancipatory boundary critique.* This concept explains how a proper use of boundary judgments can help create better argumentative chances for all those concerned, at least for critical purposes, regardless of unequal access to expertise, status, and power. The point is that for anyone who has grasped the basic idea of boundary critique, it becomes possible to challenge claims that take their underpinning boundary judgments for granted. For this it needs to become obvious to all the parties and, where necessary, to a larger public, that these claims owe their apparent objectivity and rationality to a selection of facts and values that is buttressed by non-argumentative means or is in other ways arbitrary. To achieve such transparency, one need not be able to challenge those who use boundary judgments dogmatically on an equal footing with respect to knowledge and expertise. It is good enough to offer an overtly tentative and subjective suggestion or question regarding a boundary issue. The only thing that matters is that everyone can then see there may be *options* for selecting relevant facts and values! When the mask of objectivity and rationality slips, we discover boundary judgments at war.

Unlike all other models of rational discourse currently available in the literature on practical philosophy and discourse ethics, this simple model of critical argumentation need not assume ideal conditions of rationality but works under everyday conditions of imperfect rationality. It achieves this by restricting itself to a critical purpose; but for this critical purpose, it offers a cogent form of argumentation. Therein consists the emancipatory potential that I associate with boundary critique. It can secure to all the parties a gain in *symmetry of critical competence* (Ulrich 1993, 604f).[16]

4.5 *Concluding Comment*

I cannot introduce the specific conceptual framework of critical heuristics here in any detail.[17] Nor is this really necessary for understanding the principle as such. More important is that we appreciate its (purposeful self-) limitations:

> Critical heuristics does not intend to turn boundary critique into a self-contained methodology. That would not be conducive to its aim of supporting professionals and decision makers in the quest for ethically alert practice, *whatever methodologies they may choose to rely on.*
>
> Boundary critique cannot (and does not mean to) ensure to those who master it

16 For a more comprehensive introduction to the emancipatory use of boundary critique, compare Ulrich (1983, whole Ch. 5, 265–314; also 1987, 281f; 1993, 599–605; and 2000, 257–260).

17 See the literature recommendations in note 14.

a position of superior rationality. It aims to promote reflective practice in a *living civil society* (Ulrich 2000), not to replace it by a new "expertocracy" trained in boundary critique.

Boundary critique does not mean to do away with partiality. It will not, with a happy phrase of James' (1907, 29; 2000, 37), afford us a *moral holiday.* A moral holiday would be conceivable to the extent to which an absolute, superior position of impartiality outside and above all partialities would be available – the implicit ideal of moral universalization.

Ethical boundary critique pursues a more realistic, but no less relevant, aim. It aims at revitalizing the moral and democratic vision of a society in which people – ordinary professionals and decision makers as well as ordinary citizens – regulate their conflicts in peaceful ways, through processes of decision making and conflict settling that are both argumentatively and democratically based. Reason, in the form of ethical boundary critique, can contribute to such a vision by supporting processes of meaning clarification and validity examination but *not* by telling citizens what is good and right for them. We might even expand James' phrase and say that ethical practice cannot afford us a *democratic holiday* either.

The proposal for grounding ethical practice that I associate with critical pragmatism is, then, an imperfect one – by necessity. It cannot secure moral justification, any more or less than a theoretical approach such as discourse ethics can achieve this. But at least, it can improve chances for reflective practice. Rather than dreaming the dream of perfect rationality, let us concentrate on putting ethical reflection to work on the job of dealing with everyday conditions of imperfect rationality.

References

Apel, K.-O., 1973. *Transformation der Philosophie,* 2 vols. Suhrkamp, Frankfurt a.M., 358–435. (English translation: *Towards a Transformation of Philosophy*. Routledge and Kegan Paul, London, 1980, and Marquette University Press Milwaukee, Wisconsin, 1998.)

Apel, K.-O., 1975. *Der Denkweg von Charles S. Peirce: Eine Einführung in den amerikanischen Pragmatismus,* Suhrkamp, Frankfurt a.M. (Originally published as Introductions to the German translation of C.S. Peirce's writings by K.-O.

Apel, *Charles Sanders Peirce: Schriften.* 2 vols., Frankfurt a.Main: Suhrkamp, Vol. I: 1967, Vol. II: 1970. English translation: *Charles S. Peirce: From Pragmatism to Pragmaticism.* University of Massachusetts, Amherst, MA, 1981).

Apel, K.-O., 1976. "Sprechakttheorie und transzendentale Sprachpragmatik – zur Frage ethischer Normen." In: K.-O. Apel, *Sprachpragmatik und Philosophie.* Suhrkamp, Frankfurt a.M., 10–173.

Atkin, A., 2005. "C.S. Peirce's pragmatism." In: J. Fieser and B. Dowen (eds), *The Internet Encyclopedia of Philosophy,* http://www.iep.utm.edu/p/PeirePr.htm.

Burch, R., 2001. "Charles Sanders Peirce" In: E.N. Zalta (ed.), *Stanford Encyclopedia of Philosophy,* http://plato.stanford.edu/archives/fall2001/entries/peirce/.

Carr, S. and Levidow, L., 2000. "Exploring the links between science, risk, uncertainty and ethics in regulatory controversies about genetically modified crops." *Journal of Agricultural and Environmental Ethics,* 12 (1), 29–39.

Churchman, C.W., 1968. *Challenge to Reason.* McGraw-Hill, New York.

Churchman, C.W., 1971. *The Design of Inquiring Systems.* Basic Books, New York.

Churchman, C.W., 1979. *The Systems Approach and Its Enemies.* Basic Books, New York.

Churchman, C.W., 1982. "An appreciation of Edgar A. Singer, Jr.." In: C.W. Churchman, *Thought and Wisdom.* Intersystems Publications, Seaside (CA).

Churchman, C.W., Ackoff, R.L., and Arnoff, L.E., 1957. *Introduction to Operations Research.* Wiley, New York.

Goodman, R., 2003. "William James." In: E.N. Zalta (ed.), *The Stanford Encyclopedia of Philosophy,* http://plato.stanford.edu/archives/spr2003/entries/james/.

Günther, K., 1988. *Der Sinn für Angemessenheit: Anwendungsdiskurse in Moral und Recht.* Suhrkamp, Frankfurt a.M. (English translation: *The Sense of Appropriateness: Application Discourses in Morality and Law.* 1993. State University of New York Press, Albany (NY).)

Habermas, J., 1971. *Knowledge and Human Interests.* Beacon Press, Boston (MA) (German original: *Erkenntnis und Interesse*, 1968, Suhrkamp, Frankfurt a.M.)

Habermas, J., 1973. *Theory and Practice.* Beacon Press, Boston (MA).

Habermas, J., 1975. "A postscript to 'Knowledge and Human Interests'." *Philosophy of the Social Sciences,* Vol. 3, 175–189.

Habermas, J., 1983. *Moralbewusstsein und kommunikatives Handeln.* Suhrkamp, Frankfurt am Main. (English translation: *Moral Consciousness and Communicative Action,* 1990, Polity Press, Cambridge.)

Habermas, J., 1991. *Erläuterungen zur Diskursethik.* Suhrkamp, Frankfurt a.Main. (Partial English translation: *Justification and Application.* 1993, Polity Press, Cambridge.)

Höffe, O., 1984. "Ist Rawl's Theorie der Gerechtigkeit eine kantische Theorie?" *Ratio, 26,* No. 2, 88–104.

James, W., 1898. "Philosophical conceptions and practical results: The annual public address before the [Philosophical] Union, University of California, Berkeley, 26 August." *University of California Chronicle,* 1, September 1898, 287–310. (Reprinted in F. Bowers and I.K. Skrupskelis [eds], *The Works of William James.* Vol. 1: Pragmatism. Harvard University Press, Cambridge (MA), 1975, 257–270).

James, W., 1899. "On a certain blindness in human beings." Lecture 2. In: W. James, *Talks to Teachers on Psychology and to Students on Some of Life's Ideals.* Henry Holt & Co., New York, Ch. 2. (Also in James (2000), 267–285).

James, W., 1907. "What Pragmatism Means." Lecture 2. In: W. James, *Pragmatism: A New Name for Some Old Ways of Thinking.* Longman Green and Co., New York, pp.17–32. (Also in James (2000), 24–40.)

James, W., 2000. *Pragmatism and Other Writings.* Edited with an Introduction and Notes by Giles Gunn. Penguin, New York.

Kant, I., 1781. *Critique of Pure Reason,* Translated by Norman Kemp Smith. St. Martin's Press, New York, 1965. (Original: 1929, Macmillan, New York.) Quotes refer to the second ed. (B) of 1787.

Kant, I., 1785. *Groundwork of the Metaphysic of Morals,* Translated and analyzed by H.J. Paton. Harper Torchbooks, New York, 1964. Quotes refer to the second ed. (B) of 1786.

Kant, I., 1788. *Critique of Practical Reason and Other Writings in Moral Philosophy,* Translated and edited with an introduction by Lewis White Beck, University of Chicago Press, Chicago (IL), 1949.

Menand, L., 2001. *The Metaphysical Club: A Story of Ideas in America.* Farar, Straus & Giroux, New York.

Morris, C.W., 1938. *Foundations of the Theory of Signs.* Chicago University Press, Chicago (IL). (*International Encyclopedia of Unified Science*, Vol. I, No. 2).

Oehler, L., 1968. *Charles S. Peirce: Über die Klarheit unserer Gedanken / How to Make Our Ideas Clear* (bilingual edition of the original essay, with an introduction and commentary by K. Oehler). Klostermann, Frankfurt am Main.

Peirce, C.S., 1878. "How to make our ideas clear." *Popular Science Monthly,* 12, January, 286–302. (Also in Peirce (1934), par. 388–410.)

Peirce, C.S., 1905. "What pragmatism is." *The Monist, 15,* No. 2 (April), 161–181. (Also in Peirce (1934), par. 411–437.)

Peirce, C.S., 1934. *Pragmatism and Pragmaticism. Collected Papers,* Vol. V, ed. by Ch. Hartshorne and P. Weiss. Harvard University Press, Cambridge (MA), 411–437.

Popper, K.R., 1959. *The Logic of Scientific Discovery.* Hutchison, London.

Rawls, J., 1971. *A Theory of Justice.* Belknap/Harvard University Press, Cambridge (MA).

Rorty, R., 1989. *Contingency, Irony, and Solidarity.* Cambridge University Press, Cambridge.

Schön, D., 1983. *The Reflective Practitioner: How Professionals Think in Action.* Basic Books, New York. (Paperback edition: 1995, Arena/Ashgate Publishing, Aldershot, Hants., UK.)

Schön, D., 1987. *Educating the Reflective Practitioner: Toward a New Design for Teaching and Learning in the Professions.* Jossey-Bass,San Francisco.

Singer, E.A., 1936. *On the Contented Life.* Henry Holt & Co., New York.

Singer, E.A., 1959. *Experience and Reflection.* ed. by C.W. Churchman. University of Pennsylvania Press, Philadelphia (PA).

Snow, C.P., 1959. *The Two Cultures and the Scientific Revolution.* Cambridge University Press, Cambridge. (Originally delivered as the Rede Lecture at Cambridge, 1959.)

Ulrich, W., 1983. *Critical Heuristics of Social Planning: A New Approach to Practical Philosophy.* Haupt, Bern, Stuttgart. (Paperback edition, 1994, Wiley, Chichester, UK.)

Ulrich, W., 1984. "Management oder die Kunst, Entscheidungen zu treffen, die andere betreffen." *Die Unternehmung, Schweizerische Zeitschrift für betriebswirtschaftliche Forschung und Praxis, 38,* No. 4, 326–346.

Ulrich, W., 1987. "Critical heuristics of social systems design." *European Journal of Operational Research, 31,* No. 2, 276–283. (Reprinted in M.C. Jackson, P.A. Keys, and S.A. Cropper (eds), *Operational Research and the Social Sciences.* Plenum Press, New York, 1989, 79–87, and in R.L. Flood and M.C. Jackson (eds), *Critical Systems Thinking: Directed Readings.* Wiley, Chichester, UK, 1991, 103–115.)

Ulrich, W., 1988. "Systems thinking, systems practice, and practical philosophy: a program of research." *Systems Practice, 1,* No. 2, 137–163. (Reprinted in R.L. Flood and M.C. Jackson (eds), *Critical Systems Thinking: Directed Readings.* Wiley, Chichester, UK, 1991, 245–268.)

Ulrich, W., 1993. "Some difficulties of ecological thinking, considered from a critical systems perspective: a plea for critical holism." *Systems Practice, 6,* No. 5, 583–611.

Ulrich, W., 1996. *A Primer to Critical Systems Heuristics for Action Researchers.* University of Hull, Centre for Systems Studies, Hull, UK. (Available from the author).

Ulrich, W., 1999. "An Appreciation of C. West Churchman." *Werner Ulrich's home page,* Section "A Tribute to C. West Churchman," http://www.geocities.com/csh_home/cwc_appreciation.html. (Earlier version: *Systems Practice, 1,* No. 4, 1988, 341–350.)

Ulrich, W., 2000. "Reflective practice in the civil society: the contribution of critically systemic thinking." *Reflective Practice, 1,* No. 2, 247–268.

Ulrich, W., 2001. "The quest for competence in systemic research and practice." *Systems Research and Behavioral Science,* 18, No. 1, 3–28.

Ulrich, W., 2002. "A Bibliography of C.W. Churchman's Writings from 1938 to 2001." *Werner Ulrich's home page,* Section "A Tribute to C. West Churchman," http://www.geocities.com/csh_home/cwc_bibliography.html.

Ulrich, W., 2003. "Beyond methodology choice: critical systems thinking as critically systemic discourse." *Journal of the Operational Research Society,* 54, No. 4, 325–342.

Ulrich, W., 2004a. "C. West Churchman, 1913–2004." *Journal of the Operational Research Society,* 55, No. 11, 1123–1129.

Ulrich, W., 2004b. "In memory of C. West Churchman (1913–2004): reminiscences, retrospectives, and reflections." *International Journal of Organizational Transformation and Social Change, 1,* No. 2/3, 199–219.

Wellmer, A., 1986. *Ethik und Dialog: Elemente des moralischen Urteils bei Kant und in der Diskursethik.* Suhrkamp, Frankfurt a.M.

Wolff, R.P., 1977. *Understanding Rawls: A Reconstruction and Critique of a Theory of Justice.* Princeton University Press, Princeton (NJ).

Werner Ulrich

Werner Ulrich is currently Visiting Professor at the Centre for Complexity and Change in the Faculty of Technology of The Open University in Milton Keynes, United Kingdom. He is also "Ancien Professeur titulaire" in the Faculty of Philosophy of the University of Fribourg in Switzerland. He has been a Visiting Professor at the University of Hull in England, at Canterbury University in Christchurch, New Zealand, and at the University of Lincoln, England. He has experience as a chief researcher and policy analyst in government and initiated the Lugano Summer School of Systems Design at the University of Italian Switzerland in Lugano, which he is currently directing.

Born in 1948 in Bern, Switzerland, Ulrich obtained doctoral degrees in Economics and Social Science (Dr.rer.pol., 1975) from the University of Fribourg and in Philosophy of Social Systems Design (Ph.D., 1980) from the University of California at Berkeley. At Berkeley he studied and worked during five years with C. West Churchman, noted research philosopher and pioneer of the fields of operations research, management science, and systems thinking.

Ulrich is known as a pioneer of critical systems thinking (CST), which is the use of systemic thinking in the service of reflective practice and research. Among over 150 publications, his major book is *Critical Heuristics of Social Planning: A New Approach to Practical Philosophy* (Haupt: Bern, 1983, and Wiley: New York, 1994). His current research programs on "CST for Professionals and Citizens" and on "Critical Pragmatism" explore the ways critical systems thinking can contribute to responsible professional practice and to preparing citizens for their role in a living civil society. Personal home page: http://www.geocities.com/csh_home/.

Gian Vittorio Caprara
University of Rome "La Sapienza"

Cristina Capanna
University of Rome "La Sapienza"

Moral Disengagement in the Exercise of Civic-ness

Democracy cannot survive without a populace ready to endorse the obligations that the respect of individuals and the pursuit of public good entail. Yet, a number of scholars warn against the decline of civic virtues in modern societies (Putnam, 1993; 2000), while others document the pervasiveness of violations of civic codes (such as the corruption of public officers and tax evasion) and business transgressions "by people of all statuses in all walks of life" (Bandura 2003, 102; 1990; Bandura, Caprara, and Zsolnai 2000; Gabor 1994).

Trustworthiness, generalized reciprocity, civic engagement, and related concepts have become popular in the political and sociological discourse as basic ingredients of liberal democracy and progress of nations (Putnam 2000). Yet, the psychological underpinnings of these concepts have been often disregarded, although no one would contest that individual agents are the carriers of thoughts and ultimately of reasons that determine the orientation of people toward society and that may ultimately promote both human and social capital.

Surveys that attest to significant changes in civic participation serve descriptive and comparative purposes but they can't help much in guiding interventions aimed either at promoting or discouraging behaviors that people continue to enact in their daily transactions. To do so, one needs to clarify the psychological mechanisms that embed those behaviors in a coherent network of reasons; namely, beliefs, values, and goals that assign meaning to individuals' actions and pursuits and make sense of their engagement in given domains of activity.

In this regard, social cognitive theory provides a theory of psychological functioning capable of supplying the conceptual apparatus that is needed to identify and to assess structures and mechanisms that underlie civic involvement, and eventually to guide interventions aimed at promoting desirable behaviors (Bandura 1986; Caprara and Cervone 2000).

Self-reflection and self-reactivity are core properties of human agency that enable people to capitalize upon experience and to be active agents in charting their own lives (Bandura 2001). People reflect on the consequences of their actions and accord their goals to their accomplishments. People do things that give them satisfaction and a sense of self-worth and refrain from actions that bring self-censure.

Mastery beliefs and anticipatory self-rewards and sanctions, largely derived from previous experience, keep conduct in line with personal capacities and standards. Accordingly, people do not engage in civic activities unless they believe they can master and value these activities. Both mastery beliefs and personal standards assigning value to civic commitment are critical to induce people to make the efforts and to bear the sacrifices that the endorsement of responsible citizenship may carry.

Yet, this does not exclude the fact that people, although capable and ethically committed, may violate the principles of desirable civic behavior while continuing to profess the same principles, especially when their interests are at stake. A kind of division between thought and action seems to take place when considerate people break the rules or get involved in dirty business, through a neutralization of self-evaluative reactions that habitually refrain from transgression.

What is most surprising in many cases of rule violation and misconduct in daily transactions is that people are not bothered by their conscience, do not fear any sanction and do not feel obliged to make reparations. Furthermore, their misconduct does not seem to diminish their confidence in the system of rules they are breaking, as if a divorce between thought and action would prevent them from acknowledging the conflict.

Most people would not dispute that taxes have to be paid, that workers have to be treated fairly, and that everybody is responsible for keeping cities safe and clean. Yet, many actions do not fully correspond to people's moral standards, and there is a surprising absence of accompanying personal distress.

In reality, the adoption of moral standards does not create a fixed control mechanism within the person. Self-reactive influences, carrying a sense of self-blame or self-worth, do not operate unless they are activated, and there are many psychosocial processes by which self-sanctions can be disengaged from major or minor violations. Selective activation and disengagement of internal control enable otherwise considerate people to commit transgressions without experiencing personal distress.

In this reasoning, we are indebted to Bandura, who first focused on selective deactivation of internal censure through mechanisms of moral disengagement as part of a broader self theory encompassing self-reflective, -reactive, and -regulative proactive mechanisms (Bandura 1986; 1991; 1999; 2001).

1. Civic Moral Disengagement

Mechanisms of moral disengagement, namely, the psychosocial maneuvers by which moral self-sanctions become disengaged, giving free way to a variety of misbehaviors without carrying any moral concern, were originally investigated in relation to aggression and inhumane conduct leading to the identification of eight mechanisms (Bandura 1986; Bandura, Barbaranelli, Caprara, and Pastorelli 1996). *Figure 1* summarizes schematically the four major points in the self-regulatory system at which internal moral control can be disengaged from detrimental conduct.

Self-sanctions can be disengaged by reconstructing the conduct, obscuring personal causal agency, misrepresenting or disregarding the injurious consequences of one's actions, and vilifying the recipients of maltreatment by blaming and devaluating them.

Moral justification, euphemistic labeling, and advantageous comparison are maneuvers that operate on the construal of injurious behavior itself. People do not ordinarily engage in reprehensible conduct until they have justified to themselves the rightfulness of their actions. By moral justification, detrimental conduct is made personally and socially acceptable by portraying it in the service of valued social or moral purposes.

Reprehensible activities can assume different appearances depending on what they are called. By "euphemistic labelling," deleterious conduct looks less serious and even benign, relieving those who engage in it from a sense of personal responsibility (Bolinger 1982; Lutz 1987).

Behavior can also assume very different qualities depending on what it is contrasted with. By advantageous comparison, harmful conduct can be rendered of little consequence when contrasted with flagrant behavior.

Figure 1

Mechanism through which moral self-sanctions are selectively disengaged giving free way to misbehaviors at different points in the self-regulatory process

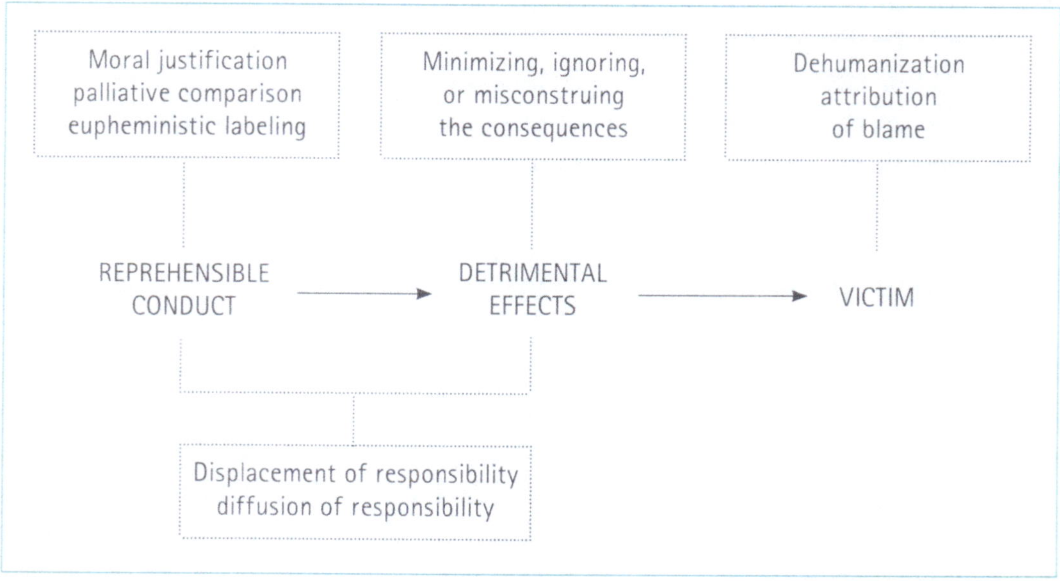

Source: Social Foundations of Thought and Action: A Social Cognitive Theory (Bandura 1986, 376). Copyright 1986 by Prentice-Hall Inc. Reprinted by permission of Prentice-Hall Inc., Upper Saddle River, NJ.

Displacement and diffusion of responsibility are maneuvers that operate by obscuring or distorting the agentive relation between actions and the effects they cause. Under displacement of responsibility, people view their actions as springing from social or others' pressures rather than as something for which they are personally responsible. Under diffusion of responsibility detrimental outcomes appear to result from joint actions, in which the contribution of each individual is undistinguishable from the contributions of others. Paradoxically, when everyone is responsible, no one really feels responsible. Disregarding or distorting the consequences corresponds to another maneuver that leads people to avoid or to weaken self-deterring reactions such as guilt or shame, by minimizing or ignoring the harm they cause.

The final set of disengagement practices operates on the recipients of detrimental acts by attribution of blame and dehumanization. For most people, it is difficult to mistreat innocent persons without risking personal distress and self-censure associated with empathetic or vicarious emotional relations. On the other hand, most people do not hesitate to withdraw sympathy from people whose sins deserve punishment or when the targets of blame and punishment have been deprived of human qualities (Kelman 1973).

The disinhibitory effects of the various forms of moral disengagement have been extensively documented in the perpetration of large-scale inhumanities (Andrus 1969; Keen 1986; Kelman and Hamilton 1989; Rapoport and Alexander 1982; Reich 1990). The power of the same self-exonerative mechanisms has been examined in the area of political and military violence, as in cases of terrorism and counterterrorism (Bandura 1990; 2003). Laboratory studies have further verified that conditions conducive to disengagement of moral self-sanctions heighten punitive behavior (Bandura, Underwood, and Fromson 1975; 1991; Diener 1977; Diener, Dienen, Endersen, Beaman, and Fraser 1975; Milgram 1974; Tilker 1970; Zimbardo 1969; 1995).

Similar self-exonerative maneuvers operate to justify reprehensible behavior and rule violations other than aggression and violence, as it has been recently documented in four famous cases of corporate transgressions and discussed in light of their implications for business ethics (Bandura, Caprara, and Zsolnai 2000).

How many people would relinquish using the arms of seduction or adulation to obtain a favor or avoid a sanction? And how many people have been able to resist? How many persons believe that stealing an ashtray, towels, or other "souvenirs" from restaurants or hotels is just a harmless habit? Who can claim to have never stolen someone else's ideas or stuff without identifying the rightful owner? How many people continue to value principles that contrast with their behavior without experiencing any embarrassment?

It is not difficult to evoke behaviors that accord with mechanisms of moral dis-engagement, and this is true not only in the sphere of aggression, violence and inhumane conduct. Likely, moral thought and behavior can be divorced from each other in the service of self-interest in a variety of contexts such as the family, work setting, and school.

Ultimately, it is an empirical task to ascertain the extent to which the same eight mechanisms that are likely to exert a disinhibitory effect on aggression are equally effective in other domains of functioning. To this end, Caprara, Barbaranelli, Beretta, Iafrate, Pastorelli, Steca and Bandura (in press), have recently proposed a scale to assess civic moral disengagement (CMD); namely, the mechanisms of moral disengagement in the exercise of civic-ness. Caprara and colleagues reasoned that the same eight mechanisms of moral disengagement that operate in justifying aggressive behavior or terrorism may serve similar self-exonerative functions in the realm of civil duties.

Table 1 reports the items used by Caprara and colleagues to assess the tendency to use mechanisms of moral disengagement in common daily transactions, when personal interests can be pursued through "minor" transgressions toward others or society.

Table 1

Items of the Civic Moral Disengagement (CMD) scale

1. Using drugs is a way of "expanding the limits of one's consciousness" EL
2. When there are no efficient refuse disposal services, there is no sense reproaching citizens who leave trash on the street DILS_R
3. Some people are real disasters DEUM
4. To forget to declare a financial error in our favor is not serious, since it is the responsibility of who suffers the error to make checks ATT_B
5. There is no reason to fine those who make "graffiti" on walls since others commit much more serious acts of vandalism AC
6. When traffic moves quickly, drivers who exceed the speed limit in order to keep up should not be fined DISL_R
7. There is no sense for the individual to worry about environmental deterioration since the harmful effects are produced at the collective level DIFF_R
8. Evading taxes cannot be considered reprehensible considering the squandering of public money DIST_C
9. Those who behave brutishly can only expect to be treated the same way by others DEUM
10. Thefts in large department stores are irrelevant compared to the stores' earnings DIST_C
11. Victims are generally unable to stay out of trouble ATT_B

12.	Thefts do not damage retail sales very much since insurance covers the losses DIST_C
13.	Drawing graffiti on walls is the expression of "creative spirit" EL
14.	There is no sense feeling guilty for damages we have contributed toward producing only in a very small way DIFF_R
15.	Those who refuse to pay fines cannot be condemned given the corruption among policemen AC
16.	A manager is not culpable if he inflates balance sheet items in order to avoid his company going bankrupt MJ
17.	Fraud in economic transactions is simply a "strategic distortion" EL
18.	Silencing those who continue to be annoying, even using hard measures, is understandable ATT_B
19.	Taking "bribes" is not serious since no one is hurt DIST_C
20.	People cannot be held responsible for crimes they commit on the instigation of others DISL_R
21.	There is no sense in blaming individuals who evade a rule when everybody else does the same thing DIFF_R
22.	Gambling is a pastime just like any other one EL
23.	For the advance of science, it is lawful to use humans as "guinea pigs" even in high risk experiments MJ
24.	If people leave their belongings around, it is their fault if someone takes them or robs them ATT_B
25.	If someone loses control during a brawl, he is not completely responsible for the consequences of his actions DISL_R
26.	Citizens who dirty the streets should not be severely persecuted since industry produces much more serious pollution AC
27.	Athletes who take stimulants should not be punished since all their companions behave in the same way DIFF_R
28.	Using force is often inevitable to protect one's own interests MJ
29.	Given the widespread corruption in society, one cannot disapprove of those who pay for favors AC
30.	In order to keep family cohesion, its members should always be defended, even when they are guilty of serious crimes MJ
31.	Those who behave deplorably deserve a cruel destiny ATT_B
32.	Whoever does not behave like a human being cannot be treated like one DEUM

33. Destroying old things is a way of convincing the state to provide new facilities DIST_C
34. It is not the fault of drivers if they exceed the speed limit since cars are made to go at high speeds DISL_R
35. Young people cannot be considered guilty if they smoke a joint since most adults use much stronger drugs AC
36. Rivals deserve being humiliated and maltreated DEUM
37. Loyalty involves not denouncing the transgressions committed by one's friends MJ
38. Employees are never responsible for executing the illegal decisions of their bosses DIFF_R
39. In order to force some people to work, they have to be treated like beasts of burden DEUM
40. Pornography is basically "cheap" eroticism EL

Note: The labels next to each item indicate the mechanism of moral civic disengagement measured.

Legend: *Moral justification* = MJ; *Advantageous comparison* = AC; *Euphemistic labelling* = EL; *Diffusion of responsibility* = DIFF_R; *Displacement of responsibility* = DISL_R; *Disregarding/distorting the consequences* = DIST_C; *Dehumanization of victims* = DEUM; *Attribution of blame* = ATT_B.

Previous studies document the validity of the scale of Civic Moral Disengagement according to the usual criteria of classical test theory (Caprara et al., in press).

Recent findings (Caprara and Capanna in press) show that resorting to mechanisms of civic moral disengagement is associated with assigning higher priority to self-enhancing values such as achievement, power, and hedonism than to self-transcendening values such as benevolence and universalism (Schwartz 1992; 1994). Moreover, people who are inclined to moral civic disengagement are less committed to civic duties such as voting and contributing actively to the well functioning of a social system, assign less importance to respecting the environment and the social order, are less inclined to obey laws and regulations and less prone to engage in activities aimed at promoting civic solidarity and welfare.

2. Conclusion

As one might guess, values dictate when self-exonerative mechanisms are appropriate, and our findings may suggest that the more people are concerned with self-enhancement goals, the more they are inclined to resort to mechanisms that permit them to disengage from the duties and obligations of civic life and to justify transgressions when their self-interest is at stake. Yet this has to find empirical support in further research.

It is a matter of fact that our society often rewards the search for power, encourages the search for achievement, and regards hedonism as a worthwhile pursuit. Thus one may wonder whether all this may lead to excessive emphasis on priorities that may ultimately clash with civic virtues. The more people become self-concerned, the more difficult it may become to contrast self-exonerative maneuvers aimed at enhancing and protecting oneself, especially when significant components of society move in that direction.

In reality civic societies need agents who are capable of caring about and pursuing both self and community interests.

References

Andrus, B.C., 1969. *The Infamous of Nuremberg.* Fravin, London.

Bandura, A., 1986. *Social Foundations of Thought and Action: A Social Cognitive Theory.* Prentice Hall, Englewood Cliffs (NJ).

Bandura, A., 1990. "Mechanisms of Moral Disengagement." In: W. Reich (ed.), *Origins of Terrorism: Psychologies, Ideologies, Theologies, and States of Mind.* Cambridge University Press, Cambridge, England, 161–191.

Bandura, A., 1991. "Social Cognitive Theory of Moral Thought and Action." In: W.M. Kurtines and J.L. Gewirtz (eds) *Handbook of Moral Behavior and Development: Theory, Research and Applications.* Hillsdale, Erlbaum (N J), Vol. 1, 71–129.

Bandura, A., 1999. "Moral disengagement in the perpetration of inhumanities." *Personality and Social Psychology Review.* Special Issue on Evil and Violence, 3, 193–209.

Bandura, A., 2001. "Social cognitive theory: An agentic perspective." *Annual Review of Psychology,* 52, 1–26.

Bandura, A., 2003. "Selective moral disengagement in the exercise of moral agency." *Journal of Moral Education*, 31, No. 2, 101–119.

Bandura, A., Barbaranelli, C., Caprara, G.V., and Pastorelli, C., 1996. "Mechanisms of moral disengagement in the exercise of moral agency." *Journal of Personality and Social Psychology*, 71, 364–374.

Bandura, A., Caprara, G.V., and Zsolnai, L., 2000. "Corporate transgressions through moral disengagement." *Journal of Human Values*, 6, 57–64.

Bandura, A., Underwood, B., and Fromson, M.E., 1975. "Disinhibition of aggression through diffusion of responsibility and dehumanization of victims." *Journal of Research in Personality*, 9, 253–269.

Bolinger, D. 1982, *Language: The Loaded Weapon.* Longman, London.

Caprara, G.V., Barbaranelli, C., Beretta, M., Iafrate, M., Pastorelli, C., Steca, P., and Bandura, A., 2004. *La misura del disimpegno morale e civile su un gruppo di adolescenti e di adulti.* (The measurement of civic and moral disengagement in a group of adolescents and adults) (in press).

Caprara, G.V. and Capanna, C., "Moral Disengagement and Values." *Ricerche di Psicologia* (in press).

Caprara, G.V. and Cervone, D., 2000. *Personality: Determinants, Dynamics and Potentials.* Cambridge University Press, New York.

Diener, E., 1977. "Deindividuation: Causes and Consequences." *Social Behavior and Personality*, 5, 143–156.

Diener, E., Dienen, J., Endersen, K., Beaman, A.L., and Fraser, S.C., 1975. "Effects of altered responsibility, cognitive set, and modeling on physical aggression and deindividuation." *Journal of Personality and Social Psychology*, 31, 328–337.

Gabor, T., 1994. *Everybody Does It: Crime by the Public.* University of Toronto Press, Toronto.

Keen, S., 1986. *Faces of the Enemy*. Harper & Row, San Francisco.

Kelman, H.C., 1973. "Violence without moral restraint: Reflections on the dehumanization of victims and victimizers." *Journal of Social Issues*, 29, 25–61.

Kelman, H.C. and Hamilton, V.L., 1989. *Crimes of Obedience: Toward a Social Psychology of Authority and Responsibility*. Yale University Press, New Haven (CT).

Lutz, W.D., 1987. "Language, appearance, and reality: Doublespeak in 1984" In: P.C. Boardman (ed.), *The Legacy of Language: A Tribute to Charlton Laird.* University of Nevada Press, Reno, 103–119.

Milgram, S., 1974. *Obedience to Authority: An Experimental View.* Harper & Row, New York.

Putnam, R.D., 1993. *Making Democracy Work. Civic Traditions in Modern Italy.* Princeton University Press, Princeton (NJ).

Putnam, R.D., 2000. *Bowling Alone. The Collapse and Revival of American Community.* Simon and Schuster, New York.

Rapoport, D.C. and Alexander, Y. (eds), 1982. *The Morality of Terrorism: Religious and Secular Justification.* Pergamon Press, Elmsford (NY).

Reich, W. (ed.), 1990. *Origins of Terrorism: Psychologies, Ideologies, Theologies, States of Mind.* Cambridge University Press, Cambridge.

Schwartz, S.H., 1992. "Universals in the content and structure of values: Theoretical advances and empirical tests in 20 countries." In: M. Zanna (ed.), *Advances in Experimental Social Psychology.* Academic Press, New York, Vol. 25, 1–65.

Schwartz, S.H., 1994. "Are there universal aspects in the structure and contents of human values?" *Journal of Social Issues* 50, 19–45.

Tilker, H.A., 1970. "Socially responsible behavior as a function of observer responsibility and victim feedback." *Journal of Personality and Social Psychology*, 14. 95–100.

Zimbardo, P.G., 1969. "The human choice: Individuation, reason, and order versus dein-dividuation, impulse, and chaos" In: W.J. Arnold and D. Levine (eds) *Nebraska Symposium on Motivation.* University of Nebraska Press, Lincoln, Vol. 17, 237–309.

Zimbardo, P.G., 1995. "The psychology of evil: A situations perspective on recruiting good people to engage in anti-social acts." *Research in Social Psychology*, 11, 125–133.

Gian Vittorio Caprara

Gian Vittorio Caprara was born in 1944 in Erba (Italy) and received his Laurea Degree in political science and his Specialization in psychology from the Catholic University of Milan. Since 1980 he has been full professor of personality psychology at the University of Rome "La Sapienza." He is a former president of the European Association of Personality and was a fellow in residence at both The Netherlands Institute for Advanced Study and The Swedish Collegium for Advanced Study in the Social Sciences.

Professor Caprara is a member of the Academia Europaea. He is also a member of scientific committees and on the editorial boards of several international scientific journals of psychology. He is author or coauthor of over 300 scientific publications, examples of which include the following:

Caprara, G.V. and G. Van Heck (eds), 1992. *Modern Personality Psychology*. Harvester Weatsheaf, London.

Caprara, G.V. and D. Cervone, 2000. *Personality. Determinants, Dynamics, and Potentials*. Cambridge University Press, Cambridge.

Cristina Capanna

Cristina Capanna was born in 1975, in Rieti, Italy. She received her Laurea Degree and her Ph.D. in psychology from the University of Rome "La Sapienza."

Cristina Capanna's publications in English include the following:

Caprara, G.V., P. Steca, A. Zelli, and C. Capanna, 2005. "A new scale for measuring adults' prosocialness." *European Journal of Psychological Assessment*, 21, (2), 77–89.

Caprara, G.V., S.H. Schwartz, C. Capanna, C. Barbaranelli, and M. Vecchione, "Personality and Politics: Traits, Values and Political Orientation." *Political Psychology* (2005, in press).

Laszlo Zsolnai
Business Ethics Center
Corvinus University of Budapest

Ethical Decision Making

The self-centeredness of modern organizations leads to environmental destruction and human deprivation. The principle of responsibility developed by Hans Jonas requires caring for the beings affected by our decisions and actions. Ethical decision making creates a synthesis of reverence for ethical norms, rationality in goal achievement, and respect for the stakeholders. The maximin rule selects the "least worst alternative" in the multidimensional decision space of deontological, goal-achievement and stakeholder values. The ethical decision maker can be characterized as having the ability to take multiple perspectives and make appropriate balances across diverse value dimensions. Modern organizations should develop a critical sensitivity to and empathy toward human and non-human beings with which they share a common environment.

1. Perverse Decisions of Modern Organizations

Modern organizations are disembedded from their environmental and social contexts and usually consider the natural environment and human persons as mere means to accomplish their own purposes and goals. The dominating *self-centered orientation* of modern organizations produces ecological destruction and human deprivation.

Perverse decisions of modern organizations appear in such phenomena as decision under risk and discounting in space and time. Prospect theory and the general theory of discount can help us in describing and analyzing these phenomena.

1.1 Risky Decisions

The *prospect theory* developed by *Daniel Kahneman* and *Amos Tversky* is an empirically well-established theory that gives us a realistic picture about the main regularities of decision making under risk (Kahneman and Tversky 1979).

Prospect theory states that decision makers display *risk aversion* in choices involving sure gains. For example, they prefer gaining $1,000 surely over gaining $10,000 with a 10 percent chance.

Prospect theory also states that decision makers display *risk seeking* in choices involving sure losses. For example, they prefer losing $10,000 with a 10 percent chance over losing $1,000 surely.

From prospect theory it follows that decision makers are *more sensitive to losses* than to gains. This means, for example, that they prefer gaining $10,000 surely and, at the same time, losing $100,000 with a 10 percent chance over losing $10,000 surely and, at the same time, gaining $100,000 with a 10 percent chance.

Risky decisions made by corporate and governmental decision makers often endanger the safety and integrity of the natural environment and human populations. The so-called catastrophic risk is a closely related phenomenon. The probability of catastrophes caused by modern, large-scale technologies is usually low but never zero. And the possible negative consequences are horrifying: irreversible destruction of ecosystems and enormous losses of human life.

The most tragic examples of this kind of ecological and human tragedy are the Chernobyl nuclear reactor explosion in 1986 that sent nuclear fallout across Europe, increasing human and animal cancers, and the wreck of the Exxon Valdez oil tanker at the Alaskan coastline in 1989 that produced the largest oil spill in American history.

1.2 Discounting in Space and Time

Decision makers usually overvalue things here and now in comparison with things far and later. This phenomenon is produced by the mechanism of *discounting*.

According to the general theory of discount, decision makers discount gains that are distant in space and time. For example, they prefer gaining $1,000 here and now over gaining $1,000 far and later. "A bird in the hand is worth two in the bush."

According to the general theory of discount, decision makers put off negative things till the morrow because they discount losses that are distant in space and time. For example, they would rather lose $1,000 far and later than here and now.

From the general theory of discount it follows that decision makers undervalue both gains and losses that are distant in space and time. For example, they prefer gaining $1,000 here and now and losing $1,000 far and later over losing $1,000 here and now and gaining $1,000 far and later.

Decision makers use discount rates to value things distant in space and time. The present value of a thing is usually calculated as follows:

$$T = t/(1 + \alpha)^x$$

where T is the present value of the thing t, x is a measure of the distance of t in space or in time, and α is the discount rate, which is usually between 5 percent and 15 percent.

If the distance of a thing in space and/or time is great enough then its present value becomes extremely small. Also, the present value depends on the applied discount rate: the greater the discount rate, the smaller the present value. The present value of a thing is determined by the applied discount rate and its distance in space and time.

Discounting in space and time may produce negative consequences in corporate and governmental decision making. Decision makers, who strongly discount things in space and time, are interested in neither the solutions of long-range ecological and human problems, nor the global impacts of their activities on the natural environment and human communities.

The international trade in hazardous wastes is an illustrative case in point. American and West-European countries transport and dump hazardous wastes in distant and less-developed Third World countries, without displaying any interest in the future ecological and human health impacts of these materials (Sing and Lakhan 1989).

1.3 Self-Centered Organizations

By combining the main lessons of prospect theory and the general theory of discount we can arrive at a better understanding of the self-centeredness of modern organizations.

Modern organizations favor sure gains here and now and unsure losses far and later while disfavoring sure losses here and now and unsure gains far and later. For example, they would rather gain $1,000 here and now for sure and lose $10,000 far and later with a 10 percent chance rather than lose $1,000 here and now for sure and gain $10,000 far and later with a 10 percent chance (Table 1).

Table 1
Self-centered Choices of Modern Organizations

	sure, here and now	**unsure, far and later**
gains	favored	disfavored
losses	disfavored	favored

Modern organizations experience a sharp distinction between themselves and their natural and social environments. In *Gregory Bateson*'s words, this state of mind can be called "non-participating consciousness " In such a state of mind the subject "in here" sees himself or herself as radically disparate from the object he or she conceptually confronts "out there " In this view the self is created by the subject-object dichotomy, the distance between nature and ourselves. (Berman 1981).

The self-centered orientation of modern organizations is deeply rooted in their non-participating consciousness, which leads to *environmental destruction* and *human deprivation*.

2. The Principle of Responsibility

The outstanding German-American philosopher *Hans Jonas* has injected the problem of moral responsibility into contemporary moral discourse. Jonas published the German version of his theory of responsibility in 1979 under the title "Das Prinzip Verantwortung. Versuch einer Ethic fur die Technologische Zivilization" The rewritten and enlarged English edition was published in 1984 under the title "The Imperative of Responsibility: In Search of an Ethics for the Technological Age" (Jonas 1979; 1984).

Jonas argues that the nature of human action has changed so dramatically in our times that a correspondingly radical *change* in *ethics* is called for as well. He emphasizes that in previous ethics "all dealing with the nonhuman world, that is, the whole realm of techne was ethically neutral. Ethical significance belonged to the direct dealing of man with man, including man dealing with himself: all traditional ethics is *anthropocentric*. The entity of 'man' and his basic condition was considered constant in essence and not itself an object of reshaping techne. The effective range of action was small, the time span of foresight, goal-setting, and accountability was short, control of circumstances limited" (Jonas 1984, 4–5).

According to Jonas new dimensions of responsibility emerged because *nature* became a subject of human responsibility. This is underscored by the irreversibility and cumulative character of the human impact on the living world. *Knowledge*, under these circumstances, is a prime duty of man and must be commensurate with the causal scale of human action. We should seek "not only the human good but also the good of things extrahuman, that is, to extend the recognition of 'ends in themselves' beyond the sphere of man and make the human good include the care of them" (Jonas 1984, 7–8).

For Jonas, an imperative responding to the new type of human action might run like this: "Act so that the effects of your actions are compatible with the permanence of genuine human life " Or, expressed negatively: "Act so that the effects of your actions are not destructive to the future possibility of such life" (Jonas 1984, 11).

Jonas argues that our duties to future generations and to nature are independent of any idea of rights or reciprocity. Human responsibility basically consists of a *non-reciprocal duty* to guarding beings.

Jonas states that the necessary conditions of moral responsibility are as follows: "The first and most general condition of responsibility is causal power, that is, that acting makes an impact on the world; the second, that such acting is under the agent's control; and the third, that he can foresee its consequences to some extent" (Jonas 1984, 90).

Jonas emphasizes the fact that prospective responsibility is never formal but always *substantive*. "I feel responsible, not in the first place for my conduct and its consequences but for the matter that has a claim on my acting." For example "the well-being, the interest, the fate of others has, by circumstance or by agreement, come to my care, which means that my control over it involves at the same time my obligation to it" (Jonas 1984, 92 and 93.).

Jonas differentiates between natural responsibility on the one hand and contractual responsibility on the other. "It is the distinction between natural responsibility, where the immanent 'ought-to-be' of the object claims its agent a priori and quite unilaterally, and contracted or appointed responsibility, which is conditional a posteriori upon the fact and the terms of the relationship actually entered into" (Jonas 1984, 95).

The parent and the statesman are presented as ideal types of natural responsibility and contractual responsibility, respectively. The parent is responsible for his or her child not because of the child's own will or even contrary to it. However, the responsibility of the statesman comes from the political contract that he or she has established with his or her constituencies.

There are important similarities between Jonas' theory of responsibility and the ethic of care described by *Carol Gilligan* in her best-seller "In a Different Voice: Psychological Theory and Women's Development" (Gilligan 1982).

Gilligan characterizes the morality of women as an *ethic* of *care*. "The ideal of care is thus an activity of relationship, of seeing and responding to need, taking care of the world by sustaining the web of connection so that no one is left alone." The ethic of care "is the wish not to hurt others and the hope that in morality lies a way of solving conflicts so that no one will be hurt." Women consider the inflicting of hurt as "selfish and immoral in its reflection of unconcern, while the expression of care is seen as fulfillment of moral responsibility" (Gilligan 1982, 62, 65, and 73).

Gilligan states that men and women represent two different moral ideologies: the ethic of rights and the ethic of care, respectively. Separation is justified by an *ethic* of *rights* while attachment is supported by an *ethic* of *care*. "The morality of rights is predicated on equality and centered on the understanding of fairness, while the ethic of responsibility relies on the concept of equity, the recognition of differences in need. While the ethic of rights is a manifestation of equal respect, balancing the claims of other and the self, the ethic of responsibility rests on an understanding that gives rise to compassion and care" (Gilligan 1982, 165).

Gilligan does not argue for the superiority of women's morality. The two disparate modes of moral experience are connected in *mature morality*. "While an ethic of justice proceeds from the premise of equality – that everyone should be treated the same – an ethic of care rests on the premise of non-violence – that no one should be hurt." In maturity "both perspectives converge in the realization that just as inequality adversely affects both parties in an unequal relationship, so too violence is destructive for everyone involved" (Gilligan 1982, 174).

An advanced concept of responsibility integrates the reverence for rights represented by men and the non-violence of care represented by women.

3. Making Ethical Decisions

In an economic context *Kenneth E. Goodpaster* offers the most operationalized model of ethical decision making (Goodpaster 1983).

3.1 Rationality and Respect

Goodpaster proposes understanding moral responsibility as a combination of two basic components, namely rationality and respect.

Rationality involves the following attributes:

(i) lack of impulsiveness;

(ii) care in mapping out alternatives and consequences;

(iii) clarity about goals and purposes;

(iv) attention to details of implementation.

Rationality described by attributes (i),...,(iv) greatly differs from the rationality postulate of mainstream economics that requires consistent utility maximization. The rationality concept used here is process oriented and does not require maximizing anything. *Max Weber*'s concept of "zveckrationalitat" and *Herbert Simon*'s notion of procedural rationality are closely related to it (Weber 1921–22, Simon 1978).

Respect is the other component of moral responsibility. For Goodpaster, respect means a special awareness of and concern for the effects of one's decisions and policies on others, beyond seeing others as merely instrumental in accomplishing one's own purposes. This is respect for the lives of others and involves taking their needs and interests seriously, not simply as resources in one's own decision making but as limiting conditions, which change the very definition of one's habitat from a self-centered to a shared environment (Goodpaster and Matthews 1982, 134).

Respect described in this way has a basic similarity to the altruistic behavior that is widely discussed in psychology, economics, and sociology. The prominent Italian economist *Stefano Zamagni* offers a clear conceptualization of altruistic behavior. He defines individuals as altruistic when they feel and act as if the welfare of others were an end in itself; that is, as something of relevance independently of its effects on their own well-being. If your concern for the welfare of others is merely instrumental in promoting your own longer-term ends and ceases once these ends can be more easily pursued in some other way, you are an enlightened self-interested person, not a genuine altruist (Zamagni 1992).

3.2 The 3 R Model

Goodpaster's model is a consequentialist system interwoven with agent-relative elements. Agent-relativity means that the model permits the decision maker to produce less than the overall best consequences for the stakeholders in order to realize her or his own goals and purposes. The model also extends to incorporating agent-relative constraints that would simply forbid certain courses of action for the decision maker.

Consequentialist models can be criticized on consequentialist as well as non-consequentialist grounds.

In complex economic and political decision situations phenomena can emerge that make the consequentialist evaluation of an act very difficult, if not impossible. The most important of these phenomena are marginal contributions, uncertain consequences, and distant effects.

There are cases where the agent's choice produces only marginally negative consequences to the stakeholders but the cumulative and/or aggregate effect of this kind of behavior is detrimental to them. Ecologist *Garret Hardin*'s famous "tragedy of the commons" model describes such situations (Hardin 1968).

If some consequences of an act are rather uncertain then the decision makers tend to neglect them in their consequentialist considerations. This may lead to inadequate accounting. Similarly, if the consequences of an act are distant in space and/or time then the decision makers discount them at a positive (and sometimes very high) rate. Hence consequences beyond the normal space and time reference of the decision makers are usually overdiscounted.

The phenomena of marginal contributions, uncertain consequences, and distant effects present *decision traps* from which there is no escape within the consequentialist framework.

Consequentialist models are also criticized from a deontological point of view. Deontological ethicists have developed strong deontological arguments that overwrite consequentialist considerations. The decision maker may have deontological reasons not to do certain things even if they would lead to good overall consequences. Deontological reasons limit what we may do to others or how we may treat them (Nagel 1986).

It is better to define respect exclusively in terms of altruistic orientation toward the affected parties. Also, we can introduce deontological considerations as a separate component into the model of ethical decision making. In this way we can get a more robust model in which ethical decision making is characterized by the making of a synthesis of deontological considerations, rationality in goal-achievement, and respect for the stakeholders. This model of ethical decision making can be called the 3 R model, since its components are reverence & rationality & respect (Zsolnai 1997). (See Figure 1)

Figure 1
The 3 R Model

Ethical Decision Making = Reverence & Rationality & Respect

3.3 Complex Decision Situations

The following features can characterize complex business or public administration decision situations. First, at least two decision alternatives are available for the decision maker; that is, she or he can choose among different courses of action. Second, in the decision situation ethical norms apply which represent duties of the decision maker. Third, the decision maker has goals that she or he wants to achieve in the decision situation. Finally, different stakeholders are present that can be affected by the outcome of the decision.

We can formalize the above listed elements of complex decision situations as follows:

(1) $\mathbf{A_1, \ldots, A_i, \ldots, A_m}$ $\qquad (\mathbf{m \geq 2})$

This means that at least two decision alternatives are feasible for the decision maker.

(2) $\mathbf{D_1, \ldots, D_k, \ldots, D_p}$ $\qquad (\mathbf{p \geq 1})$

This means that at least one ethical norm applies in the choice situation.

(3) $\mathbf{G_1, \ldots, G_j, \ldots, G_n}$ $\qquad (\mathbf{n \geq 1})$

This means that the decision maker has at least one goal that she or he wants to achieve.

(4) $S_1, ..., S_q, ..., S_r$ $(r \geq 1)$

This means that at least one stakeholder is present in the choice situation.

Ethical decision making involves finding and implementing the decision alternative that best corresponds to the idea of moral responsibility in the given context. Which is the appropriate decision rule for making an ethical decision?

(5) $A^* = \Omega (A_1, ..., A_i, ..., A_m)$

where A* refers to the selected alternative.

Deontological value can be defined as the value of a decision alternative seen from the perspective of the applicable ethical norms. The deontological values of the decision alternatives $A_1, ..., A_i, ..., A_m$: can be represented by a vector as follows:

(6) $\underline{d} = [D(A_1), ..., D(A_k), ..., D(A_m)]$

$D(A_i)$ can be measured on the ordinal scale [1, 0, –2]. This means that **D(Ai) = 1** if A_i is right regarding the ethical norms; $D(A_i) = 0$ if A_i is neutral regarding the ethical norms; and $D(A_i) = -2$ if A_i is wrong regarding the ethical norms.

The deontological values of decision alternatives depend on two things:

(i) Which are the considered ethical norms?

(ii) How are the importance weights assessed?

The answer to these questions is that an ideal third party, the so-called impartial spectator, should define the set of applicable ethical norms and assess the corresponding weights in the given situation. That no such ideal third party exists necessitates a real world surrogate. Possibilities include some of the newer institutions of deliberative democracy such as the citizens' jury, for example.

It is natural that the decision maker considers the value of the decision alternatives with a view toward the achievement of her or his own goals. In classical decision theory this was the only dimension in which courses of action were evaluated and decided upon.

Goal-achievement value can be defined as the value of a decision alternative seen from the locus of the achievement of the decision maker's goals. The goal- achievement value of the decision alternatives $A_1, ..., A_i, ..., A_m$ can be represented by a vector.

(7) $\underline{g} = [G(A_1), ..., G(A_i), ..., G(A_m)]$

$G(A_i)$ is measured on the ordinal scale [1, 0, –2]. This means that $G(A_i) = 1$ if A_i is useful regarding the goals; $G(A_i) = 0$ if A_i is neutral regarding the goals; and $G(A_i) = -2$ if A_i is useless regarding the goals.

The important question is to what extent the decision maker is free to choose her or his goals and the weights she or he attributes to the chosen goals.

Decision makers are embedded in interpersonal relations and the social context, so it is realistic to presuppose that decision makers set goals and assign weights to them with reference to those communities and organizations in which they happen to exist and function.

Stakeholder value can be defined as the value of a decision alternative seen from the perspective of the stakeholders. The stakeholder values of decision alternatives A_1, ..., A_i, ..., A_m can be represented by a vector:

(8) $\underline{s} = [S(A_1), ..., S(A_i), ..., S(A_m)]$

$S(A_i)$ can be measured on the ordinal scale [1, 0, –2]. This means that $S(A_i) = 1$ if A_i is good regarding the stakeholders; $S(A_i) = 0$ if A_i is neutral regarding the stakeholders; and $S(A_i) = -2$ if A_i is bad regarding the stakeholders.

Weighing of the stakeholders poses difficult questions. Any distribution of weights generates some form of justice or injustice among the stakeholders. We can agree with *Michael Walzer* that an adequate conception of justice is necessarily plural, that is, multidimensional (Walzer 1993).

Two variables can be considered as means by which stakeholders can be weighed against one another. One variable is their stake while the other is their size. The greater the stake and the size of a stakeholder, the greater the weight that should be attributed. Notice that there is no such thing as an absence of weighing if at least two parties are present. If one does not attribute weights to the parties then she or he considers them as being equal. Having no weights means having equal weights.

Holding (6), (7), and (8) together we can get a *multiple evaluation* of the decision alternative A_i.

(9) $\underline{v} = [D(A_i), G(A_i), S(A_i)]$

The first component of the vector is the deontological value of the decision alternative; the second component is the goal-achievement value of the decision alternative, while the third component is the stakeholder value of the decision alternative.

The vector **v** represents a simultaneous evaluation of the same course of action from different perspectives. The deontological value is assessed from the perspective of an impartial observer; the goal-achievement value is assessed from the perspective of the agent; and the stakeholder value is assessed from the perspective of the affected parties (Figure 2).

Figure 2
Multiple Perspectives in Evaluation of an Act

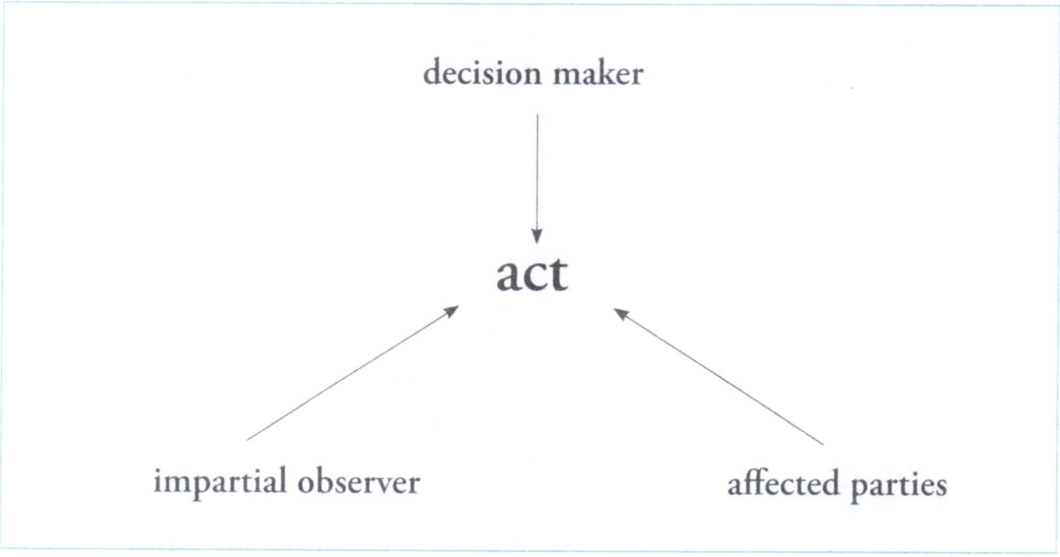

The "ethical calculus" advanced here is close to *Amartya Sen*'s ideas about the moral evaluation of acts. In his influential book "On Ethics & Economics" he writes "To get an overall assessment of the ethical standing of an activity it is necessary not only to look at its own intrinsic value (if any), but also its instrumental role and its consequences on other things .... The advantages of consequential reasoning involving interdependence and instrumental accounting, can then be combined not only with intrinsic valuation, but also with position relativity and agent sensitivity of moral assessment" (Sen 1987, 75 and 77). Our moral accounting system tries to do exactly this job.

3.4 The Maximin Principle

A matrix that contains multiple evaluations of all the decision alternatives available for the decision maker can provide an overall picture about the choice situation.

$$(10)\ \underline{V} = \begin{matrix} D(A_1), \ldots, G(A_1), \ldots, S(A_1) \\ D(A_i), \ldots, G(A_i), \ldots, S(A_i) \\ D(A_m), \ldots, G(A_m), \ldots, S(A_m) \end{matrix}$$

The matrix $\underline{V}$ may present *value conflict*. The best strategy is to maintain the complexity of the decision situation and try to find an *optimal compromise* among diverse value dimensions. Trying to balance different values against one another is an essential strategy in complex choice situations. The *maximin rule* can do the required job quite well. It implies the maximization of the minimum payoff of decision alternatives.

Austrian logician *Earnest Zermello* first described the maximin rule in 1912. In their groundbreaking book "Theory of Games and Economic Behavior", *John Von Neumann* and *Oscar Morgenstein* developed the rule further (Von Neumann and Morgenstein 1944).

In complex decision situations the rule of making ethical decisions is stated as follows:

$$(11)\quad \mathbf{A^* = maximin}\ [D(A_i), G(A_i), S(A_i)]$$

Ethical decision making demands the selection of the *least worst alternative* in the decision space of deontological, goal-achievement, and stakeholder values – in the sense that the minimum value of the selected alternative is greater than the minimum value of any other alternative available for the decision maker in the given situation. The comparability of $D(A_i)$, $G(A_i)$, and $S(A_i)$ is provided by the fact that they are measured on the same ordinal scale [**1, 0, –2**].

If there are two decision alternatives A_1 and A_2, then the responsible decision is A_1 if and only if:

$$(12)\ \mathbf{min}\ [D(A_1), G(A_1), S(A_1)] > \mathbf{min}\ [D(A_2), G(A_2), S(A_2)]$$

The underlying principle of responsible decision making is that the decision maker should find an optimal compromise among the applicable ethical norms, her or his own goals, and the interests of the stakeholders.

The ethical decision defined by (11) provides a *Pareto optimal result* in the multidimensional decision space. This means that given the set of decision alternatives it is not possible to increase their value in one value dimension without decreasing their value in at least one other value dimension. In this sense the alternative chosen by the maximin rule dominates all the other alternatives.

4. Analyzing the World Bank Case

A provocative case concerning the World Bank environmental policy is useful in demonstrating how the ethical decision making model works.

In the early 1990s, some economic advisors of the World Bank were proposing that the organization should encourage increased migration of dirty industries to less-developed countries. The argument was as follows: "The measurement of the costs of health-impairing pollution depends on the foregone earnings from increased morbidity and mortality. From this point of view a given amount of health-impairing pollution should be done in the country with the lowest cost, which will be the country with the lowest wages .... The costs of pollution are likely to be non-linear as the initial increments of pollution probably have very low cost .... The demand for a clean environment for aesthetic and health reasons is likely to have very high income-elasticity. The concern over an agent that causes a one-in-a-million in the odds of the prostate cancer is obviously going to be much higher in a country where people survive to get prostate cancer than in a country where under-5 mortality is 200 per thousand. Also, much of the concern over industrial atmospheric discharge is about visibility-impairing particulates. These discharges may have very little health impact. Clearly, trade in goods that embody aesthetic pollution concerns could be welfare enchanting" (*The Economist*, February 8, 1992, 66).

In this case, there are a wide variety of stakeholders because not only citizens of developed and less-developed countries are affected by the World Bank environmental policy, but also the natural environment and future generations. The *policy options* (alternatives) are as follows:

A_1 = encouraging the migration of dirty industries to LDCs

A_2 = not encouraging the migration of dirty industries to LDCs

The most relevant ethical norm that applies here is fairness. **(D)** It is formulated by *Hausman* and *McPherson* as the pay-your-way principle, which requires locating dirty industries so that those who derive the largest benefits from industries endure most of the pollution costs (Hausman and McPherson 1996, 204).

The declared goal of the World Bank is to enhance global welfare. (**G**)

The most important stakeholders can be identified as citizens of the developed countries (S_1), dirty industries in the developed countries (S_2), citizens of the less developed countries (S_3), the natural environment affected by dirty industries in the developed countries (S_4), the targeted natural environment in the less developed countries (S_5), and future generations (S_6).

From a deontological perspective alternative A_1 is certainly *wrong* while alternative A_2 is certainly right because the latter corresponds to the norm of fairness and the former violates it. Using the ordinal scale of [**1, 0, –2**] we can calculate the deontological values of A_1 and A_2 as follows:

$D(A_1) = -2$

$D(A_2) = 1$

Alternative A_1 can be useful for the goal of enchanting global welfare with probability **p**. Alternative A_2 might be useless for the achievement of this goal with probability **q**. Using the ordinal scale of [**1, 0, –2**] we can calculate the goal-achievement values of A_1 and A_2 as follows:

$G(A_1) = 1(p)-2(1-p) = 3p-2$

$G(A_2) = 1(1-q)-2(q) = 1-3q$

Migration of dirty industries to LDCs would be good for the citizens of developed countries (S_1), for the industries themselves (S_2), and for the natural environment affected by those industries in the developed countries (S_4). However, it would be bad for the citizens of less developed countries (S_3), for the targeted natural environment in the less developed countries (S_5), and for future generations (S_6) since environmental pollution is much more controllable in the developed countries than in the less developed countries.

Using the ordinal scale [**1, 0, –2**] the stakeholder values of A_1 can be calculated as follows:

$S_1(A_1) = 1$

$S_2(A_1) = 1$

$S_3(A_1) = -2$

$S_4(A_1) = 1$

$S_5(A_1) = -2$

$S_6(A_1) = -2$

This policy option is neutral for stakeholders $S_1, \ldots, S_5$ since it does not change the present status quo. However, future generations (S_6) could benefit from keeping dirty industries in the developed countries by forcing them to innovate and to become more environmentally friendly.

For this reason the stakeholder values of alternative A_2 can be calculated as follows:

$S_1(A_2) = 0$

$S_2(A_2) = 0$

$S_3(A_2) = 0$

$S_4(A_2) = 0$

$S_5(A_2) = 0$

$S_6(A_2) = 1$

The question remaining is how to weight stakeholders $S_1, \ldots, S_6$:

Let $v_1, \ldots, v_6$ be importance weights attributed to the stakeholders. On the basis of inter-species and inter-generational justice we can argue that equal weights should be attributed to nature, society, and future generations. This implies that $v_1 + v_2 + v_3 = v_4 + v_5 = v_6$. We do not discriminate between citizens of the developed countries and citizens of the less developed countries, consequently $v_1 = v_3$. Similarly, we do not discriminate between the natural environment in the developed countries and the natural environment in the less developed countries, consequently $v_4 = v_5$. Considering that almost everybody is served by dirty industries, they can get a weight similar to citizens of the developed countries: $v_1 = v_2$.

It is required that

$$\sum v_i = 1 \qquad (i = 1,\ldots,6)$$

Hence we get

$$v_1 = 1/9;\ v_2 = 1/9;\ v_3 = 1/9;\ v_4 = 1/6;\ v_5 = 1/6;\ v_6 = 1/3$$

Aggregate stakeholder values of the two alternatives are as follows:

$S(A_1) = -5/6 \approx -0{,}83$

$S(A_2) = 1/3 \approx 0{,}33$

Table 3 shows the different payoffs of the two policy options.

Table 3

Payoffs in the World Bank Case

	deontological value	goal-achievement value	stakeholder value
A_1 alternative	–2	3p–2	–0,83
A_2 alternative	1	1–3q	0,33

Multiple evaluations of the alternatives are provided by the following vectors:

$V(A_1) = [-2, 3p-2, -0{,}83]$

$V(A_2) = [1, 1-3q, 0{,}33]$

According to the maximin rule A_2 is better than A_1 because **min** $V(A_2) >$ **min** $V(A_1)$. The worst component of $V(A_1)$ is –2 while the worst component of $V(A_2)$ is always greater than –2, holding that $1 > q > 0$.

The World Bank *should not encourage* migration of dirty industries to less developed countries. Encouraging migration of dirty industries to less developed countries is unacceptable from the deontological perspective and also negative from the stakeholder perspective, so some questionable welfare improvement cannot compensate for the violation of ethical norms and vital stakeholder interests. The rejection of the policy option is also justifiable even if citizens of the less developed countries get full monetary compensation from citizens of the developed countries.

5. Conclusion

The *procedural model* of ethical decision making can be summarized as follows:

(I) Framing of the decision situation by
- (i) identifying the applicable ethical norms;
- (ii) mapping out the affected parties;
- (iii) defining goals and generating alternatives.

(II) Multiple evaluation of the available alternatives regarding
- (i) the ethical norms;
- (ii) the goals to be achieved;
- (iii) the affected parties.

(III) Finding the least worst alternative in the multidimensional space of deontological, goal-achievement, and stakeholder values.

The ethical decision maker can be characterized as having the ability to take *multiple perspectives* and make *optimal balances* across diverse value dimensions. He or she is a properly socialized individual who has developed reflexivity regarding the ethical norms of her or his society and displays empathy toward others.

The components of the 3R model of ethical decision making, namely reverence for the ethical norms, rationality in goal achievement, and respect for others can be considered as virtues. These are motivational dispositions that determine ways individuals tend to act in certain sorts of circumstances. The view of reverence, rationality, and respect as virtues is consistent with the Aristotelian notion that virtues are "aretai," that is, excellencies that result from a person's self-cultivation (Pincoffs 1992, 1286).

Perverse decisions of modern organizations can be avoided by employing ethical decision making. The preservation of the natural environment and the provision of the good life for present and future generations require critical sensitivity to the ethical norms of society and caring for human and non-human "beings."

References

Berman, M., 1981. *The Reenchantment of the World.* Cornell University Press, Ithaca & London.

Dawes, R.M., van de Kragt, A.J.C., and Orbell, J.M., 1990. "Cooperation for the Benefit of Us – Not Me, or My Conscience." In: J.J. Mansbridge (ed.), *Beyond Self-Interest.* The University of Chicago Press, Chicago & London, 97–110.

Goodpaster, K.E., 1983. "The Concept of Corporate Responsibility." *Journal of Business Ethics,* 1983. No. 1., 1–22.

Goodpaster, K.E. and Matthews, J.B., 1982. "Can a Corporation Have Conscience?" *Harvard Business Review,* 1982. No. 1., 132–41.

Hardin, G., 1968. "The Tragedy of the Commons." *Science,* 1968. (December), 1243–48.

Jonas, H., 1984. *The Imperative of Responsibility: In Search of an Ethics for the Technological Age.* University of Chicago Press, Chicago & London.

Kahneman, D. and Tversky, A., 1979. "Prospect Theory: An Analysis of Decision Under Risk." *Econometrica,* 1979 (March), 263–91.

Nagel, T., 1986. *A View from Nowhere.* Oxford University Press, New York.

Pincoffs, E.L., 1992. "Virtues." In: L.C. Becker and C.B. Becker (eds), *Encyclopedia of Ethics.* Garland Publishing, Inc., New York & London, 1283–88.

Sen, A., 1987. *On Ethics and Economics.* Blackwell, Oxford.

Simon, H.A., 1976. *Administrative Behavior.* The Free Press, New York.

Simon, H.A., 1978. "Rationality as Process and as Product of Thought." *American Economic Review,* 1978. No. 2., 1–16.

Sing, J.B. and Lakhan, V.C., 1989. "Business Ethics and the International Trade in Hazardous Wastes." *Journal of Business Ethics,* 1989. No. 2.

Von Neuman, J. and Morgenstein, O., 1944. *Theory of Games and Economic Behavior.* Princeton University Press, Princeton.

Walzer, M., 1993. *The Spheres of Justice.* Basic Books, New York.

Weber, M., 1921–22. *Economy and Society.* G. Roth and C. Wittich (eds), 1968. Bedminster Press, New York.

Zamagni, S. (ed.), 1992. *Economics of Altruism.* Edward Elgar, Cheltenham.

Zsolnai, L., 1997. *Responsibility and Choice: Decision Making in Multiple Value Perspectives.* The Netherlands Institute for Advanced Study, Wassenaar (Manuscript).

Laszlo Zsolnai

Laszlo Zsolnai is professor and director of the Business Ethics Center at the Corvinus University of Budapest. He is chairman of the Business Ethics Inter-faculty Group of the Community of European Management Schools (CEMS). He is editor of the Frontiers of Business Ethics book series at Peter Lang Academic Publisher in Oxford.

Laszlo Zsolnai was born in 1958, in Szentes, Hungary. He has a master's in finance and a doctorate in sociology from the Budapest University of Economic Sciences. He received his Ph.D. and DSc degrees in economics from the Hungarian Academy of Sciences.

Laszlo Zsolnai is editorial board member of the *International Journal of Social Economics, International Journal of Spirituality and Management, Business Ethics: An European Review, Finance and the Common Good, Society and Economy*, and *Society and Business Review.*

Laszlo Zsolnai's books include the following:

The European Difference. 1998. Kluwer Academic Publishers, Boston/Dordrecht/London.

Ethics and the Future of Capitalism. 2002. Transactions Publisher, New Jersey/London (with Wojciech Gasparski).

Ethics in the Economy: Handbook of Business Ethics. 2002. Peter Lang Academic Publisher, Oxford and Bern.

Spirituality, Ethics and Management. 2004. Kluwer Academic Publishers, Boston/Dordrecht/London.

Business Within Limits: Deep Ecology and Buddhist Economics. 2005. Peter Lang Academic Publisher, Oxford and Bern (with Knut Johannessen Ims).

PART 2

Innovative Practices and Policy Reforms

David Boyle
New Economics Foundation
London

Authenticity

Anita Roddick is no longer co-chair of the Body Shop, at one stage Britain's biggest international retailer, but she has studiously continued to shock and irritate the mainstream business world.

Shock because she is probably more antipathetic than ever to the moral vacuum that now passes for "free trade" policy. *Irritate* because – although she is endlessly invited to marketing conferences to expound on modern marketing – she is obviously deeply skeptical about the whole idea.

Body Shop actually won a string of marketing awards, but it was at a time when they had no marketing department. And except briefly in North America – where one shopper fainted while watching the Body Shop ad with a man with a tanning lotion bottle down his crotch – they have always shunned advertising.

The Roddick approach to marketing is that you have to tell stories, about real people in real places behind your products. If you step back from the rather self-congratulatory theories of brand management – the assertion, for example, by advertising agency Young and Rubicam that brands are the new religion – the importance of storytelling becomes much more apparent.

In practice, people are almost immune to the 12,000 or so advertisements they see every day – they have to be to stay solvent. In practice, the sheer smoothness of brands – the element of mind control that is just discernable behind the hype – is disconcerting and disappoints very quickly.

That is one reason big brands have been suffering around the world. This decade has seen major crises of confidence among giants such as Coca-Cola, Ford and McDonalds; and in most years since 2000, the annual Interbrand survey has shown more than half the world's biggest brands losing value.

It is a period that has also witnessed the strange theater of the giants HSBC and Interbrew fighting over the right to call themselves "The World's Local ...," which they manifestly are not.

Anita Roddick's stories allow companies to bypass some of this growing suspicion of marketing, spin and manipulation. But it is not a solution open to any global multinational. Body Shop's stories were about real people: if the stories behind your products are actually about sweatshops, semi-slavery and anonymity, that path is closed to you.

All these are symptoms of a much bigger trend, a reaction against marketing – more obvious in some countries than others, but the UK is one of them – and a demand for what is real, unmediated, unspun and human. In short, it is a demand for authenticity.

There are an estimated 12 million Europeans – many with well-paid jobs and young children – who are now downshifting by cutting salary or hours in search of more "authentic" living. There is a parallel phenomenon concerning the way we all spend our money. The annual Ethical Purchasing Index in the UK, published by the Co-op Bank and the New Economics Foundation, which tracks spending patterns during the year, shows that nearly £20 billion a year is spent ethically in the UK. This includes £6.9 billion on ethical goods and services, £3.9 billion on ethical banking and rising fast, with ethical investment roaring ahead of the market. That is small compared to the whole of British expenditure of course, yet some products – A-rated energy efficient appliances and free range eggs, for example – now account for 40 percent of their respective markets.

Of course this is not a universal phenomenon – the last few years have also seen a number of parents naming their babies after the Swedish furniture chain Ikea – but there is a powerful minority for whom authenticity increasingly matters.

Often it stems from a deep-seated unease with the lies we are expected to swallow from companies and governments alike. The lies that underpinned the Iraq war, and the constant lies behind marketing, sap the spirits just by encountering them. The demise of Coca-Cola's Dasani brand – purporting to be rather more than what it actually was: water from the taps – is evidence that truth matters to people.

But actually they are turning against lies even in a more subtle form – the big corporate lie that artificial food, artificial intelligence, virtual sex, virtual teachers and bank managers are somehow every bit as good or as real as the real thing. And one area where this is especially obvious is food.

Those of us who remember such things will recall that, in the historic Apollo 11 mission to the moon in 1969, one of the main stories was about the food the astronauts took with them. The meal of beef and vegetables in a translucent plastic pack, which would turn to soft mush when they added a little hot water, became world famous. At the time, consumers were assured by the media that this was the future of food. All meals would soon come in tubes or plastic bags, without fuss or effort.

The following year, the presenters of the BBC program *Tomorrow's World* – Raymond Baxter and James Burke, both familiar faces from moon-shot commentating – published a vision of what Britain would be like in 2120. This is how they saw the inevitable future of food: "Much of the food available will be based on protein substitutes and, as with a book club today, a family will contract with a company to supply it with part-cooked daily menus which will be delivered once a month in disposable vacuum packs," they wrote. "The most complicated dish will need only a few seconds under a microwave heater to make it ready for the table. As a result of this development, modern homes will no longer have kitchens for food preparation, and the resulting saving in space on a national scale will provide room for a million and a half extra full-sized living units."

But this has still not happened. There is fake food in abundance. We do buy ready meals in their plastic-packaged millions, but it is clear that the culture is also going another way entirely. We are not seeing the last gasp of authentic eating in a flurry of what used to be called "analogue" food (the word "artificial" was thought to frighten people). Nor are we embracing the brave new world of artificial smells, tastes and consistency.

Quite the reverse. Organic food is enjoying an explosion of interest on both sides of the Atlantic. Cookery TV programs and books are some of the most popular. Farmers markets, stuffed with fresh produce straight from the farm, are emerging profitably all over the country. The Campaign for Real Ale has transformed our drinking habits. The market for fast food is increasingly powerful, but it has spawned a growing demand for what is authentic, local and trustworthy.

What is true for food is also true for other areas. Despite the predictions, especially over the past decade, that the future is entirely global and virtual, there is increasing commitment to real food, real culture, real politics, real schools, real community, real medicine, real culture, real stories. This is apparent in the rise of local brands, real ale, reading groups, organic vegetables, complementary medicine, slow food, poetry recitals, unmixed music, materiality in art and unbranded vintage fashions; they are all symptoms of the same thing – a demand for human-scale, face-to-face institutions and real experience.

But most of all, they are symptoms of the creeping exhaustion that comes from dealing with constant manipulation. Almost every public discourse, from magazines to television news, is subtly attempting to cajole, shame or fool us into some kind of action, and we want a break.

If you are rich enough you can avoid it – the U.S. cable channel HBO has no advertisements; McDonalds is banned from the Bahamas. The rest of us get tired of having our defenses up all the time.

Paul Ray's concept of "cultural creatives" – which seems to encompass this consumer group, set out in his book of the same name – suggests that anywhere between 25 and 50 percent of the population is committed to authenticity. They may eat fast food sometimes but will defend their right to an authentic option with increasing passion, yet most of them believe they are almost alone.

The branding think-tank known as the Medinge Group has recognized the basic issue behind this long-term trend, which is that brands must become "more human and more humane" or they will fail. Humanity is indeed the essence of authenticity, and it is why the big brands have such difficulty meeting this demand. They are one-dimensional non-human approximations. This makes it hard for big brands, which are using technology to deliver services to a wide range of people around the world. Small companies, in other words, can be authentic, but can their big competitors?

This disconnection will probably mean increasing segmentation in the market, but there are ways in which the big brands are also trying to board the authenticity bandwagon. In a relatively free market – despite the increasing monopolization of some sectors by a few names – what enough people demand, they will get.

The open source software Linux is one example of a big phenomenon that borrows some authentic clothes. It is the product of a virtual community of debuggers and is increasingly eating into Microsoft's market share – the number of server computers loaded with Linux is growing at 50 per cent a year. That human community at its heart is one of the main sources of its trust, and it is somehow not regarded as being shared with Microsoft.

It is the same with some other major surviving dot.coms. Like Google, eBay is fast, accurate, doesn't overwhelm you with selling messages, and treats you like a real person, rather than a selling opportunity. Like Amazon, they deliberately eschew traditional aspects of branding, spending their money instead on the service itself. Like Starbucks, they simply provide a venue for new communities, and a highly efficient search engine that you can use however you want. eBay provides a system whereby people can interact and create the experience for themselves.

These are just aspects of authenticity. There are no genuine communities here, and people do still seem to have a need for authentic geographical roots. In fact, over half the British population now lives within a 30-minute journey of where they were born. That is why geographical roots are increasingly valuable to companies, and why Champagne, Stilton or Parma ham have successfully defended their rights to use their own historic names. The Slow Food campaign – itself a successful symbol of authenticity – is in the process of promoting others like them: Siennese pigs, Vesuvian apricots, Pietmontese cows – real in a way packaged international brands can never be.

The means to access this whiff of authenticity is also going to be a valuable business proposition in the future. Go into Neal's Yard Dairy in London, for example. Or the new store brand launched in Richmond called Source – slogan: "real food for real people." It is true that these cater to the upper end of the market, but the appeal to geographical roots is obvious: every product is labeled according to precisely where it has come from.

One of the obvious symptoms of demands for authenticity has been the way companies are rowing backwards from the Coca-Cola ideal – exactly the same everywhere – to one where every package tells a story of its own. Café Direct has pictures of some of their growers. Some crisp companies give the name of the fryer that made the packet. Lush packaging even has a picture of the employee who made the box. These mini-stories are the stuff of authenticity: the real people and the real places that made them.

So what can companies do now to be authentic? It is certainly going to be difficult, but some of them are already trying to put into practice some or all of these four authenticity principles:

(1) Eschew glitz and rationalized delivery systems, and garner trust by telling simple stories and wandering off-message as needed.

(2) Connect with what is human – either because the brand is an expression of a single personality, or because it reveals the personalities of the range of people behind it, or because the service is genuinely personal.

(3) Have genuine roots to a specific place, or provide a portal to ordinary producers or sellers in specific places.

(4) Allow customers and employees to feel better connected to their own ideals and values.

What is most difficult for corporate marketing is that authenticity has imperfection at its heart. That is why people tend to trust those with the humanity to risk being off-message. The manifesto of the Glasgow-based consultancy Erasmus says: "Imperfection carries a story in a way that perfection can only dream about."

This is how people seem to recognize authenticity in an instant, even though they may find it difficult to define. They recognize it because it is human: it is made by people, mediated by people, and is three-dimensional like human beings. It is not a shiny, perfect experience delivered by automatons or computer programs, delivered in an identical way from here to Seattle. It is real because it has depth. And 3-D means being imperfect, because it's real.

David Boyle

David Boyle is the author of a series of books about history, social change and the future. His book *Authenticity: Brands, Fakes, Spin and the Lust for Real Life* (Flamingo, 2003) helped put the search for authenticity on the agenda as a social phenomenon. *The Tyranny of Numbers* (Flamingo, 2001) and *The Sum of Our Discontent* (Texere, 2001) predicted the backlash against the government's target culture. *Funny Money: In Search of Alternative Cash* (Flamingo, 1999) launched the time banks movement in the UK.

David Boyle is an associate of the New Economics Foundation, a pioneering think-tank in London, and has been at the heart of the effort to introduce time banks to Britain as a critical element of public service reform.

His work on the future of money has also been covered in books and pamphlets such as *Why London Needs its Own Currency* (NEF, 2000), *Virtual Currencies* (Financial Times, 2000), *The Money Changers: Currency Reform from Aristotle to e-cash* (Earthscan, 2002) and *The Little Money Book* (Alastair Sawday, 2003).

He has written for many national newspapers and magazines, stood for Parliament, and edited a range of magazines including *Town & Country Planning* and *Liberal Democrat News*. He is currently the editor of *Radical Economics*. His first medieval history book, *Blondel's Song: The Imprisonment and Ransom of Richard the Lionheart* was published in 2005 by Viking Penguin.

Robert Earhart
Brooklyn Bridge/TBLI Group
Amsterdam

The Maturation of Sustainable Investment

1. Sustainable Investment: Current Drivers

Over the past few years, *socially responsible investment* (SRI), *triple bottom line investing* (TBLI), *clean technologies* (CleanTech), and *corporate social responsibility* (CSR) have become buzzwords, used in both optimistic and derogatory terms. However, at the same time, these interrelated aspects of sustainable investment are contributing to an emerging field of specialized financial practice, indicating that this relatively new field of finance is going mainstream. Several drivers have played a role in bringing this about.

First, many investors have grown impatient with the role of politics in bringing about significant change in the improvement of social and environmental conditions. The political sector seems to be increasingly disconnected from scientific, social, and economic activity. The ability to bring about adaptation and change from economic and investment-based activism has become appealing. The growing popularity of engagement methods to achieve social and environmental change serves as a quintessential example of how these sectors are blending into the political realm. Moreover, mainstream multinational companies such as GE, Ford, BP and Shell have all begun to implement social and environmental reforms without the prompting of legislation or political control. At a time when the political climate in North America and Europe is moving away from regulation, many companies are choosing to self-regulate and invest in social and environmental projects.

Second, some businesses are discovering that waste reduction and energy savings in their manufacturing processes, as well as the adoption of more sustainable technologies, provide more than public relations benefits. Such measures increase profitability and enhance long-term competitive advantage. Much of this is not a result of investment activism, but more a result of seeing the opportunity in looking at capital investments in the long term. General Electric CEO Jeff Immelt recently said, "We plan to make money doing it. We're at a tipping point where energy efficiency and emission reductions also equal profitability" (CNN/Money, 2005).

Publicly available information about corporations and their financial practices has increased drastically in recent years because of new information technologies. As a consequence, the third driver of sustainable investment growth comes from this enhanced knowledge on the part of investors about the non-financial attributes of companies and how they impact risk, profitability, and investment return. Many mainstream investment analysts are beginning to adopt the methods developed by the SRI profession to examine and evaluate their portfolios for non-financial risks and opportunities.

Another catalyst has been the corporate and accounting scandals, which have become more visible since the economic boom period of the late 1990s. Shareholders, government, labor groups, and financial institutions are the groups calling most loudly for better corporate governance and more responsible business practices in the interest of reducing risk and enhancing long-term stability.

Finally, the growing sophistication of high-net-worth, institutional, and retail investors presents another dimension for the growth in sustainable investment. There has been an ever-increasing demand for new financial investment products that better reflect the values of investors, from religious and moral values to environmental and social values. The financial industry is scrambling to mimic the mass customization already mastered by consumer-product companies.

These trends are also reflected in the developing world, where calls for greater accountability and crackdowns on corruption in many countries are rapidly changing the business environment. As sustainable and ethical investment become more prevalent in developed countries, new trends and practices are emerging in developing economies. Part of this is due to the new investment and aid policies of multinational companies and multilateral treaty and development aid organizations, such as the World Bank and the IFC. Many developing countries see the value of avoiding the social and environmental mistakes made during past economic growth. Moreover, there are significant financial, social and environmental gains to be made by including economically marginalized populations in the economic equation. The emergence of micro-finance as a viable and profitable investment strategy has gained momentum, and we are seeing more working capital placed in the hands of the most economically disadvantaged populations.

A final point worth noting is the subtle shift that underlies the changing methodology for investment decisions. As more collaboration takes place as a result of new technologies and innovative thinking, there is an increasing interdependency among government, corporations, and non-governmental organizations. The societal roles and responsibilities of these sectors are becoming less segmented and more intertwined. As a result, the focal point of social and environmental activism is moving from street protests to corporate boardrooms and shareholder resolutions. There are more partnerships between sectors to realize specific economic, social and environmental outcomes. While some of this may reflect the perception that the traditional political routes are growing more irrelevant in changing the behavior of business, there is a quiet undercurrent altering the way finance and investment interact with other disciplines. The boundaries between the formerly discrete disciplines of economics, politics, sociology, natural sciences, and business administration are breaking down, resulting in new hybrids of organizational practice and investment methodology. Many companies are recognizing this and choosing to move towards more ethical, social and environmentally conscious policies. Looking beyond the silos of organizational practice allows new methods to gain competitive advantage and financial opportunity outside of the longstanding idea that "if it's good for the environment and society it's bad for business."

2. Sustainable Growth for Sustainable Investing

The past couple of years have seen explosive growth in the areas of CSR, SRI, and CleanTech. However, financial professionals and journalists are rigorously questioning the significance of many of these developments. Are these indicative of an ongoing trend that indicates the growth of a viable investment class, or is sustainable investment simply the "flavor of the month" which will be discarded for the next hot thing, much like the Internet start-ups of 1999?

Based on several growth indicators of the past year, I believe that we are seeing the development of an ongoing trend towards sustainable investment practices going mainstream and maturing into a field of regular practice. These indicators include the following:

Growth in non-financial reporting

The increasing proliferation of sustainable investment methods and practices is reflected in the growth of the number of companies that are reporting their social and environmental outcomes. In 2000 over half of the top 250 Fortune 500 companies issued a social and/or environmental report (KPMG 2005). However, the significance of this increased level of reporting is questioned. William Baue observes: "One interpretation of the link between these two releases is it is simply another example of a company promoting corporate responsibility on one hand while acting irresponsibly with the other" (KPMG 2005). Other interpretations laud the efforts on the part of large corporations to report their positive and negative social and environmental outcomes. Both perspectives on this issue are probably valid and vary widely based on specific company reports. A more comprehensive look into the reasons why companies are reporting may reveal which perspective best reflects corporate reporting behavior.

Competitive advantage within the financial services industry

The growth of available information over the Internet and through other forms of media has significantly reduced the ability of financial service providers to distinguish themselves from one another. Many have moved from developing and marketing their own funds and advice to an "open architecture" structure. Online brokerages and research tools have also served to undermine the traditional investment services models. Even private banks that cater to high-net-worth and institutional investors are having a hard time competing on performance and service alone. The next wave of competition may very well be on more customized and individualized services to customers. Mass customization has existed in retailing and manufacturing for quite some time, and it has already emerged in financial services. Sustainable investments, faith-based investing, and values-oriented investing offer a significant advantage in acquiring new investors, and maintaining relationships with current clients, to the early adopters.

Asset growth

More assets are flowing into SRI investments. From 1995 to 2003, the number of public equity assets under management subjected to some form of social and/or environmental screening grew by 240 percent. As of 2003, 11.3 percent of assets under management, $2,164 billion, were covered under some form of screening in the United States. Moreover, SRI assets are growing 40 percent faster than traditionally managed assets (SI Forum 2003). The depth of screening is also increasing as more SRI funds apply positive screening and engagement methods. Negative screening eliminates companies in specific sectors (such as tobacco, weapons, and gambling) or those companies with poor ethical practices (such as child labor, pollution, and bribing government officials). Positive screening focuses on investing in companies with the best practices in a particular industry. Nevertheless, most SRI funds still rely heavily on negative screening for the composition of their portfolios. Engagement, the other strategy, involves advocacy and shareholder activism with companies to improve their social and environmental practices. This takes the form of voting shares, introducing stockholder resolutions, and advocacy work with corporate boards and managers. Engagement as an SRI investment strategy continues to grow, a phenomenon criticized by some for its lack of accountability to ethical and socially responsible principles demanded by investors in SRI funds and equities (Hawkins 2004).

Growth of available asset classes

A significant recent development in the growth of sustainable investment practices is within the subset of alternative asset classes, specifically in the area of CleanTech private equity investments. This sector had grown to 7.26 percent of total investment in private equity by the second quarter of 2005 (Cleantech Network Venture 2005). Renewable energy, in particular, has experienced a remarkable expansion as traditional forms of fossil-based energy have increased in price because of growing demand, dwindling supplies, and security concerns. As the price of oil and natural gas rise, renewable energy technologies become more competitive. Furthermore, the emergence of screened bonds, sustainable real estate, micro-finance funds, and carbon trading instruments are opening up new opportunities to investors and providing attractive returns. Carbon credits, in particular, have allowed some sustainable business ventures to gain additional revenue on top of their other core activities.

Growth of "anti-SRI" sentiment

Oftentimes, a measure of success is the degree of pushback, defined by the intensity of criticism and resistance to a concept or new idea in scale and scope. Despite the advancements made by the advocates of sustainable investment, the past year has also seen a number of harsh criticisms. This often has included the three related fields of CSR, SRI, and CleanTech. There are a few recent high profile criticisms that stand out. *The Economist* questioned the fundamental benefits and overall usefulness of CSR with a special survey (2005). On the flip side, a study authored by Chris MacDonald and Wayne Norman indicated that the term Triple Bottom Line (TBL) implies a fundamentally flawed methodology that is impossible to objectively evaluate and unable to deliver promises of improved social and environmental performance (Norman and MacDonald 2004).

Practices diametrical to SRI take the criticism a step further. A couple of years ago, stocks that appeal to "antisocial sentiments" emerged as an investment strategy. So-called sin investing looks for high returns in such "recession proof" areas as tobacco, alcohol, firearms, and companies with poor environmental and social practices. A fund that utilizes this strategy has also been issued (the Vice Fund or VICEX). This past year has also seen the emergence of a fund, the Free Enterprise Action Fund (FEAF), that supports those companies and industries that maintain consistency with right wing or nationalistic ideologies. However, it is likely that these investment strategies will not exceed the returns of the mainstream SRI funds over the long term.

While some of this criticism has merit, much of it is simply a reaction by interests that are threatened by the growth of responsible investment. Ultimately, most of these criticisms will be held to the test of time. One of the primary aspects of socially responsible investment requires a long-term outlook on investments, often having to abandon short-term performance expectations. In the short term, such reactionary investment strategies may show higher performance, and indeed may be "recession proof" in a single instance. However, when considerations of legal, environmental, social, and reputation liabilities are taken into account, the higher risks presented with such funds and strategies do not present a favorable outlook for ongoing returns.

3. Barriers to Future Development

While sustainability and CSR have become more widely accepted, there are some barriers to the mainstream acceptance and maturation of this industry specialty. Often CSR programs overreach the abilities and scope of the companies implementing them, are poorly implemented, and in many cases, the terms are misunderstood to begin with. SRI suffers from many of the same problems, especially since there is a lack of standards in quantitative methods, and qualitative methods currently lack transparency to all but the most sophisticated investors in this area.

If the fields of SRI, CSR and CleanTech are to fully develop and mature, rather than be relegated to the status of artifacts in the future, several barriers need to be better managed. Some of these include the following:

Single Standards

Frequently, CSR reports contain few or no audited statements and often they resemble public relations efforts rather than any meaningful information about social and environmental performance. Although several standards were developed during the past decade to address specific areas of practice (such as GRI, AA1000, SA8000, and ISO14000), a single definitive and auditable standard has yet to emerge. Few companies have their CSR or sustainability reports audited, and of the companies that do, few are willing or able to audit all of their statements.

What is CSR, exactly?

Unfortunately, CSR is often confused with charity or public relations, as is the case with the January 2005 survey presented in *The Economist*. However, the numerous companies that house a "CSR department" under their public relations division indicates that media are not the only source of this confusion. This structural condition tends to indicate that sustainability or CSR is not a company-wide priority and probably will have little or no effect on day-to-day operations.

Short-term vs. long-term financial performance

As more investors are beginning to understand, CSR and SRI are more about reducing risks and enhancing performance in the long term than about seeing high returns in the short term. Many portfolios have seen a large reduction due to single events such as lawsuits, boycotts, slumping consumer demand, or a change in social or environmental legislation that severely complicates current business practices. As a long-term strategy, SRI looks at those companies that have the lowest possible risk over time for enhanced performance. Companies that adapt to social and environmental risks have a higher likelihood of outperforming those that refuse to adapt in the long term. The concept of evolution is not limited to biology. Over time, we consistently see that companies that adapt to adverse conditions and maintain lower risks tend to be the ones that survive over time (de Geus 1997).

Marketing basics

In terms of SRI, banks that offer or manage SRI funds do little to market them to their retail or institutional customers. An informal survey conducted on the five largest financial institutions in the Netherlands revealed that in eight out of the ten inquiries, customer service representatives and financial advisors were either not aware that their institutions offered SRI funds or refused to recommend them over other funds.[1] In one case, the two funds that were strongly recommended had experienced poorer performance over the previous 24 months than all of the SRI funds offered by that same institution. While the results of such a survey are not statistically significant and cannot be considered representative of the industry, they do hint at a potential barrier to ongoing growth-sustainable investment. Furthermore, at most brokerage sites, very little non-financial information about their equities and mutual funds is readily available.

1 Survey conducted by Brooklyn Bridge/TBLI during July 2004. Included the five largest financial institutions based in the Netherlands based on assets under management. Subjects were contacted using publicly available customer service phone numbers for both retail and institutional market segments. Results are not statistically significant, nor are they intended to be representative of the industry.

Politics is relevant

As activists, corporations and investors have circumvented the political process through lobbying, CSR, and SRI, the growing level of cynicism about the political sector needs to be examined with a greater level of scrutiny and addressed with a greater level of vigor. Without a better system of regulation, economic reforms, and alignment of politics with other sectors, the gains made by CSR and SRI will stagnate. In particular, the persistent existence of perverse incentives and ease of externalizing social and environmental costs continue to punish the SRI equities and reward unethical and exploitative practices. Nowhere is this more revealing than in the financial calculations that result in the death of many sustainable business ventures, particularly in renewable energies. Fossil fuels are substantially less expensive. Many emerging clean technologies and socially responsible practices cannot compete, in terms of financial performance, with "business as usual" in the current regulatory structure. The short-term perspective, with its limited focus that is both socially and environmentally damaging, will continue to have an advantage in terms of financial performance as long as governments subsidize these practices and place no value on the services provided by a clean natural environment and a stable and just society. Drivers mentioned above are already putting pressure on governments to change the regulatory landscape.

4. Sustainable Investment, Sustainable Longevity

Based on the drivers that SRI and CSR have been seeing throughout the last few decades, it is clear that we have not yet reached the peak of this type of investment or the trend for companies to have socially responsible practices. Individual activism, corporate activism, and the increase in information technology, combined with recent scandals and the need to cater to individual investors, are current drivers for the increase in SRI and CSR practices in the corporate and financial world. Trends in developing countries designed to prevent repeating mistakes from the past are showing the clear effects that SRI and CSR are having on politics and government in the world.

Of course, the existence of these drivers does not answer whether this is an overall trend or whether our societies and economies are adopting a new language or expectations for our economic growth. Certain signs such as the intensification of non-financial-related information reports, asset growth, increase in subsets of certain asset classes, and a backlash against SRI seem to indicate that SRI is beginning to gain momentum.

The obstacles SRI is facing in this growth are based on the definition of what socially responsible investing is, how it is defined by financial institutions, how it is regulated, and ultimately, how it can be presented to the consumer. Politics will also determine how quickly or slowly the SRI becomes an integral part of our economies, as governmental and regulatory policies affect the true financial cost or benefit of these investments.

The outlook for sustainable investment is promising, but tenuous. Strong drivers and the promise of interesting and effective SRI and CSR are leaving their marks on our economies, governments, and society. The growth of the past decade is poised to continue as long as investors, financial professionals, and corporate managers can maintain the momentum of recent trends. However, as considered, there are multiple factors that will either positively or negatively influence investor demand, corporate motivation, and political will. The influence of significant events, such as corporate scandals, environmental catastrophes, technological breakthroughs, and political shifts, still has the ability to propel or slow sustainable investment growth.

References

Baue, W., 2005. "KPMG Finds More Than Half of Fortune 250 Issuing Standalone Sustainability Reports." 22 June 2005, http://www.socialfunds.com.

CleanTechVenture, http://www.cleantechventure.com.

CNN/Money, "GE discovers it's easy being green." 9 May 2005, http://money.cnn.com/2005/05/09/news/fortune500/ge_environment/.

De Geus, A., 1997. *The Living Company: Habits for Survival in a Turbulent Business Environment.* Harvard Business School Press, Boston.

The Economist (Print Edition), 20 January 2005.

Hawkins, P. and The Natural Capital Institute, 2004. "Socially responsible investing: How the SRI industry has failed to respond to people who want to invest with conscience and what can be done to change it." October 2004, www.naturalcapital.org/docs/SRI%20Report%2010-04_word.pdf.

KPMG International Survey of Corporate Responsibility Reporting 2005; University of Amsterdam and KPMG Global Sustainability Services, June 2005, http://www.kpmg.com/Rut2000_prod/Documents/9/Survey2005.pdf.

Norman, W. and MacDonald, C., 2003. "Getting to the Bottom of Triple Bottom Line," *Business Ethics Quarterly* 2003 March.

Social Investment Forum, "2003 Report on Socially Responsible Investing Trends in the United States." December 2003.

Robert Earhart

Robert Earhart joined Brooklyn Bridge/TBLI Group in 2003 and is now the consulting director, providing strategic management and SRI program development services to clients, as well as project management for service partnerships. During this time, he has developed the curriculum for academic and corporate training courses on SRI, CSR and corporate governance.

Robert Earhart has been working in CSR for the past ten years in a variety of different capacities in the private, NGO and political sectors. From 1994–95 he worked at the State of Oregon Legislative Assembly, where he provided policy and budget analysis, specializing in social and environmental legislation. He has also served as a treasurer and political finance consultant for several statewide political action committees. In 1998 he became the founding financial manger of SE Works, a community-based NGO, providing financial, human resources, and operations coordination for the organization and engineering of several public/private partnerships to support local area economic development objectives. In 2000, he was elected chair of the Foster Target Area Project, a local government initiative to provide economic revitalization to Southeast Portland.

Robert Earhart originally comes from San Francisco, but he has also lived in Iran and Greece. He currently resides in the Netherlands. Robert has a bachelor of arts degree in philosophy and a bachelor of science degree in psychology, both from Lewis & Clark College in Portland, Oregon. He has an MBA in international management from the Rotterdam School of Management. He is currently working on his doctorate of business administration at the University of Humanist Studies in Utrecht, Netherlands, with a topical research focus on CSR and the management consulting industry.

Zsolt Boda
Corvinus University of Budapest

Emese Gulyas
Corvinus University of Budapest

The Ethical Consumerism Movement

Corporate scandals undermine the reputation of companies. This is particularly serious for them now, when they are involved more than ever in branding: building up brands which are easy to recognize and to identify with. The most important asset for many companies is their brand; it is an intangible asset, heavily dependent on the recognition and assessment of the social environment. This is especially true for companies producing consumer goods, but for others as well – partly because they may become a consumer-goods-producing company at any time, as the example of Caterpillar suggests. Now, the reputation acquired among consumers is particularly important: they should know, love, identify with, and finally choose brands.

But can we love a brand that is associated with child labor, environmental destruction and other corporate misbehaviors? Klein (1999) suggests that branding carries an inherent paradox. While it reflects the desperate will of corporations to get rid of their "dirty backyard" (smoky factories, pollution, conflicts with workers, trade unions, etc.) by outsourcing the production activities and creating a "spiritual identity" for the firm, at the same time it contributes to the growing inquiry of consumers about the real meaning of a brand. What is it exactly that I am supposed to identify with? Are the values that brands convey real ones, or just PR constructions?

Indeed, many studies show that people are increasingly driven by inherent value considerations when making their consumer choices. For instance, according to the Cooperative Bank's report (2003) the total value of ethical consumption was £19.9 billion in the United Kingdom. The Ethical Purchasing Index (EPI), also elaborated by the Bank to measure ethical consumption, showed a 13 percent increase from 2001 to 2002.

Recent poll data show that even in Central and Eastern Europe, where ethical consumerism is supposed to be a new phenomenon, after 40 years of economic centralization, people are convinced that by their shopping decisions they can influence corporate behavior. According to our own research 47 percent of Hungarians state that if consumers preferred the products of environmentally and socially responsible companies, companies would intend to satisfy such consumer needs. Also, 27 percent of consumers believe that boycotts can be an effective means for communicating their commitments and lobby for their interest.

According to the referred study of the Cooperative Bank 57 percent of UK citizens claim to have boycotted at least one product in the past twelve months.

The Fair Trade Labelling Organisation International recorded a 42 percent increase in the sales of Fair Trade-labelled products around the world between 2002 and 2003.[1]

And if 88 percent of environmental organizations believe that individual consumers can have a major impact on the direction of the economy (Hilton 2003, 317), they may be right. After all, isn't it the basic promise of consumer society that our opinion counts for companies?

Hilton states that ethical consumerism movements are recognizable as definite social phenomena of growing importance in the past three decades. In his brief definition he describes ethical consumption as a linkage of personal consumption

1 http://www.fairtrade.net/sites/impact/facts.html

with environmental, human and animal rights concerns. According to Hilton ethical consumerism can be seen as a means for expressing social and individual identities. Expressing identities became a right and finally a basis for political action (Hilton 2003, 315). That is, ethical consumerism is an expression of personal identities in the era of "consumer society," and at the same time it is a new political movement, by which people seek to consciously influence economic and social institutions.

1. The Beginnings of Ethical Consumerism

But is ethical consumerism really a brand new development as Hilton suggests?

If we follow the approach of anthropologists, we may argue that ethical consumerism is just a new expression of an old phenomenon. Mary Douglas and Baron Isherwood state that consumption activities are special communication processes which inform people about one another's beliefs, values, and the way the world is viewed. Goods provide subsistence, but at the same time they draw the lines of social relationship (Douglas and Isherwood 1996, 39). In this sense consumption has always had a cultural, social determination and value orientation: consumer decisions have always been based in part on deeper meanings; not only do they involve needs and preferences as economists state, but additionally, "choice between goods is the result of, and contributes to culture" (Douglas and Isherwood 1996, 52). Thus consumer decisions derive from and contribute to the formulation of norms and values and make consumption one of the most important organizing forces of society.

However, consumption should be differentiated from consumerism. Consumption is the purchase and use of goods, which is, according to Douglas and Isherwood, a universal human activity, while consumerism is a political-social movement, which needs the conditions of modernity. First, consumerism needs some kind of democratization of the society, where individual freedom is important and consumption activities are not deeply embedded in, and totally determined by, social order. Second, consumerism needs the condition that most of the goods be purchased on the market (instead of being made at home by people themselves), where supply is assured by several producers competing with one another. These conditions give place to value-driven individual consumer choices, which, in turn, may influence producers and traders.

Consumerism as a political-social movement or an extended political activity of ordinary citizens expressing shared beliefs and ideological commitments can be traced back to at least the middle of the 19th century in North America and Western Europe, or even earlier (Micheletti 2003). Organized boycott activities of that time showed new ways for ordinary people to exercise their collective influence on local and national policy issues.

Friedman (1999) distinguishes early boycotts according to their orientation. Most of the time consumer boycotts focused on the availability or the price of such basic consumer goods as meat or sugar. Traders being accused of creating an artificial scarcity and raising prices unfairly were boycotted. But we should not forget about those consumer movements that were organized around more general values, such as patriotism, human rights, workers rights, women's rights, or later, peace and ecology.

Some of the typical and popular early ethical consumer initiatives were the ones which expressed patriotism and struggled for political independence of the emerging nation-states. Maybe the most well known of such initiatives were the Mahatma Ghandi-led Swadeshi movement, which helped to build Indian national unity and identity by promoting domestic products and industry, and the protest of American consumers against British goods after the launch of the Stamp Act in 1756 and the tax on tea. But we can find similar examples from all around the world, including Central and Eastern Europe. In the first half of the 19th century the Hungarian Association of Patriots (Védegylet) promoted Hungarian products in order to achieve economic and political independence from the Habsburgs.

Probably the first significant linkage of human rights issues and ethical consumption was the organized protests against slavery in the US in the first half of the 19th century. Consumers initiated boycotts against tea, sugar and other goods produced by slaves. According to their beliefs they were actually boycotting slavery and promoting freedom of workers (Glickman 2004, 23). Later, from the 1930s through the sixties grassroots, local boycotts were organized in the United States protesting against segregation and the discrimination of the black minority. For instance, during the Great Depression urban African Americans reflected their unemployment by organizing the "Don't Buy from Where You Can't Work" campaign. In the 1930s they organized on-the-spot campaigns against stores (and their customers) that refused to employ black employees (Friedman 1999).

Not only have corporate misbehavior and political issues been targeted by consumer movements. Micheletti brings an early example of positive political (ethical) consumerism from the turn of the 19th century: the National Consumers' League in the United States organized the so-called "White Label Campaign." The campaign was one of the early labelling initiatives, which encouraged cotton underwear manufacturers to adopt more progressive labor policies than were demanded by law. For example they only recommended the product if the manufacturer guaranteed that he did not require overtime or employ children under the age of 16.

Why initiate consumer movements? According to Micheletti citizens turn to organized consumer actions when they consider them to be the only, or the relatively most efficient, way to influence politics and consider other means to be hopeless. This might be true especially for the early form of ethical consumer activities from the 18th century to the beginning of the 20th, when even voting rights were limited to nobles or to males. The fact that many times organizers or leaders of local boycott activities were women or women organizations seems to support this idea.

2. Ethical Consumerism Today: Objectives and Means

Today the goals of ethical consumer movements are more complex, moving beyond the logic of single-issue movements. Of course, boycotts are still launched against individual companies, and "specialized" NGOs exist which focus their activities on one particular topic (e.g., animal welfare). However, more and more organizations emphasize complex objectives promoting social and environmental sustainability, global justice and fairness towards society, nature and future generations. More importantly, people are more aware of the issues of ethical consumerism and they seem to increasingly support them. Let us just cite the result of one more survey: According to the results of the first-ever Europe-wide survey on corporate social responsibility in all of the twelve countries surveyed, over half of the population stated a company's social responsibility was an important factor when making a purchase (Crane and Matten 2004, 290). If half of the adult population knows and approves of a movement, it cannot be seen as a marginal one any more.

It would go beyond the scope of this study to analyze in depth the underlying causes of these new developments. Some of the most important – and mutually interrelated – factors are the following: identity politics; the rise of new political activism; growing anti-corporate feelings; and the problems of globalization.

We already referred to the importance of expressing one's cultural and political identity. In a "consumer society" personal identities are to a large extent shaped by, and expressed through, commercials, consumer activities and popular culture, and therefore consumerism can easily become a means to reflect commitments and shared beliefs.

Second, as Inglehart noted, the legitimacy of traditional political institu-tions is decreasing, but at the same time, trust in civil society movements is increasing. Making committed consumer choices is certainly one of the easiest forms of civil activism.

Third, the unprecedented growth of the power and influence of multinational companies fuels the growing anti-corporate feelings, as testified by such publications as Korten's (1995) or Klein's (1999) books, among others. Anti-corporate boycotts may provide a sense of capability for people in influencing these huge and powerful organizations.

Fourth, the complex problems of globalization – which include those created by multinational companies – certainly contribute to the growth of the ethical consumerism movement. Globalization criticism has become a discursive platform of major importance where the issues of global ecology, fair trade, the problems of poverty, the power abuses of multinational companies, job insecurity, and (un)sustainable development are treated together. The anti- or alter-globalization movement builds on, and integrates, the experiences of different kinds of civil movements, and at the same time fuels new kinds of activism. These new kinds of activism include the organization of alternative world forums, joint international campaigns, the extensive use of new media (Internet) – and ethical consumerism.

Now, what are the tools in the hands of ethical consumer movements? During the past decades tools supporting ethical-consumption decisions have become more complex and based on a wider range of information.

One of the classical means of protest ethical consumers have is organized *boycotts*. Friedman refers to a US survey showing that senior managers consider boycotts the most effective tool for consumers seeking to influence companies. Friedman defines a boycott as "an attempt by one or more parties to achieve certain objectives by urging individual consumers to refrain from making selected purchases in the market place." (Friedman 1999, 4) He emphasizes three important characteristics of boycott initiatives: (1) focus on convincing individuals, (2) using the dynamism of the marketplace to achieve goals which are outside the marketplace such as environmental or human rights improvements, and (3) selective withdrawal of consumers from the marketplace.

Friedman states that contemporary consumer boycotts differ from early initiatives in many aspects. First of all they target new issues. While a century ago the main issues were pricing, the availability of goods and labor issues, today boycotts relate to ethnic concerns, animal rights, antiwar activities, and environmental matters (Friedman 1999, 216–22).

For instance in 1997 *The Ethical Consumer* magazine made a survey among its readers and asked them if they joined boycotts. According to their report 93 percent of their readers had joined different boycotts.[2] The most popular boycotts were the Nestlé,

2 http://www.ethicalconsumer.org/boycotts/popularboycotts.htm

McDonalds and Shell Company ones. Though the Nestlé boycott had been going on for 20 years at that time, 78 percent of their readers refused to buy the products of the company targeted because of its aggressive marketing strategies of infant formula in the developing world.

Beginning in the 1980s boycotts became more media oriented than the early marketplace boycotts (Friedman 1999). They not only changed their strategy by using the mainstream media to approach consumers, but in recent years many of the boycott organizers have developed their own media outlets. Today many of the boycott calls have developed their own websites and electronic and printed newsletters in order to continuously inform consumers and the mainstream media about the progress of the initiative. Here we can cite the *National Boycott News*, the *Boycott Action News*, the *Boycott Quarterly* or the *Boycott Monthly*, which have all been published in the US. The first of such newsletters, the *National Boycott News*, achieved a circulation of 15,000 before its cessation in the mid-1990s.[3] According to Friedman the third significant difference in recent boycotts is comprised by the new boycott tactics. This means that the main considerations of selecting media-oriented campaign targets are visibility, good reputation, economic instability, and the absence of a long-established market position of the given company. Boycott organizers also have to use dramatic devices and techniques to attract media attention. Finally, the success of a boycott also depends on the choice of the goods to boycott. Boycotts that call for refraining from the consumption of goods that are easy to substitute are more likely to succeed.

Other, but quite rarely, used tools are *buycotts or positive boycotts*, which "attempt to induce shoppers to buy the products or services of selected companies in order to reward them for behavior consistent with the goals of the activists" (Friedman 1999, 201). Buycotts are not advertisements as they do not have any profit-making intention, and they are similar to boycotts in the sense that they use market means to achieve goals that are beyond the marketplace. Hilton (2003) claims buycotts are more similar to modern ethical consumer behavior. He considers green consumer movements as a shift from ascetic, self-denying, anti-materialistic and single-issue initiatives towards a new lifestyle, which is the projection of alternative identities. Hilton links the herald of modern ethical consumerism to the publication of the *Green Consumer Guide* by Elkington and Hailes in 1988.

One of the first buycott campaigns was the already mentioned "White Label Campaign" of the National Consumers' League in the United States. The most popular

3 http://www.washingtonfreepress.org/09/Spike.html

buycott initiatives are the "buy local" or "buy national" campaigns that we have found in almost every country since the foundation of nation-states. In 2002 7.9 percent of all ethically bought products and services were selected on the "local" criteria in the United Kingdom (The Ethical Consumerism Report 2003).

Friedman makes a detailed classification of buycotts from several aspects. He distinguishes between direct and indirect buycotts. Direct ones call for buying specific products from particular companies. Indirect calls urge the labelling of approved products that correspond to the criteria of the labelling organization. In this case there are several products that meet the purpose of the call.

Micheletti, who considers *labelling schemes* an independent institution of ethical consumerism (political consumerism as the author phrases it), highlights five general areas that are covered by labelling schemes: ecology, fair trade, organic food, forestry and marine life. We should add animal welfare as a sixth area since the labelling of "cruelty free" products is fairly well developed and such products are very popular. The author typifies three different kinds of labels and states that the most advanced labelling schemes are basically managing risks "through transparent market-based instruments that stimulate the supply and demand of alternative and less hazardous products" (Micheletti 2003, 90).

It is telling about the progress of labelling schemes that www.eco-labelling.org, which provides information on private and government labels, can identify 137 different eco-labels. Also a remarkable fact is that fair trade organizations felt the need to harmonize and coordinate different labels, and therefore founded Fairtrade Labelling Organisation International to fulfill that task.

Micheletti also considers *stewardship certification schemes* to be an increasingly important institution of ethical consumerism. Stewardships are for common pool resources that do not have defined owners and are easy to abuse or overuse such as forests, air, and water, etc. The users of such goods develop rules for the management of the goods. Those actors meeting stewardship criteria are certified. Micheletti mentions that the first stewardship initiatives were raised by consumer boycotts, when consumer groups called for action against the overuse of tropical rainforest woods. According to their 2005 report, the Forest Stewardship Council certified 65 million ha forests worldwide.[4] Their logo appears on wooden goods coming from forests managed according to sustainability criteria.

4 http://www.fsccanada.org/pdf_document/FSCstatus_WorldCanada_September05.pdf

We can conclude from most of the early examples that consumer actions were concentrating on one single issue and they used boycotts or buycotts as their means. These are still popular and widely used tools for ethical consumers but we can observe a definite change in recent times. As production schemes have become more complex and difficult to monitor by consumers, ethical consumer decision making is also becoming more sophisticated. Ethical consumer decisions have more aspects today and natural beauty has moved from joining single-issue boycotts or buycotts to making ethical consumer decision an everyday practice, based on more complex criteria.

The most popular tools guiding ethical consumers are the different *databases and guides* providing various information on the environmental, social, economic and ethical profiles of companies, brands or products. Guides and databases are interfaces through which consumers can communicate their expectations of companies and influence their corporate behavior in an ethical direction.

Since the 1980s there have been single-issue guides covering one area, such as environment, animal welfare, or human rights issues. Here we can mention the database of the British Union for the Abolition of Vivisection (BUAV), which compiled a guide for cruelty-free products, or green guides. But what makes the contemporary databases and guides novel is that they provide information on all these different aspects at the same time.

We compared five popular databases that provide information on the following records of companies.[5]

Environment: Positive evaluations are given for those companies that have environmental policies, environmental management systems, environmental reports, eco-labels, and which made efforts at energy efficiency and selective waste management. Companies involved in nuclear energy, pollution, organized PR campaigns against environmental groups, and those that engage in environmentally unsustainable practices, have negative ratings.

Those guides providing data mostly on international corporations' group information on *employees*, and general *human rights* issues, are lumped together, since human rights conflicts usually occur in third world employment. The main issues that companies are rewarded for include these: creating new workplaces, applying

5 The Ethical Consumer: www.corporatecritic.org (United Kingdom); Responsible Shopper: www.responsibleshopper.org (USA); L'Observatoire de L'Éthique: Le Guide Éthique du Consommateur, Albin Michel SA, Paris, 2001 (France); Buy Blue: www.buyblue.org (USA); Tudatos Vásárló (Conscious Consumer): www.tudatosvasarlo.hu (Hungary). The Hungarian database is under construction and not available yet on the Web.

and meeting International Labour Organization (ILO) standards, having supportive schemes for the employment of discriminated groups (young, women, disabled, minorities, etc.), having supportive policies for families, having a fair distribution of male and female managers, having widely accessible education programs, supporting local communities, and having fair living wages and benefit packages. Negative evaluation is given for abuse of employees, contracting sweatshops, exploitation of employees, applying child labor, restricting working unions, not respecting workers' rights, discrimination, unhealthy and unsafe working conditions, having subsidiaries in countries with oppressive regimes, using irresponsible marketing practices, and involvement in the manufacturing or commerce of arms.

In the case of *animal rights* the negative issues mentioned in different guides are animal testing for cosmetic purposes, distributing animal-tested products, applying or serving factory farming, and being the owner of a slaughterhouse or user of its byproducts. A positive rating is given for producing or distributing cruelty-free products, and for applying natural farming methods.

Some databases (e.g., Guide Éthique du Consommateur, Tudatos Vásárló) also evaluate the *trade and commercial practices* of the companies. They give lower scores for those employing any of the following: having unfair contracts with suppliers; using market dominance for unfair pricing; engaging in commerce with questionable or hazardous goods such as GMO food or radioactive, poisonous items; having an unfair relationship with competitors, and involvement in corruption. Higher scores are given for monitoring the whole life cycle of products, preferring local suppliers, and having fair contractual terms with suppliers.

We can find *transparency* as a preferable and often-evaluated corporate behavior. Guides such as the Guide Éthique reward the appropriate information on product labels and packaging, ethical advertising, involvement of different stakeholders in decision making and publicly accessible information on the management, committees and management salaries.

The Guide Éthique and the Buy Blue score *corporate social responsibility*, or *corporate citizenship*, separately, which means charity contributions, shareholder rights, community participation, product safety and liability issues, sponsorship, contribution to the local welfare through education programs, and creation of workplaces supporting discriminated groups.

Other often-published information includes the involvement of the company in GMO issues (participation in production or patent, commerce with GMO products), whether or not the company was the target of boycott calls, the ownership of the company (preferably local), taxpaying ethics and relationship with local communities.

Those guides that provide *data on the product itself* gather information on the compounding, packaging, life cycle, origin and the labelling of the products.

The main sources of information in all cases are the media, reports of civil organizations, court decisions, authority registers, dialogue with companies, and data from research institutions.

It should be clear that these guides and databases give quite complex pictures of the companies. Moreover, the different aspects of evaluation are not necessarily homogeneous; that is, we may have companies which have relatively good performance in, say, the environmental dimension, but which score poorly in terms of other criteria. Other companies may have contradictory profiles. If so, and no "best" or "worst" companies can be identified – or not necessarily – what is the potential use of these databases?

In our opinion, such databases may have at least four different uses. First, they can obviously help consumer decision making, especially if the consumer has a clear preference: for instance, she wants to avoid the products of companies accused of using child labor. In this case other aspects of corporate ethicality are of second-order importance. Second, such databases may contribute to raising awareness about the ethical challenges of today's business. That is, they may have an indirect effect on consumer attitudes. Third, such guides and databases target companies as well. They report what is (or may be) important for consumers and provide a rating of a given company compared to its competitors. Then a company may decide to try to improve its performance in critical areas. Fourth, such databases may be used by ethical investment funds that provide portfolios in which no companies with ethically, socially or environmentally questionable practices are included.

3. Conclusion

Ethical consumerism is one among many social movements that reflect today's conflicts between business and society. It should not be seen as isolated from anti-corporate protests, the alter-globalization movement, CSR initiatives and developments in ethical investment. It may significantly contribute to raising the ethicality of business, since consumers are supposed to be the most important stakeholders of firms, upon which the companies' survival depends. Ethical consumerism has certainly gained considerable strength in the past decades and we can predict that it will continue to effectively organize itself, using new communication means and building on new sensibilities.

Issues such as GMOs, chemical safety, animal welfare or dislocation of production easily combine selfish motivations concerning perceived threats to health, jobs, etc., with more general and generous claims for a safe environment, animal rights, local development and fair trade.

An important development is that ethical consumerism also has an effect on the activities of mainstream consumer protection organizations. Some of the classical consumer organizations whose activity traditionally consisted of – simply speaking – quality testing and price comparison started to move in new directions. For instance, the agenda of Consumers International, the most important global consumer organization, already includes the issues of corporate social responsibility (CSR), ethical management standards and labelling, fair trade, and GMOs. Ethical consumerism is becoming part of the usual social landscape. And companies should increasingly take this into account.

References

Crane, A. and Matten, D., 2004. *Business Ethics*. Oxford University Press, Oxford.

Douglas, M. and Isherwood, B., 1996. *The World of Goods – Towards an Anthropology of Consumption.* Routledge, London.

The Ethical Consumerism Report 2003. The Cooperative Bank, 2003.

Friedman, M., 1999. *Consumer Boycotts: Effecting Change through the Marketplace and the Media.* Routledge, London.

Glickman, L., 2004. "Consommer pour réformer le capitalisme américain. Le citoyen et le consommateur au début du XXe siécle." In: *Marché et politique. Autour de la consommation engagé.* Science de la société, Vol. 62., May, 17–45.

Hilton, M., 2003. *Consumerism in Twentieth-Century Britain.* Cambridge University Press, Cambridge.

Ingelhart, R., 1997. *Modernization and Postmodernization. Cultural, Economic, and Political Changes in 43 Societies.* Princeton University Press, Princeton.

Klein, N., 1999. *No Logo*. Picador, New York.

Korten, D.C., 1995. *When Corporations Rule the World.* Kumarian Press , West Hartford and Berrett-Koehler Publishers, San Francisco.

Micheletti, M., 2003. *Political Virtue and Shopping: Individuals, Consumerism and Collective Action.* Palgrave Macmillan, New York.

L'Observatoire de L'Éthique: Le Guide Éthique du Consommateur, 2001. Albin Michel SA, Paris.

Pruzan, P., 2001. "Corporate Reputation: Image or Identity?" *Corporate Reputation Review*, Vol. 4, No. 1, 47–60.

Zsolt Boda

Zsolt Boda was born in 1969 in Budapest, Hungary. He graduated from the Budapest University of Economic Sciences (BUES) in 1993 and has an MA in economics. He also received his Ph.D. in political science from BUES in 2000.

Zsolt Boda is research fellow at the Institute of Political Science, Hungarian Academy of Sciences, and associate professor at the Business Ethics Center, Corvinus University of Budapest. He teaches "Business Ethics" and "Ethics of the International Economy" at the Corvinus University of Budapest. He is also active in the Hungarian green movement and has worked as an expert for environmental NGOs.

He has co-edited two books in Hungarian: one on corporate ethics and another on political theory. His book on global ecopolitics was published in 2004. He has published several papers, in academic journals, and books on international ethics involving the fair trade problematic, trade and environmental issues, and the politics of global environmentalism.

His publications in English include the following:

Conflicting Principles of Fair Trade, Business Ethics Papers, No. 3, Business Ethics Center, Budapest University of Economic Sciences, January 2000.

"Globalization and International Ethics." In: Laszlo Zsolnai (ed.): *Ethics in the Economy: Handbook of Business Ethics.* Peter Lang, Oxford, 2002, 233–258.

"Global Environmental Commons and the Need for Ethics," *Society and Economy*, Fall 2003, 213–224.

Emese Gulyas

Emese Gulyas has a Master's Degree in sociology from the Budapest University of Economic Sciences. Currently she is working on her sociology Ph.D. thesis, also at the Corvinus University of Budapest. Her research focuses on the theory and practice of ethical consumerism. She is the co-founder of the Association of Conscious Consumers, an NGO promoting sustainable and ethical consumerism in Hungary.

Frank Dixon
Senior Advisor
Innovest Strategic Value Advisors, New York

Gross National Happiness
Improving Unsustainable Western Economic Systems*

Bhutan's interest in developing a Gross National Happiness index (GNH) reflects great wisdom. GNH is intended to be a more accurate measure of social well-being than Gross National Product (GNP), the primary indicator of social well-being in Western nations. GNP is a crude measure that counts many social negatives as positive (e.g., incarceration). It also fails to count services that enhance social well-being (e.g., parents caring for children), degradation of critical assets (forests, water, air, etc.) and

* This is a shorter version of the paper presented at the GNH Conference in Thimphu, Bhutan, February 2004. The original paper can be downloaded at: <en.wikipedia.org/wiki/Gross_national_happiness>.

intangible factors, such as happiness (the ultimate goal of many people). It probably is no coincidence that Western economies are rapidly degrading environmental life support systems and making many unhappy (as indicated by growing obesity, anti-depressant drug use and other factors). What doesn't get measured doesn't get managed.

1. Western Economic Systems

Western economic systems have produced great improvements in many areas including technology, medicine and the provision of essential and non-essential goods and services. However, as industrial economies continue to grow in a finite world the overall impact is increasingly negative. Inefficient use of resources, high levels of pollution and numerous social disruptions resulting from industrialization have caused human society to be grossly unsustainable.

Studies by the World Resources Institute and many others show that, with some regional exceptions, every life support system on the planet is in decline (i.e., clean air, clean water, forests, topsoil, aquifers, fisheries, wetlands, biodiversity, etc.). Social pressure and turmoil are increasing around the world, driven by population growth, a widening gap between rich and poor and other factors. Social distress is evident even in prosperous regions. Americans, for example, medicate themselves with food (two-thirds are overweight, one-third are obese), television (four hours per day on average), and anti-depressant drugs (rapidly growing use).

Systems Perspective

Unsustainability is driven largely by the failure to adopt and act from a systems perspective. A cell cannot survive apart from the body. So the relevant perspective for human health is at the total body level. In the same way, a human cannot survive apart from the Earth. So the relevant perspective for human survival and prosperity is global. Every person, plant, animal and thing on this planet is part of one interconnected system. This total system is too complex for any one person to understand. As a result, systems are broken into parts (reductionism) and studied in isolation rather than in relation to one another.

Modern economic and business theories were developed from this limited perspective. Firms are seen as being separate from one another and the rest of society.

It is believed that they must compete with one another for scarce resources. Modern economic theory also says profits must grow indefinitely – failure to grow equals death. However, in the real world, failure to restrain growth equals death. Encouraging subcomponents of a system to compete with one another and grow indefinitely is analogous to cancer in the human body. Ultimately, the cancer kills the host, then dies itself. Despite the best of intentions, this is exactly what modern economic systems are doing to the Earth.

This shortsighted action on the part of humans is completely understandable. Nearly all academic knowledge has been developed from the perspective of the individual human mind (since that is the mechanism doing the contemplating). However, as noted above, this is not the relevant perspective for human survival and prosperity. The wisdom of Buddhism is in seeing beyond the illusion that the individual is separate from the rest of the world (fostered by the five senses) to the reality that everything is interconnected (a reality being shown by quantum physics and other branches of science). Through the experience of millions, Buddhism and other traditional religions have shown that expanding one's perspective from being an isolated individual to being part of one interconnected system leads to a more fulfilling, sustainable and effective existence.

The wisdom of Buddhism is as relevant for business and other human organizations as it is for the individual. Businesses actually are part of one interconnected system (whether they realize it or not). Raising business consciousness means helping firms understand and act upon this knowledge of interconnectedness. From this perspective, firms maximize their own well-being by working to maximize the well-being of the overall system. (A paper called "Total Corporate Responsibility" by this author describes a model by which firms can improve financial performance through adoption of a systems perspective.)

Short-Term Thinking

Another key element of perspective is time frame. To the individual human mind, seventy years seems like a long time. But from the perspective of this planet (again, the relevant perspective for human survival and prosperity), seventy years is almost instantaneous. From the human perspective, firms competing with one another and generating some negative environmental and social impacts appears rational and acceptable, though perhaps suboptimal. However, from a global perspective, this action is irrational and suicidal. Seen from a larger perspective, business (as currently operated) appears to be a cancer on the planet.

Another illusion caused by the short human time frame is the idea of one person or business prospering relative to another. Under the current economic system, it is thought that groups of people and firms can prosper relative to others. In the short-term, this appears to be true. But if this "prospering" destroys the environmental and social systems that support humanity over the long term, are these groups really prospering? This would be like dining in a luxury cabin on the Titanic as it sinks.

It is more realistic to think of human prosperity from the perspective of the human race over the long-term rather than from the individual perspective. Thinking from the individual perspective would be like thinking from the perspective of a cell in the body. In reality, the cell can only prosper if the body prospers. It is the same for humans in relation to the Earth – humans can only prosper if the Earth prospers.

Natural Wisdom

The short-term, narrow, survival-oriented perspective of the human mind is a key driver of unsustainability. From this perspective, it appears logical to maximize one's well-being at the expense of others. However, as noted above, this "logic" is highly irrational when seen from a larger perspective. In a sense, the human ability to think has made humans the least intelligent creatures on the planet, as evidenced by the fact that life support systems are being destroyed while many are made unhappy.

All other creatures act on intuition and always do exactly the right thing, as evidenced by the fact that they are sustainable. Humanity has become quite arrogant. It is surrounded by infinitely greater intelligence, but nevertheless fails to recognize its lack of sophistication. The simplest of natures' creations is infinitely more complex than the greatest of human inventions. Humans have access to this level of wisdom through greater use of the intuitive function. Unfortunately, the so-called rational, scientific human mind often discounts or discredits information that it does not understand, in part because of the human ego's need to understand and control.

More traditional cultures such as Bhutan that value contemplation have greater access to this intuitive wisdom, the wisdom of nature. Cultures such as these have lived sustainably for hundreds, even thousands of years, often with much higher levels of happiness (as indicated by family stability, lack of violence, etc.).

The US-Led Global Economy

The global economy is led by a young and immature nation, the United States. Like most young people, the US culture values physical beauty, physical strength and youth. Whereas older, more mature cultures value the elderly, wisdom that comes from a life well lived, peaceful coexistence, and inner rather than outer prosperity.

The principles upon which the US was founded are excellent – for example that each person has the right to life, liberty and the pursuit of happiness. The US has brought great benefits to the world over the years in supporting peace, democracy and human rights. US-led advances in technology and medicine have also brought great benefits. However, the large negative environmental and social impacts of the US are less obvious, especially to many Americans.

It is clear that the founders of the US believed the primary obligation of government was to protect and provide for future generations. The founders often used the word posterity. In his inaugural address, Thomas Jefferson spoke of preserving the Union for the ten thousandth generation.

However, economic and political systems have evolved in such a way that the US and other Western governments are forced to focus on the short term. In what appears to be a logical economic strategy (from a short-term perspective), the US-led global economy is damaging, and in some cases destroying, the environmental and social systems needed for long-term prosperity.

Western System Flaws Driving Unsustainability

Perhaps the largest flaw of Western economic systems is the failure to hold firms fully responsible for their negative environmental and social impacts. Failing to hold firms responsible in a competitive market essentially forces them to be irresponsible and unsustainable. This occurs because firms attempting to fully mitigate impacts would probably put themselves out of business (costs would become too high relative to peers).

Given the immense complexity of the overall Earth system, it is understandable that firms are not held fully responsible. It is difficult to quantify negative impacts (especially intangible impacts) and include them in prices. Nevertheless, greater efforts must be made to hold firms fully accountable if human society ever hopes to achieve sustainability.

Economic System Flaws

Economic system flaws include failure to incorporate externalities into prices, failure to consider limits to growth and the discount rate. Coal-fired electricity illustrates one of many failures to incorporate externalities into prices. It is known that burning coal causes premature deaths, various types of illness, birth defects (from mercury), acid-rain-damaged forests and many other negative impacts. These are real costs paid by society that are not included in electricity prices. This creates the illusion that coal-fired electricity is cheap, when it actually may be the most expensive form of power generation. This subsidization of coal (and other fossil fuels) causes over-consumption and significantly drives humanity's unsustainable state. From society's perspective, it is inefficient to not incorporate externalities into prices since it is usually much more expensive to clean up pollution than to prevent it (assuming cleanup is even possible).

Failure to consider limits to growth illustrates the simplistic and unsophisticated nature of human economic theories and systems. Natural systems are infinitely more sophisticated than human systems. Modeling human economic systems after nature would make humanity sustainable. In nature, systems such as forests grow then level off, forming a sustainable balance with other systems. The idea that a business or national economy should grow indefinitely in a finite world is unrealistic. A more sophisticated economic system would recognize that firms also have optimal sizes. Companies would be rewarded for achieving and maintaining optimal size. Growth beyond this would be penalized.

The discount rate is based on the idea that today's money is more valuable than the future's. This is of course true in the sense that today's money can be invested and earn a return. However, this concept also says that tangible assets (forests, clean air, clean water, etc.) as well as intangible assets (human life, quality of life, etc.) have lower value as time goes on. In other words, the discount rate says people today are worth more than those in the future. Beyond fifty years or so, the discount rate says most people and things are nearly worthless. As a result, when making economic decisions at the firm and national level, business and political leaders are often compelled to act as if their grandchildren are nearly worthless. The overall goal of an economic system should be to maximize the well-being of society over the long term. The discount rate is one of many system flaws causing Western economic systems to work in opposition to this goal.

Political Systems Flaws

Political system flaws include the ability of companies to financially influence politicians (in effect, bribery). When politicians must rely on funding from corporations and their owners to get elected, the government becomes primarily focused on serving short-term corporate ends. This focus is illustrated by an 1872 mining law in the US that allows companies to buy rights to minerals on federal lands for five dollars an acre. For many years, firms have lobbied and provided funding to politicians who vote to maintain this law. As a result, Chevron was able to pay $10,000 for rights to platinum and palladium worth an estimated $30 billion on 2,000 acres near Yellowstone Park.

Natural resources belong to current and future citizens, not to government. The government is supposed to manage resources fairly on behalf of owners by selling them at market prices. When government receives campaign contributions from firms then sells resources to these firms at deep discounts, it lowers revenues that could have been used to reduce income taxes.

Another major political/legal system flaw is the limited liability corporate structure. This structure is intended to facilitate corporate investment by not holding firms and their owners fully responsible for negative impacts on society. As a result, taxpayers often must pay to remediate environmental and social problems caused by firms. As noted above, this process is grossly inefficient since remediation is virtually always far more expensive than prevention. Also as noted above, failing to hold firms responsible essentially forces them to be irresponsible.

The government is supposed to hold firms fully responsible when they negatively impact society, in the same way that government holds individuals responsible when they commit crimes. However, when firms are allowed to give money to politicians and when legal findings limit corporate and investor liability, it becomes impossible to hold firms fully responsible. This causes many negative impacts on society, such as over-consumption of resources (from under-pricing), increased pollution and related public health impacts (from not holding firms fully responsible for the negative impacts of pollution), and corporate welfare.

Corporate welfare occurs when taxpayers must pay for the negative impacts of firms and when national resources are sold below market value. Allowing these policies implements a reverse Robin Hood situation where wealth is taken from poor and middle-income taxpayers and given to the wealthy. Ending the ability of anyone to financially influence politicians and implementing complete public funding of political campaigns would make it much more difficult for companies to avoid being held responsible. It also would reduce taxes more than any other tax reduction activity. For example, ending the thousands of corporate welfare abuses, such as the Chevron example above, probably would reduce taxes in the range of hundreds of billions of dollars.

Social System Flaws

System flaws in the social area include the largely unregulated ability of firms to influence public opinion and values through advertising and media. Being focused on maximizing sales and earnings, companies view citizens primarily as consumers of goods and services. Advertising is used to create a perceived need and prompt a purchase. This is frequently done by taking advantage of human needs for self-esteem, love and connection to others. Advertisements often use strong emotional appeals to imply purchasing a product will meet these non-material needs.

A common and intended consequence of advertising is that consumers feel inadequate without the product. Widespread use of this type of advertising creates a pervasive sense of emptiness and low self-esteem in society. Emotionally false advertising does not tell consumers that non-material needs are met through activities such as being a good spouse, parent and neighbor, doing fulfilling work or being in nature, since firms don't make money on this. Conventional advertising is one of the most destructive influences in society. It is a root cause of increasing compulsive behavior and depression.

With overwhelming financial resources, relative to other stakeholder groups, and control of many media outlets, firms have the ability to unfairly influence and mislead public opinion. The founders of the United States were concerned about this abuse of power. They often spoke of the evils of democracy. The founders were concerned that the uninformed public could be whipsawed by sound bites. As a result, they structured the country to be a republic, where politicians study complex issues and make expert decisions on behalf of current and future generations, rather than a democracy, where the uninformed majority rules, often through opinion polls.

Because politicians are often seen as serving corporate interests rather than the public good, they do not receive the public trust and support needed to make tough decisions. In this environment, public opinion is highly vulnerable to corporate misinformation campaigns. In pursuit of profit maximization, some firms seek to confuse the public about key issues in an effort to avoid being held responsible for their negative impacts. A good example is when oil companies publish ads questioning the reality of climate change, even though nearly all scientists not receiving funding from firms agree climate change is largely induced by human activities and will have significant negative impacts on society.

Gross National Product

Another flaw of Western economic systems is the method of measuring social well-being (GNP). In all fairness, GNP was never intended to be a measure of overall social well-being. Instead, it was intended to be a measure of economic growth. Western economic theory holds that economic growth will enhance social well-being. In some ways this is true, for example when basic human needs are better met. However, GNP is an incomplete measure. It does not account for the environmental and social degradations that often accompany economic development.

Economic growth is intended to be the means to the end of social well-being. However, as society focuses on what is being measured, the means become the end. In other words, Western nations make the mistake of equating economic growth with social well-being.

Social well-being is a complex measure consisting of many tangible and intangible factors. The measure cannot be reduced to one quantitative, monetized number. GNP is a misleading indicator of social well-being because it counts growth of many social negatives as positive, such as incarceration, medical costs, anti-depressant use, environmental damage and related remediation, etc. The measure also does not value many of the services which contribute most to social well-being, such as parenting, mentoring and volunteer work.

GNP also fails as a measure of social well-being since it does not account for assets. Businesses gauge financial condition and performance by using a balance sheet and income statement. Using GNP to measure social well-being (or even economic performance) would be like a firm using only an income statement to measure financial condition. A more accurate indicator of social well-being would decline when assets, such as forests, clean air and clean water, were consumed. Finally GNP fails as an indicator of social well-being since it does not measure intangibles, such as inner peace and happiness (factors that many consider to be the ultimate goal of life).

It is critical that an alternative to GNP be developed, in large part because society tends to manage what is measured. If humanity does not measure the state of its life support systems or the happiness of people, these issues will continue to be low priority (in relation to what is measured – GNP). Failing to measure environmental and social conditions will drive further declines and cause humanity to become even more unsustainable.

2. Developing and Implementing Gross National Happiness

In perhaps the most important areas, Bhutan appears to be ahead of many Western nations. The country is one of the few regions where humans live at or near a sustainable level. In addition, the country seems to have higher levels of happiness as measured by family stability, lack of violence and other metrics. However, life is hard for many Bhutanese. Western technology, products and know-how could help improve living conditions and better meet basic needs in many cases. The difficult part will be gaining these benefits while avoiding the environmental and social degradations that nearly always accompany Western-style development.

Development is a misleading word since it implies improvement. Countries often wind up worse off in many ways from their exposure to Western ideas, marketing, technology and business practices. For example, Western business models force companies to focus primarily on growth. To increase sales, advertising is used to get people to buy products, often by making them feel inadequate without the product. In many cases, this type of advertising causes young people in developing countries to lose interest in their parents' values – values that have sustained these cultures for many years. As a result, young people often move from villages to cities where they frequently cannot find work. Through this process, advertising and Western media can cause social degradation by divorcing a country from its traditional values.

Economic development is often prompted by Western corporations seeking new markets and new sources of raw materials. Financial institutions, such as the World Bank, provide funding for infrastructure construction, which in turn provides revenues to Western firms. To pay off debt, developing countries are often compelled to adopt an export-oriented economy, which is usually built upon export of their natural resources. Through corruption, weak legal systems and intense economic pressure, countries often wind up selling their resources for much less than market value. This infrastructure-debt-export cycle can cause living conditions to worsen as economies shift from meeting internal needs to generating foreign exchange through exports. In addition, this process frequently results in severe environmental degradation and disruption of indigenous cultures.

GNH can be the measurement component of an overall plan to maximize social well-being. The first step in developing GNH would be to identify a preferred society in the greatest detail possible. This information would be used to identify the relevant components and metrics of GNH. Finally, a practical plan for achieving GNH goals would be developed and implemented.

Establishing Goals

With input from all stakeholder groups in Bhutan, the components and goals of a preferred society should be identified. Social goals and priorities are implicitly known and conveyed through cultural processes in Bhutan. However, it will be important to make these goals more specific as Bhutan considers development. Having more specific social goals and priorities will help Bhutan decide which development actions would actually enhance social well-being, rather than degrade it.

Social goals should be established in great detail. The process would comprehensively look at all tangible and intangible aspects of society. Goals would be established in areas including education, health care, housing, clothing, food and nutrition, shelter, environmental and habitat protection, parents spending time with and raising children, arts, business practices, infrastructure, legal and regulatory issues, reported levels of happiness, etc.

This process could be achieved through various mechanisms. For example, an interdisciplinary group of experts might develop a report that addresses all these issues and makes proposals over the short, mid and long term. This would serve as a starting point for dialogue among Bhutanese stakeholder groups. Over time, a consensus document could be produced that would guide development of GNH.

Developing GNH Metrics

Using the ideal state defined above, specific metrics can be identified to measure performance on every tangible and intangible aspect of social well-being. For each metric, current performance would be quantified and short-, mid- and long-term goals would be established. This process may be highly complex as many intangible factors will be difficult to quantify. As a result, proxies will be needed to track performance for some intangible factors.

Complexity will be further increased by the likely need to develop alternative means of measuring success. Literacy and education provide good examples of this. Illiteracy is high in Bhutan. This would be seen as bad from a Western perspective. However, Bhutanese children may be far better educated on the most important aspects of life than American children. Bhutanese children spend much more time with their parents. In doing so, they learn cultural values, social skills, and the agricultural and other practical skills needed to sustain them over their lives.

In the US educational system, children must learn the same set of knowledge (math, science, English, etc.). A competitive grading system teaches children to see peers as obstacles to their success (which weakens social skills). It also makes children feel inadequate if they are not good at a subject in which they may have no interest. This system encourages conformity, rather than encouraging children to find their own unique passions and interests, then build their lives upon them.

In addition, children are made to sit for up to seven hours per day, five days per week and listen to an adult talk to them, something few adults would want to do. Children are meant to be moving around and learning by doing. To an increasing degree, when children won't sit still in class (i.e., when they act naturally), they are given drugs such as Ritalin that numb their minds into obedience and passivity. Giving drugs to a young developing mind may permanently impair brain function.

Add to this obesity, drug use, teenage pregnancy, depression, suicide and weak academic performance relative to other nations and it appears Bhutanese children are far better educated than American children. This illustrates why it is critical to identify the preferred state of society and use this to guide selection of performance metrics. Simply accepting Western social performance standards might be a mistake.

Once metrics and performance standards have been established, they can be assembled into an overall GNH measure. Rather than attempting to render the state of society down to one number like GNP, GNH would provide a suite of performance indicators. The performance of society is highly complex and needs to be expressed on many dimensions. By following this approach, GNH would be an accurate measure of social well-being.

3. Conclusion

Western economic systems are unsustainable because they were developed from a short-sighted reductionistic perspective. From a broader perspective, one sees that the economy and business are not separate from any other part of society or the total Earth system. From this perspective, it is understood that all impacts must be considered and factored into prices. This is true capitalism. The system now operating in the West is a destructive form of capitalism that sends grossly distorted price signals causing market players to make suboptimal, unsustainable purchase decisions.

Bhutan could greatly benefit other nations by demonstrating that it is possible to develop an economy based on a total system perspective. Wisdom must increase if humanity is to become sustainable. Wisdom involves recognizing that all things are interconnected and acting from this perspective. Bhutan can help Western nations recognize this by showing how a more effective and sustainable economy can be developed.

Western economies have demonstrated great creativity and progress in technology, medicine, business and other areas. In addition, Western nations have sacrificed greatly to support democracy, human rights and freedom from oppression and tyranny around the world. In the US, business and political leaders appear to be strongly committed to doing what is best for society. However, economic and political systems often force well-intentioned leaders to do the wrong thing for children, the environment and society overall.

Western economies are so large and entrenched that it will be difficult to improve their destructive, unsustainable systems. However, these systems can only negatively impact the environmental and social realms for so long before there is a price to pay. There is no free lunch. Sooner or later system change will be forced upon Western nations if they cannot develop the wisdom to act first.

Frank Dixon

Frank Dixon is an author and consultant specializing in sustainability, system change and enhancing financial performance through increased corporate responsibility. He is also a senior advisor to Innovest Strategic Value Advisors, the largest firm in the world analyzing corporate sustainability performance. Formerly, as head of research at Innovest, he oversaw the sustainability analysis of more than 2,000 corporations around the world for six years. Through this experience, he noticed that no company is close to being sustainable (largely because economic and political systems essentially compel firms to act unsustainably by not holding them fully responsible for negative impacts on society).

To address the need for system change and provide the real possibility of achieving sustainability, he developed the Total Corporate Responsibility methodology. TCR is a practical, incremental, profit-enhancing method of driving system change and addressing systemic barriers to sustainability. The approach is used to develop investment products with superior financial and sustainability performance as well as implement advanced corporate sustainability strategies (TCR is being implemented by a subsidiary of one of the largest corporations in the world).

Before Innovest, he worked as a management consultant in the energy and manufacturing sectors. Earlier he worked in the financial area, arranging venture financing for early-stage manufacturing companies. He has an MBA from the Harvard Business School.

PART 3

Opinions: Ecological Sustainability of Business

Ecological Sustainability of Business

Ecological sustainability is one of the most popular catchwords of our times. Business, including the largest corporations, seems to be embracing it. However, corporate critiques argue that all this is mere window dressing. Today's business is inherently unsustainable.

What are the features of ecologically sustainable business? What makes a sustainable business possible? Can a company alone achieve ecological sustainability? What are the main hindrances to companies becoming sustainable? What are the effects of economic globalization in this respect?

These are the questions that we addressed to our distinguished panel of academics and practitioners, all renowned experts in the field of environment and economy. Professor John M. Gowdy of Rensselaer Polytechnic Institute, USA; Ananda Das Gupta of the Indian Institute of Plantation Management, Bangalore, India; Professor Richard B. Norgaard of the University of California at Berkeley, USA; Diana Schumacher (Schumacher Projects, UK) and Professor Karl-Henrik Robert, the founder of The Natural Step, Sweden, all shared their views with us.

Zsolt Boda
Associate Editor

John M. Gowdy
Rensselaer Polytechnic Institute
Troy, New York

Sustainable Business Requires a Social Support System

A sustainable business monitors and controls its production process from "cradle to cradle." The environment should be the same at the beginning and the end. Care should be taken to protect the environment from the point of raw material extraction to the point of final disposal of the product the firm is producing. So a sustainable business means having ecologically sustainable production processes, recycling wastes from the production process, and minimizing the environmental impact of the final product.

A sustainable business also recognizes that work is a social as well as a money-making activity. Wages must support a decent standard of living. Businesses should encourage the full development of human potential at work including involvement in production design and the mission of sustainability.

Sustainability requires understanding the physical nature of production processes and available alternatives to achieve environmentally benign production. In some cases a single company can achieve ecological sustainability, but any company is subject to the current socioeconomic framework where growth is almost a necessity for firm survival. Also, the product itself should contribute to the well-being of society. Sustainably produced weapons, for example, are not in the same category as sustainably produced children's vaccinations.

Sustainable businesses require a support system of pro-environmental and pro-social regulations. Achieving sustainability depends on the surrounding social and environmental regulations. Sustainability is best achieved within a framework of an adequate social safety net that includes health care and social security as public policy.

In the US the nature of corporation laws and regulations is a critical hindrance to sustainability. Corporations are defined as "legal persons" yet they are exempt from basic checks and balances controlling their behavior. In the US it is actually illegal for firms to consider "social responsibility" as an investment criterion. A critical issue is the lack of public and private incentives for sustainability.

In general, IMF and World Bank policies work against sustainability as well. The bottom line of these organizations is promoting economic growth. The assumption is that human well-being can be equated with market consumption. Even worse, these organizations assume that per capita income is a good measure of social welfare, taking no account of income distribution. It is important to realize that the market system is not a "natural" outcome of an "invisible hand" but rather is imposed by laws and regulations to protect the existing power structure and prevailing free market ideology.

John M. Gowdy

John M. Gowdy is professor of economics at Rensselaer Polytechnic Institute, Troy, USA. He was past president of the U.S. Society for Ecological Economics. He holds a Ph.D. in economics from West Virginia University, and a master's in community planning from the University of Rhode Island. He is a member of a number of editorial boards including Ecological Economics, Environmental Ethics, and Environment and Planning. He is the author of over 120 academic articles and has authored or edited 8 books.

Professor Gowdy's main publications include the following:

Economic Theory for Environmentalists. St. Lucie Press, Delray Beach (with Sabine O'Hara), 1995.

Paradise For Sale: A Parable of Nature. University of California Press (with Carl McDaniel), 2000.

Limited Wants, Infinite Means: A Reader on Hunter-Gatherer Economics and the Environment. Island Press, 1998.

"The Revolution in Welfare Economics and its Implications for Environmental Valuation." *Land Economics*, 80(2), 2004, 239–257.

"Toward a New Welfare Foundation for Sustainability." *Ecological Economics* (with Jon Erickson), in press, 2005.

"The Approach of Ecological Economics." *Cambridge Journal of Economics* (with Jon Erickson), in press, 2005.

Ananda Das Gupta
Indian Institute of Plantation Management
Bangalore

Sustainability and Business from an Indian Perspective

Our present society has fundamental structural and institutional problems that we must recognize and manage in order to resolve. We must change the basic operating principles and values of the structures of our society if we are to move in a more moral, ethical and spiritual direction. For instance, because the economic system only values what is marketed or traded, everything else is considered an externality of no importance to economic analysis. A fundamental problem with economics is that it maintains inadequate accounts. Paying attention only to what has monetary value, economic analysis misses much of what is happening in society. It is like trying to take care of an automobile by only keeping the tank filled and ignoring everything else necessary to keep it running safely. Moreover, society also follows the wrong economic guidelines. Take a measure like gross domestic product. GDP is widely equated with prosperity: higher GDP means greater prosperity. However, GDP also grows when more people suffer from the ill effects of pollution; it grows if more automobile accidents requiring repairs, replacements and medical treatment occur. So GDP is not an accurate measure of prosperity and should not be used to measure it. The use of monetary measures is similarly inadequate. Too often people say, "More money equals prosperity." But you cannot eat money. If food runs out, money has no value at all. Neither money nor profit can measure human happiness and well-being.

The drive for increased productivity is another issue in which the logic of individual decisions has a perverse collective impact on society. Raising productivity is an economic imperative. A company must raise its productivity and reduce its labor costs to increase its profitability. Yet this ignores the fact that employees are also consumers. If the number of people earning wages declines, there are that many fewer consumers to buy products and services. It is a case of sawing off the branch you are sitting on. To benefit the economy in a real sense, why not seek to make everybody a consumer by ensuring total employment? Instead, decision making in the corporate system moves in the opposite direction. This is encouraged by another structural problem in Western economies: the privatization of employment and the socialization of unemployment. In other words, companies reduce their labor costs in the short term by transferring to the government the cost of maintaining the redundant workers. Such a shortsighted system ignores the importance of work as a contribution to society and a spiritual obligation.

. Then, of course, the economic system ignores the poor. Since they are insignificant consumers, the poor are excluded or forgotten. Their presence illustrates a series of fundamental failures in present mechanisms for redistributing wealth within society. Any truly developed society considers extremes of wealth and poverty to be unacceptable. The poor cannot be left to die while the rich walk over their bodies, of course; so at least some effort is made to put the poor out of sight in some way. There is, however, a greater moral principle that requires some level of wealth sharing, and taxation systems are designed to do that. Yet, it is possible to escape taxation. With globalization, wealth creation is increasingly reported not in the countries with strong tax systems, but in the Cayman Islands, Vanuatu and other so-called tax havens. Such avoidance of taxation is logical within a system in which the first priority is to maximize profit. Multinationals increasingly shift their real wealth creation out of places where taxation is heavy, escaping the mechanisms that allow restoration of the social balance. One of the most fundamental crises of globalization today is the breakdown of the mechanisms for redistributing wealth.

With respect to environmental sustainability, the economic system fails to deal effectively with most environmental problems. It works at the wrong scales in time and space. The economic system is very short term, while most environmental problems are long term, planetary, and occur on a very large scale. Businesses only deal with small fragments of such problems. No mechanism puts together individual forms of corporate behavior to enable us to look at the larger picture. The result is a fundamental mismatch when it comes to dealing with such large-scale problems as carbon-dioxide accumulation, the ozone hole, persistent organic pollutants, soil and water management, and the like. Too often, the economic system fails to come to grips with the essential issues because it tries to deal with them at the wrong scales in space and time.

The questions posed by these problems are fundamentally ethical: How do we foster a new moral, ethical and spiritual foundation in business? How do we establish new ground rules for business to help it contribute to a more ecologically sustainable society? How can we create a broader legal and institutional framework in which business can work to overcome the problems of fragmentation of responsibility and inadequate or absent moral and ethical accountability? The root of the problem lies in the way in which economic institutions are structured. We need to explore how we can maintain the vitality of corporate structures and their ability to evolve quickly, but within a framework built around ethical, moral and spiritual values that will help the system work effectively for society as a whole.

Ananda Das Gupta

Dr. Ananda Das Gupta has been engaged in teaching and research for more than eighteen years in different universities and institutes across India in the following capacities: professor at North Eastern Hill University (Central University), head of the Department of Commerce at Aizawl, academic counselor at Indira Gandhi National Open University (North Eastern Regional Centre), associate faculty member at Vivekananda Centre for Indian Management (VCIM) in Indore, and currently, professor in organizational development, human resources development and business ethics at Indian Institute of Plantation Management, Bangalore.

He was born in 1955 in Patna, India. He has a Master's degree in commerce with a specialization in personnel management and he received his doctorate from the University of Patna as a UGC research fellow. A "life fellow" of Indian Academy of Social Sciences and a member of the Indian Society of Labor Economics, he is a doctoral supervisor of the following universities: Manipur University (the erstwhile Post Graduate Campus of JNU), Imphal; Aligarh Muslim University, U.P.; Vidyasagar University, West Bengal; and Amaravati University, Maharastra.

Ananda Das Gupta's books include the following:

Human Values in Management. Ashgate Publishing Limited, England, 2004.

Working Environment and Health Aspects of the Women Workers in Tea Plantation in India: Towards Sustainable Development. Edwin Mellen Press, USA, 2005.

Ethics in Business. Rawat Publications, Jaipur/New Delhi, 2005.

Corporate Citizenship: Perspectives in the New Economy. Springer, Heidelberg, (forthcoming).

Richard B. Norgaard
University of California at Berkeley

Corporate Sustainability: Impossible Alone, Participation Essential, Leadership Needed

The sustainability of any one corporation depends on the sustainability of our whole economic system. Corporations depend on suppliers, laborers, capitalists, and customers; all must be sustained for any particular corporation to be sustained. All are in this together; no corporation can sustain itself. Being the last surviving corporation is no consolation.

That said, business leaders are choosing among multiple paths. Reasoning that others will "free ride," some corporate leaders figure they might as well "free ride" too. If too many follow this path, we are all doomed to suffer an environmentally degrading world until it collapses around us. A few other corporate leaders seem to be reasoning that, if collapse is near anyway, "it is better to fail trying" with the hope of getting others to follow. Of course, it is more complicated than this. Between these extremes, few corporations pass up the opportunity to invest in a strategic innovation favorable to the environment if it will give them a market advantage. And new environmental protection regulations, as well as incentives to do environmental good, are opening up new environmental markets that only an environmental curmudgeon among corporate leaders would pass up. Corporations also see tighter environmental regulations and larger incentives to move toward sustainability in the future, and these are affecting their investment decisions today, making rational decisions from a purely economic perspective look like environmental leadership. And as more corporations respond, some see a trend that they must keep ahead of to stay competitive, a wave to ride or be rolled in. Lastly, green washing, fooling consumers and stockholders, surely pays in the short run. Most of these are purely economic strategies that intermingle with corporate citizenship, good and bad. The strategies of most corporations are a bundle of contradictions, reflecting the distribution of leadership and opportunities within the modern corporation in a rapidly changing world.

Though the direction of corporate leadership is difficult to read, there seems to be a significant shift toward the idea that "it is better to fail trying." A primary reason for this is tied to energy. The industrializing world that began only about 150 years ago initiated a shift from renewable energy sources, energy derived from current and recent flows from the sun, to fossil hydrocarbons representing solar energy accumulated over millennia. This transition appeared to be freeing humanity from the constraints of nature in a way that facilitated unbounded growth in material transformation. In fact we became dependent on a limited stock of natural flows that had accumulated over the past. And in the process we initiated a reversal in the balance of carbon dioxide around our globe that determined the amount of solar radiation re-radiated back to earth. With global temperatures rising, species and natural systems as we have known them are both adapting and going extinct, mostly to the detriment of long-run human well-being overall.

All are aware that energy prices are high because petroleum production is now recognized as being beyond its peak and in decline while demand continues to soar. Nor is the political disruption in major producing regions about to stabilize. Furthermore, the scientific consensus based on empirical evidence that climate change is upon us is stronger than ever. Indeed, scientists have shifted their concern from understanding the problem in general to getting a grip on worst case scenarios where sudden shifts in ocean currents or stores of carbon trigger catastrophic rates of change in the environments on which we depend. We do see the economy responding. Investments in energy efficiency and renewables are paying off more than ever before while renewable portfolio standards and other policies guarantee market shares. Carbon markets are up and working, though still somewhat experimental. These are the directions in which we will have to go, and go together, to solve a fundamental problem of sustainability. In many countries, even with petroleum and automobile companies dragging their heels, corporations are ahead of government.

Energy is not the only way to see the human predicament. The Millennium Ecosystem Assessment, a four-year project of some seven hundred scientists from around the world and another seven hundred external reviewers, was completed during 2005. The findings are grim. Think of ecosystems as natural capital with the flows of their services being comparable to interest when drawn at sustainable rates. Of the twenty-four types of ecosystem services examined, the ecosystems, or natural capital, of fifteen are being degraded or used unsustainably. The degradation has resulted in lower flows of ecosystem services. Only four ecosystem service flows, three of which provide agriculture, have increased over the past fifty years, but these increases do not appear to be sustainable. Excessive nutrient flows from artificially fertilized modern agricultural lands to sensitive ecosystems present a major problem. A rapid increase in invasive species associated with globalization is another. Problems multiply. Invasives, for example, typically do better in disturbed ecosystems. Thus the assessment makes a strong case that we are rapidly diminishing the natural capital on which the future of humanity depends. The scientists who participated in this study also began to see that the resilience of ecosystems was lower than expected and declining while the pressures upon them were increasing. Thus they foresaw a greater likelihood of ecosystem crashes in the future. While the Millennium Assessment (or MA for short) does not wallow in the worrisomeness of the human prospect, the implications are indeed grim.

The Millennium Assessment is highly qualitative because the data available for the magnitudes of different types of ecosystem capital and flows are very weak. We need much better data to derive multiple and more sophisticated "ecological footprint" measures. Simply having better measurement opens up business opportunities. As these measurements become increasingly applied, and applied to corporations themselves, there will be both new opportunities and new pressures for corporations to respond. Switching toward energy efficiency and renewables will help on net, but the energy transition will also introduce new ecological problems. Stemming the decline in ecosystem capital will entail serious advances in our knowledge about how to manage ecosystems, new institutions to guide corporate choice, and serious efforts to work with ecosystems rather than exploit them. As with energy efficiency and renewable energy, those corporations that begin to explore the transition to sustained ecosystem management will ultimately be in a position to help design and insist on effective institutions as well as develop the new technologies we will need.

The Millennium Assessment details a whole new set of challenges for corporations. New changes are ahead. And in a changing environment, we can expect corporate leaders to read their options in different ways. Thus we can expect to see some exciting new forms of leadership, some interesting investment decisions, and wholly novel green-wash as well. Let's hope that on net, however, we will see an ever clearer and accelerating shift toward the philosophy of "it is better to fail trying," for the changes needed are truly staggering.

Richard B. Norgaard

Richard B. Norgaard has been a professor at the University of California, Berkeley (energy and resources and agricultural and resource economics) since he earned his Ph.D. in economics at the University of Chicago in 1971. He is recognized within his discipline for both his critiques of and contributions to neoclassical environmental economics, but he spends most of his time working across disciplinary ways of understanding. His research emphasizes the contradictions between neoclassical economic theory and multiple biological and social science approaches to understanding complex natural and social systems.

His current work stresses how the collective understanding of complexity challenges modern beliefs about science and the policymaking process. He also writes on development as a process of coevolution between social and environmental systems. His writing is informed through work on energy, environment, and development issues around the globe, especially Brazil, as well as through work in both Alaska and California.

Recent publications

Richard B. Norgaard (chapter 8). In *The Changing Face of Economics: Conversations with Cutting Edge Economists.* David Collander, Richard P.F. Holt and J. Barkley Rosser, Jr. (eds). University of Michigan Press, 2004.

"Collectively Seeing Complex Systems." Special Roundtable Section with four articles. In *BioScience* 55 (11), 953–82, November, 2005.

"Sustainable Development in a Post-Bruntland World." *Ecological Economics* (with Christopher Sneddon and Richard Howarth) September, 2005.

Development Betrayed: The End of Progress and a Coevolutionary Revisioning of the Future. Routledge, London, 1994.

"Intergenerational Choices Under Global Environmental Change" (with Richard Howarth). In: Daniel W. Bromley (ed.) *Handbook of Environmental Economics.* Basil Blackwell, Oxford, 1995.

Diana Schumacher
Schumacher Projects, UK

The Principles of Sustainability

There is now an increasing awareness of the importance of ecological sustainability within the business community around the world. However, this is by no means matched by the numbers of companies actually implementing policies "that make a real difference" in mitigating the ecological crisis now upon us. That task is formidable and in order to succeed will require nothing less than a worldwide change of culture by millions of businesses and the people who work in them. From being a society driven by ever-increasing "wants," the change will have to be towards a culture of conservation and ever-increasing simplicity of lifestyle.

Features

To become ecologically sustainable is probably the biggest task facing businesses today so that global warming and the many other symptoms of the ecological crisis can be alleviated. Awareness that there is a crisis is a welcome first step but it is not nearly not enough. Companies throughout the world will have to become ecologically sustainable in deeds as well as in words.

To become sustainable in practice, we suggest that companies should first and foremost adhere to the seven principles of sustainability in every aspect of business. This is in itself not an arduous task and can be achieved within the current market economy without threatening the overall profitability of business. On the other hand, taken together, these principles provide a powerful framework for right actions. Repeated over a period of time actions become habit; and habit eventually becomes the cornerstone for a new culture.

The seven principles of sustainability are as follows:

1. The Principle of Efficiency: Sometimes called the principle of conservation, all companies turn inputs (energy, raw materials, etc.) into outputs (products and/or services). The principle of efficiency ensures that the consumption of inputs is minimized per unit of output.

2. The Principle of Human Scale: A company seeking ecological sustainability must be of a size such that all of its employees can recognize and relate to each other both socially and professionally. When a company becomes too big its employees splinter into cliques and it becomes very difficult to sustain a consistent policy across the board.

3. The Principle of Autonomy: Otherwise known as the principle of subsidiarity, this dictates that a company's authority structure is such that decision making is delegated to the lowest possible level. Without real delegation, authority becomes over-centralized and removed from those people on the shop floor or in the office whose commitment and skills are essential if ecological sustainability is to be achieved.

4. The Principle of Evaluation: Achievement of ecological sustainability cannot come about unless everyone involved possesses and fully understands the targets that must be reached. For this there needs to be a full portfolio of available measures and standards and a system to monitor performance against set goals. Transparency

is obligatory. Part of this would be to adopt a "cradle to grave" accountancy policy particularly in the fields of energy, materials and waste management. This should involve everyone.

5. The Principle of Complementary Parts: This states that companies can only achieve ecological sustainability if they are fully in control of all the component parts required to complete a "whole work process." Many companies nowadays are organized into narrow functional silos based on common skills or tasks; e.g., all engineers are in one department, all process chemists in another. In such organizations no one sees the whole picture. Organizational monocultures are not sustainable.
6. The Principle of Integration: To achieve ecological sustainability requires a high degree of cooperation from all employees in a company. There needs to be a common strategy aimed at encouraging teamwork throughout the company. A starting point may be to publicize the company's ecological objectives in a mission statement or annual report. As a powerful symbol of the cultural shift towards greater ecological sustainability the company should consider rephrasing its objectives in terms of a "triple bottom line" (financial, social and environmental) rather than simply a "bottom line" (financial only).
7. The Principle of Authority: As the current debate on global warming is showing, voluntary sustainability cannot be maintained indefinitely. It must be buttressed by legally enforceable sanctions to overcome resistance to its less popular aspects. Executive authority presupposes a management hierarchy. A first step might be for all companies to be required by law to appoint a senior manager responsible for overseeing the discharge of the company's environmental obligations.

Hindrances

Some of the more common hindrances are itemized below. However, they must be put into context. First, it is almost a truism to say that achieving ecological sustainability is not an event, it is a process. Each process has several steps or stages and it is erroneous to judge the first step as if it were the last.

The structural changes consequent upon applying the seven principles of sustainability are only first steps. At first sight they may appear to have little to do with achieving ecological sustainability as such. Indeed, it could be argued that they could equally be the basis for any cultural change. This is, in fact, the case. The seven principles merely prepare the ground for further change. Yet without due preparation the hindrances may become insuperable obstacles.

Typical hindrances are the following:

- Shareholders demanding short-term gains at the expense of longer term, and more costly, conservation policies.
- Lack of popular understanding of the seriousness of the current ecological crisis.
- Unwillingness of the public to undertake austerity measures, which it perceives will lower the standard of living in the face of future uncertainties.
- Unrealistic expectations that as-yet-untried science and technologies will painlessly solve both the environmental and financial problems; e.g., nuclear fusion.
- Inability of nation states to agree on common and effective policies for ecological sustainability – "too little, too late."
- A growing belief that the ecological problem is unsolvable since the negative effects on the environment are irreversible and accelerating.
- Lack of imagination, hope and a sense of community in an industrial/urban setting.
- A failure to see that globalization and the removal of trade barriers, which stimulate economic growth, inevitably puts even greater pressure on the environment.

Diana Schumacher

Diana Schumacher has been an activist for peace (including peace with nature) since the late 1970s. She has passionately worked in a voluntary capacity to make connections among energy, environment and economics and to investigate educational, international and practical transformations in these areas, which are prerequisites for peace and social justice. She has been a founding member of the Schumacher Society, The Gandhi Foundation, TOES (now The New Economics Foundation), and vice president of the Environmental Law Foundation. She is also vice president of the Environmental Action Group for Europe, a trustee of the India Development Group (UK) and Schumacher Center in Delhi, and co-director of Work Structuring Ltd, an organizational consultancy striving to bring holistic and spiritual values into the world of work, industry and institutional life.

Diana Schumacher was runner-up in the European Woman of Achievement Award "in recognition of an outstanding contribution to Pan-European understanding and progress that provides an inspiration to others." Unity and compassion are her twin inspirations.

Karl-Henrik Robert
Founder of The Natural Step

Social, Ecological, and Economic Sustainability – Risks, Challenges and Strategies

Sustainable development is about planning for a future that can be. A sustainable society, as well as a sustainable organization, is about running economies that do not systematically erode the social and ecological fabrics on which society is based. No trend will put higher demands on strategic leadership than this challenge.

Today, global human society is moving deeper and deeper into a "funnel" of declining opportunities to sustain prosperity, and in the end civilization itself. Our habitat, the biosphere, is exposed to ever higher concentrations of "left-over-matter" in the biosphere, smaller areas of remaining ecosystems, shrinking biodiversity, and fewer healthy cultures where people are glued together by trust in each other and by vital stories of meaning. To successfully avoid hitting the walls of the funnel is more about understanding and competence amongst leaders of business, than about their values. It's about enlightened self-interest.

Today, most organizations are part of the un-sustainability problem, systematically contributing to pollution, encroaching on ecosystems, and eroding the social fabric. Soon there will be 11 billion people, no longer 6, laying bids on the remaining natural resources in the biosphere. It can be shown, with scientific rigor, that this leads inevitably to increased financial risks for those who are part of the problem rather than the solution. The risks are associated with costs for natural resources, waste management, insurance, taxation, and flawed investments. And vice versa. Systematic innovation and design to provide human services without contributing to the funnel problem implies systematically lowering risks of hitting its walls.

Through an NGO I have founded, The Natural Step, I have been part of a scientific consensus process aimed at defining a rigorous framework for sustainability, with basic principles for the objective, social and ecological sustainability, as well as basic guidelines for the process to strategically approach the principles of sustainability. It is a unique planning methodology for design and innovation and tackles problems at the root causes of un-sustainability. It allows for a rich diversity of cultures and technical solutions. To imagine success in the future, defined all the way down to the basic principle level, and then to plan systematically to arrive at that imagined point is called "backcasting from principles" (as opposed to "forecasting from trends"). The framework is designed to do this in a strategic way. This means identifying such investments that not only stand a good chance of generating a good return on investment but also lay the ground for such investments tomorrow. Or in other terms – linking the short term with the longer term to avoid the walls of the funnel.

At the moment, a crisis is the most common route to increased awareness. Companies with which we have made progress include those that have hit a major problem – financial, competitive, or PR related – over environmental or social issues. Examples are Ikea, McDonald's, and Nike. We are working with many in the construction industry who also realize they need a better understanding and response to the impact of their activities, and with producers of materials. An example is a large producer of PVC in Sweden, Norway and the UK – Hydro Polymers. After years of experience in fighting Greenpeace and feeling increasing threats from the EU legislation, the company has come out as a very clever and strategic forerunner towards sustainable polymers. Business in general needs to get ahead of the game.

If top management buys in, everything moves much faster. It is then possible to inform all "programs" – CSR, health, risk management, security, quality, etc. – with basic principles of sustainability. Companies we have worked with at the highest level, Ikea and Interface for example, have made fundamental changes in their corporate culture. With others, we work with managers running a change agenda. We help frame analysis, arguments and policies to shift the company's direction towards sustainable development. For all organizations this is probably the most important leadership challenge of our times.

The strategic dimension of the sustainability game is about investing in "flexible platforms"; i.e., investments that are both economically feasible in the short term and can serve as strategic stepping-stones to a sustainable future. Each step needs to systematically become more and more compliant with basic sustainability principles. Companies investing in sustainable strategies can see a good return. They save by avoiding the walls of the funnel i.e. increasing costs for energy, tax, insurance, waste management and material resources and they earn money through product and service innovation, competitive advantage, customer and employee loyalty and increased shareholder value.

What is needed is less about new technology than changing traditional thinking. Businesses today are often delaying solutions that are actually very close at hand. But a growing number of companies are not only proactive but also strategic, demonstrating that this works. There are no constraints as regards renewable natural resources or energy, technique, economy, or even selfish motives. The whole world can increase its life-quality within the constraints set by ecological sustainability, if we only de-couple real value from physical flows (e.g., by getting rid of GNP as an indicator of our economic performance). But there is a possible constraint: will we get enough competent leaders in time?

Karl-Henrik Robert

Professor Karl-Henrik Robert is one of Sweden's foremost cancer scientists who, in 1989, initiated an environmental movement called The Natural Step. He headed the Division of Clinical Hematology and Oncology at the Department of Medicine at the Huddinge Hospital from 1985 until 1993. Dr. Robert has authored numerous scientific publications concerning leukemia, lymphoma, lung cancer and their clinical implications. His research on damaged human cells provided a platform for his interest in environmental questions. Later, with Dr. John Holmberg, he developed first order principles, the "system conditions," for ecological sustainability. Together with a growing network of scientists and decision makers in business and politics, the system conditions have been elaborated into a concrete framework for strategic planning towards sustainability.

At the launch of The Natural Step (TNS), Dr. Robert edited educational material and distributed it to every household and school in Sweden. Thereafter, he initiated a number of independent professional networks to support the framework of The Natural Step. Business executives from major Swedish companies such as, IKEA, Electrolux, and Swedish McDonald's; construction companies, the leading supermarket chains of Sweden, insurance companies, banks and a large number of other business corporations and municipalities have begun to incorporate the TNS framework into their business practices.

In 1999 Dr. Robert received the Green Cross Millennium Award for International Environmental Leadership and in 2000 he won the Blue Planet Prize for scientifically laying out the systems perspective needed to plan strategically for sustainability and for changing the environmental awareness of business, municipalities and other groups.

Dr. Robert has written many books, articles and scientific publications on the environment and sustainability that encourage an understanding of the linkage between ecology and economy. Web site: *www.naturalstep.org.uk.*

PART 4

Debate: The Ethics Management Paradox

Luk Bouckaert
Centre for Economics and Ethics
Catholic University of Leuven

The Ethics Management Paradox*

Postwar Europeans are proud of their model of social market economy. Although they pay a price for less flexibility, lower rates of employment, and the lack of competitiveness in global markets, the model remains morally attractive because of its capacity to create social stability and distributive justice. We may debate the limits of government intervention, but few European citizens are willing to give up their European way to combine business and humanity in the framework of a social market economy.

We no longer live in the postwar era, where business and social partners had the challenging task of building up national welfare states. As we all know, business today operates in the global context. The Internet is a worldwide information market.

* This article is based on the author's lecture "Humanity in Business" presented in the European Ethics Summit in Brussels on August 29–30, 2002.

Competition in the labor and consumer markets is a game with global actors. Financial markets are short-lived, and the pressures of greed on business conduct are transnational. The question of my paper is, How can we save the genuine ethics of the European model of business and humanity in this new context? Even further, How can we increasingly develop the ethical potential of the European way to combine economic prosperity with social welfare?

As a starting point, I take the Green Paper of the European Commission Promoting a European Framework for Corporate Social Responsibility (2001). The Green Paper and the synthesis of its follow-up consultation process (Communication from the Commission, 2002) are worth reading and studying. The document puts business ethics and the central concept of corporate social responsibility (CSR) on the political agenda. It provides a regulative, political framework for an ethically driven economy, which goes beyond the logic of the social market economy. Whereas the dynamics of the social market economy rested on a clear separation between economic and social institutions operating mainly within national boundaries, the new regulative structure is built on voluntary partnerships among business, government and civil society. But we have to ask what kind of ethics is at work through this document.

My contribution has a double aim. First, I want to show that the European document of CSR policies is written under the veil of a rational and technocratic conception of ethics. In this perspective, CSR is a rational reaction to the ecological and moral sensitivity of global markets and to the failure of national governments to keep the international market economy socially accountable. My second aim is to explain why this rational conception of CSR is unable to overcome through its own logic the problems of opportunism in business and politics.

The Green Paper defines CSR as "a concept whereby companies integrate social and environmental concerns in their business operations and in their interaction with their stakeholders on a voluntary basis." This definition contains the credo of business ethics, which can be summarized in three points:

(i) the need to integrate the economic, social and environmental impact in all business operations to create sustainable economic growth,

(ii) a focus on stakeholder management and manager's accountability to all the stakeholders,

(iii) a commitment to go over and above explicit legal requirements to respect the implicit social contract between business and society so that the firm's "license to operate" goes with social responsibility to create sustainable value for all its stakeholders.

Many business leaders, policymakers and other stakeholders agree today on this definition of CSR because it is the expression of a long-term rational management perspective. It is a necessary condition to remaining a trustworthy company for investors, for highly skilled and competent employees, for potential partners in a joint venture and so on. It is part of good reputation and communication. So CSR has a rational and instrumental function in a set of accepted goals and objectives. The only remaining question is how to make it operational. A list of actions is proposed in the paper and in the follow-up document, of which the most important may be the launching of a "Multi-stakeholder Forum" at the EU level. This forum has the aim of promoting transparency and convergence of all CSR practices and tools (ethical codes, audit systems, labels, participation schemes, etc.). Another important step is the integration of CSR into the other policies of the EU such as trade, development agreements, public procurement policies, public administration and so on.

To avoid ideological, philosophical or religious discussions on moral and historical substance, all concrete questions and moral dilemmas are presented as problems of rational choice, social engineering or instrumental efficiency. It is striking that in the Green Paper, and even more in the follow-up document on CSR, the label of ethics is avoided. CSR is not perceived as a genuine ethical matter, but as a rational management problem on micro and macro levels. In the same line we see that ethical concepts such as equity, trust, responsibility and integrity become part of rational management science and of professional, socio-engineering consultancy practices.

By reducing ethics to a functional and instrumental management concept we lose something vital. We are crowding out genuine moral feelings and genuine moral commitment, substituting them for rational and technocratic management tools. This substitution fails. Although business ethics took off in the late 1970s and has flourished for two decades, ethics management has failed in recent times to overcome the emergence of new, more sophisticated and hidden forms of opportunism in business. It is important to understand the nature and limits of ethics management to prevent new irruptions of irresponsibility. We must be aware of the unavoidable paradox of ethics management.

The core idea of this paradox is the following: By creating new regulations to temper opportunistic behavior in and among organizations, we may temper the symptoms but often reinforce the underlying roots of opportunism. We introduce economic incentives like benefits, such as premiums or tax relief for those who respect the new regulations, but by doing this, we substitute economic calculations for moral feelings. Preaching moral concepts such as trust, responsibility or democracy on the basis of calculative self-interest or as conditions of systemic functionality is not wrong but ambiguous.

It opens the door for suspicion and distrust because calculations and systemic conditions can easily be manipulated. When the fox preaches, guard your geese.

It is fascinating to see how trust, value-driven leadership and democratic stakeholding have become part of Western management theory. My point is that we must be aware of its paradoxical characteristics. The more economic democracy can be sustained by a rational and economic discourse, the more it risks crowding out the spiritual and moral commitment, which is a necessary condition for sustaining genuine entrepreneurship and stakeholding. Thus we must put forward not only the question of how to make business ethics operational, but also the question of how to make it genuinely ethical.

Henk van Luijk
Professor Emeritus of Business Ethics, Amsterdam

Facing the Ethics Management Paradox

Luk Bouckaert's position on The Ethics Management Paradox deserves approval, comment, and elaboration. To put it succinctly: I share his analysis, and his diagnosis in part, but I am dubious of the remedy he proposes. This implies that, for my part, I will have to be explicit about the suitability of alternative remedies.

I share Luk's analysis. Not only the Green Paper of the European Commission, but the whole field of business ethics as a discipline and a practice, has evolved, at least in Europe, from the classroom to the executive suite, and from cases to codes. The process started with guided moral discussions of business cases in the relatively safe environment of the faculties of philosophy and business administration. Gradually, steps into the real world of business became inevitable. Questions, along with vocabulary, changed from "Which is morally the most defensible decision to take under the given circumstances?" to "Which tools are available to increase alertness and competence with regard to corporate social responsibility on the work floor?" Codes of conduct, key performance indicators, and systems of monitoring, auditing and reporting turned business ethics into a toolkit for keeping upright the "Triple P" of People, Planet and Profit. Business ethics entered its operational phase.

So much for the analysis (see also Henk van Luijk 2006), but what about the diagnosis? Luk Bouckaert is worried. Business ethics today is talking more and more the language of the market, he notices. The leading principle in the field appears to be that "it pays to be honest." Opting for a practice of corporate social responsibility is a sensible thing to do. In order to guarantee, at least in the long run, the continuity of the corporation and its profits, a company willy-nilly has to adapt itself to an increasing set of societal requirements. But by reintroducing economic incentives into the language of morals, opportunism replaces moral feelings by means of economic calculations.

Here some comments are due. First, although experimental psychology and evolutionary biology do not rank among the most favorite auxiliary sciences of ethicists, these sciences do teach us that opportunism and self-interest are not the natural tendency of mankind that they often are supposed to be (Frank 2004). Second, let it be that, on the level of motives, business ethics as a practice has lost some moral depth. Let it be, as Bouckaert puts it, that "ethical concepts such as equity, trust, responsibility, and integrity become part of rational management science and of professional, socio-engineering consultancy practices." It nevertheless remains true that one generation ago, these concepts were strikingly absent in management science and practices. So there is a gain to be noticed on this point. Undoubtedly, the moral quality of motives in present-day business can be improved. But given the fact that, by definition, the average seldom rises above the mean, any increase in moral awareness is to be welcomed, rather than judged according to how much more could have been achieved ideally.

So, what is the remedy? And why do we need a remedy in the first place?

The answer is partly a matter of estimation. We need a remedy if, in the course of time, something of great value has been lost, or risks getting lost shortly. Luk Bouckaert seems to cherish the idea that the loss is already there. A rational and economic discourse is "crowding out the spiritual and moral commitment, which is a necessary condition for sustaining genuine entrepreneurship and stakeholding." To me, this sounds like an all-too-purist view, as if moral motives are only of value as long as they are pure and uncontaminated. Pure motives are an exception. The normal state of affairs is a mix of motives, the moral value of which is determined by the extent to which some form of moral inspiration is clearly recognizable as part of the mixture.

This, obviously, has consequences for the remedy we are looking for. An appeal to a spiritual and moral commitment, as Bouckaert proffers, sounds firm and forthright. It is not. For one thing, the black box, in which the transformation has to take place from appeal to execution, remains to a large extent impervious to direct intervention. And what is more, ethics in business is too serious a matter to make it depend on the morality and spirituality of individuals. The same counts, by the way, when it comes to integrity in business. An appeal to personal integrity, to the high standards somebody raises for himself, remains forceless. It is social integrity that is needed – a set of values and standards that we design in a common understanding, and to which we hold ourselves and others equally accountable (Henk van Luijk 2004).

This leads us to a far-reaching conclusion. To the extent that remedies and improvements are needed – and they always are, given the law of averages and the innate social conservatism of the market – it is not primarily on the personal level that we should expect a gain, but on the social and institutional level. Personal moral and spiritual excellence is something we can hope for, but we can hardly influence it. When it comes to active interventions in the moral domain, the domain of business for instance, it is the conditions that we should tackle, the institutional configurations that define the range of behavioral alternatives. Only at that level can sustainable improvements be furthered. For business ethics as a discipline and a practice, this entails a substantial broadening and deepening of the field of action – as is always the case, when we really try to keep things going.

References

Frank, R.H., 2004. *What Price the Moral High Ground? Ethical Dilemmas in Competitive Environments*. Princeton University Press, Princeton and Oxford.

Luijk, v. H., 2004. "Integrity in the Private, the Public, and the Corporate Domain." In: G. Brenkert (ed.), *Corporate Integrity and Accountability*. Sage Pubications, Tosand Oaks, London, New Delhi, 38–54.

Luijk, v. H., 2006. "Business Ethics: How Far Have We Come? A European Perspective." In: M. Epstein and K. Hanson (eds) *The Accountable Corporation*. 2006 (forthcoming).

Ronald Berenbeim
Principal Researcher
The Conference Board, New York

Finding Space to Discuss Ethics

Luk Bouckaert's "ethics management paradox" correctly identifies the tendency of social responsibility and sustainability proponents to present moral dilemmas "as problems of rational choice, social engineering or instrumental efficiency." If, as these concepts suggest, good ethics is good business, does it not then follow that business success affirms the virtue of the methods used to achieve it? The equation of success with virtue is an old argument that has never been persuasively made. It has been presented most recently to U.S. juries that for the most part have not found it convincing.

The sustainability concept is a good first step in alerting decision-makers to the potential ethical considerations of a business choice. Most business ethics problems confront the practitioner with a choice of whether or not to exploit certain kinds of temporary or permanent market failures such as monopolies or information asymmetries. An ethical decision in this context entails the exercise of moral restraint – a practice that corporate social responsibility and sustainability advocates counsel in certain situations. Yet they do not appear fully cognizant of all of the alternatives and of the significant losses that the exercise of moral restraint can entail. If such risk did not exist, the actor would not be confronted with an ethical problem, and there would be no need for further discussion.

Thus, although the corporate social responsibility and sustainability arguments are presented as ethical concepts, they do not confront the decision-maker with the full range of consequences that ethical reasoning requires. Indeed, the implication of these rationales is that ethical problems do not really exist. Instead, such situations are presented as strategic rather than moral dilemmas. For adherents of these views, ethical issues are like any other business process concern, such as marketing, sales, or finance. They are problems to be solved through the exercise of rational analysis – another job for consultants, as Bouckaert nicely puts it.

Bouckaert is rightly concerned that however successful sustainability and social responsibility arguments may be in conferring legitimacy on the importance of nonprofit considerations in making decisions, they leave no opportunity for real ethics discussion. The concept of prudence also encroaches on the ethics space. Prudence is the exercise of an extra measure of caution above and beyond "explicit legal requirements." Beginning with the Talmudic sages ("building fences around the law"), prudence has an ancient and honorable pedigree. Given the calendar's vicissitudes, the prudent man celebrates a holiday for two days – just to make sure that he gets it right. Is prudence a substitute for ethics in business choices? Many would say so. Bouckaert is right to be skeptical on this point.

If sustainability, social responsibility, and prudence are not substitutes for ethics, where can we find the ethics space? Business ethics is not vague speculation on how to achieve the betterment of mankind. It is a method for dealing with discrete problems to be solved – a means for an individual person or group of people to make choices. For example, does a company leave a potentially dangerous product on the market or take it off? The first question to ask is whether the decision-maker is confronted with an ethical choice. Product recall problems are potential market failure situations due to information asymmetries. Most of the time, information asymmetries deserve significant financial reward. I am glad that pharmaceutical companies know more about making aspirin than I do. I would not have it any other way. But when what they know is information about the product's potential harm, and they withhold that knowledge from me, continued silence threatens my health and safety.

Social responsibility, sustainability, and prudence are inadequate problem solving rationales in this kind of situation. Much as a broken clock occasionally tells the right time, their application can result in good outcomes, but as methods they are fatally defective because they have as their ultimate objective the company's self-preservation, rather than ethically defensible conduct. To be sure, such approaches acknowledge the existence of ethical considerations, but their priority is clear – they will help the company to survive and prosper.

In contrast, the ethicist accepts the possibility of a stark choice between business success and doing the right thing. What remains to be discussed is how to make that choice. At the outset, ethics problem solving demands rigorous insistence on factual accuracy. The reliability of data is not just critical in its own right. Decisions must often be based on limited information. It is thus all the more important that the facts used be true.

Often the decision-maker will need more information about the company in order to weigh and determine the data's relevance and relative importance. Key factors in this regard include the company's history, its own particular constitutional tradition of existing policies, procedures, decision-making precedents, and its aspirations as to what kind of company it would like to be.

These considerations were critical in Johnson & Johnson's celebrated decision to remove Tylenol from the market. A process that adheres to the requirements of justice is also a critical element in an ethical decision-making process. U.S. Supreme Court Justice Robert H. Jackson said that justice is "the tribute that power pays to reason." Only the highest standards of fairness, diligence, and good faith can merit such a tribute.

I do not know if Bouckaert is among the skeptics who argue that no prescription for moral reasoning can include the inclination to moral behavior that ethics requires, but if there is a place in business for ethics discussion it must be within the realm of process, not belief. After all, commercial practice is a project of reason, not faith. "Spiritual and moral commitment" for business professionals is the outcome, not the departure point, of an ethical dilemma. To achieve this result, a person's moral imagination must prevail over the natural inclination to pursue self-interest.

For this to happen, business people must heed Pascal's dictum to "think as men of action and act as men of thought." Only then can we find the space for business ethics and work to enlarge it.

G.J. Rossouw
University of Pretoria
South Africa

A Response to Bouckaert's Ethics Management Paradox

Bouckaert states in his article on "The Ethics Management Paradox" that the "Green Paper of the European Commission Promoting a European Framework for Corporate Social Responsibility" (2001) is written under what he calls "the veil of a rational and technocratic conception of ethics." The way ethics is conceptualized in the said Green Paper raises, according to Bouckaert, a serious concern, which is that if business ethics is conceptualized in this manner, "we substitute economic calculations for moral feelings." In doing so he believes that we run the risk of "crowding out the spiritual and moral commitment, which is a necessary condition for sustaining genuine entrepreneurship and stakeholding."

What seems to bother Bouckaert is that the above conceptualization of business ethics can seriously undermine a sustained ethical imperative in business. He is undoubtedly correct in his assessment that if ethical behavior is merely premised on rational and technocratic considerations, it runs the risk of being eliminated should business not find rational and technocratic reasons for attending to ethics. Ethical considerations in business are thus relegated to the domain of opportunism and will only be considered by business for tactical or opportunistic reasons. By framing the problem (or paradox as Bouckaert calls it) in this manner, he does two things that I wish to challenge. Firstly he places the emphasis on the motive for the ethical behavior of business and secondly he contrasts ethical behavior with self-interested behavior.

The Motive for Ethical Behavior

A legitimate question could be raised about whether it makes sense to introduce the aspect of "motive" into ethical discourse. The first problem surrounding motives is that they are notoriously difficult to trace. Do we have access to the motives that underlie our ethical behavior? The school of psychoanalysis has drawn our attention to the fact that the motives that drive our behavior are often hidden from us and therefore difficult to access or understand. At times we might not even understand our own motivations because they are hidden in our subconscious. A second and related problem is that if the discourse on motives is hampered by our lack of access to them, then it becomes very difficult to defend oneself when others ascribe dubious motives to actions in an attempt to discredit or "unmask" them. The same applies to business. If the focus is on the motives that drive the ethical conduct of business, then there is inexhaustible scope for cynicism about the "real" motives behind seemingly socially responsible behavior by corporations. It opens up an indeterminable debate. A third problem with motives revolves around the question of whether actions can only be considered moral if they originate from an appropriate moral motivation. Kant took this line of reasoning when he argued that actions can only be considered moral if they originate from a sense of obedience to the natural law. Should actions be motivated by considerations of expedience, they fail to qualify as moral actions. In the ethics of Aristotle and Mill, to give only two examples, this very strict criterion for the moral status of actions is not required.

Actions that are beneficial to one and that promote one's own well-being are not excluded from the domain of ethical behavior. A moral motive, in the non-self-interested and non-expedient sense that Kant proposed (and as Bouckaert seems to endorse), is thus not, according to thinkers such as Aristotle or Mill, required for actions to be considered moral.

Self-interested vs. Ethical Behavior

Bouckaert's view on the relation between ethical behavior and self-interested behavior also invites comment. He says that "preaching moral conceptions such as trust, responsibility or democracy on the basis of calculative self-interest or as conditions of systemic functionality is not wrong, but ambiguous." He seems to be concerned that such considerations do not provide a sufficiently stable or solid basis for sustained moral behavior. "When the fox preaches, guard your geese," he writes.

Bouckaert is correct in his assessment that self-interest provides a very thin and unstable basis for sustained moral behavior. A reliance on self-interest as the only basis for moral behavior suffers the same fate as reliance on Adam Smith's "invisible hand" and runs into the same conceptual and practical difficulties as the theory of moral egoism. Something more is required to ensure that business sustains its moral obligations – and that something more is respect and consideration for others who are affected by the corporation; i.e., for its stakeholders.

Although an overemphasis on self-interest as the basis for moral behavior is problematic, a lack of emphasis on self-interest in ethics is equally problematic. In my definition of business ethics, which is developed around the three core concepts of the "self," the "good" and the "other," the imperative of finding an appropriate balance between what is good for oneself and what is good for others is emphasized. Ethical behavior is not non-self-interested or altruistic behavior. It is about not only considering what is good for oneself, but balancing that with what is good for others.

Bringing both self-interest and the interests of others simultaneously into play is vital for business ethics. A lack of recognition of the role that self-interest plays in business in general, and in business ethics in particular, will inevitably result in imposing unrealistic moral demands on business. It will treat business as a set of pseudo-public institutions that are merely supposed to serve the public interest, while neglecting their obligation to create value for shareowners and employees and to ensure their own sustainability.

Based on the above argument, I would like to rephrase the problem that Bouckaert identifies. The problem does not reside in the fact that self-interest is presented as the basis for the European Green Paper on CSR, but the fact that it does not go beyond it. The element of self-interest is important and should be an integral part of the business considerations for CSR, but it should be supplemented by other considerations that emphasize the role and moral responsibilities of business in society. Documents like the "United Nations Global Compact" and the "Second King Report on Corporate Governance in South Africa" succeed to some extent in marrying these two sets of considerations as a basis for CSR.

Robert Allinson
Soka University of America and
The Chinese University of Hong Kong

The Paradox of Business

Bouckaert's contribution is important and provocative. His idea, if I understand him rightly, is that co-opting ethical language into rational and economic discourse runs the risk of ethics being subverted by business goals such as calculative self-interest and systemic functionality, since by so doing, one is reinforcing opportunistic roots of business. Ethics becomes a tool for its opposition. It is similar to following a diet that produces weight gain. His point is welcomed.

However, though his solution is a noble one, I think the problem cannot be solved by keeping ethics separate from business and emphasizing moral and spiritual commitments. I think that the problem is due to a more general cause, which is the conception of business to begin with as based on calculative self-interest. In my opinion, the problem is not so much an "ethics management paradox" as a "business paradox."

The business paradox is the understanding of business as a wealth-producing enterprise for owners that simultaneously creates value for stakeholders. In a recent paper published in the *Journal of Business Ethics* (Vol. 53, Nos. 1–2, August 2004), and also in a chapter in "Spirituality and Ethics in Management" edited by Laszlo Zsolnai (Kluwer, 2004), I have attempted to present a sustained argument for my ideas. The conclusion to the lengthy and detailed arguments provided in these pieces is that the concept of business as activity for profits for the owners is already inherently unethical. One man's profit is another man's loss. There is no way to make business, understood as activity for profits for the owners, ethical. The conditions for an ethical business enterprise do not currently exist. This was the idea behind the title of the article for the Journal of Business Ethics, "Circles within a Circle: The Condition for the Possibility of an Ethical Business Enterprise inside a Capitalist System." The "circles" represent individual business enterprises striving to be ethical. The singular "Circle" represents the capitalist economic system inside which all businesses must operate. While it seems to be more politically correct to refer to this as the "market system," this label does not identify different forms of economies such as a state socialism that functioned within its borders as a socialist economy but outside of its boundaries as a state capitalist enterprise.

The European economy, no matter what ethical goals it might set for itself and its stakeholders, must still operate competitively inside the world capitalist system. Hence, the business paradox remains. It does not matter if ethical language is co-opted by business leaders or if one attempts to keep moral and spiritual commitments. If European business, for example, is to remain competitive in the world capitalist system, it may operate at a business disadvantage to other business groups that neither employ ethical discourse nor conform to moral values.

One way to begin to see some light at the end of this tunnel is to consider the entire idea of a "stakeholder" more carefully. Either the entire world is a stakeholder or one's stakeholders are confined to one's community, say, the European community. If the entire world is a stakeholder, and globalism suggests this, then the term "stakeholder" becomes too wide to be of special merit. If the idea of a stakeholder is confined to members of the European community, then one's business strategies might be hampered in that by paying attention to one's own stakeholders' interests, one may be at a competitive disadvantage. Alternatively, if one's business strategies include the entire world as stakeholders, one might also be at a competitive disadvantage. The idea of a stakeholder is neither efficient nor effective.

This mini-analysis of the popular stakeholder theory reveals the wider problem. Business, perceived of as a profit-making enterprise for its owners, is inherently unethical since it sides with its owners. If it tries to shore this up by paying attention to stakeholders, this is unethical unless the idea of a stakeholder includes every person in the world. But if stakeholders include everyone in the world, how can one make a profit at the expense of one's stakeholders? On the other hand, on what basis can anyone be ruled out as a stakeholder?

There is still a business paradox in any case. For Bouckaert, business is at once conceived of as a profit-making enterprise for its owners and a value-generating enterprise for its stakeholders. In fact, Bouckaert's concern that ethical language (and thence behavior) will be swallowed up by operational business language is no less true in the co-opting of the stakeholder language by opportunistic businesses (this phrase is redundant in a capitalist system). In other words, his inclusion of value generation for stakeholders (an ethical concern) is an example of incorporating ethics inside rational business discourse. It is exactly the offense he counsels against.

The solution is to develop a new definition of business that focuses on the creation of social value as the motivation and mainstay of business enterprise. Profit making must be perceived of as a side effect, not as the main goal of business enterprise. In the Chinese language, a businessperson is literally a "buying-selling" person. A businessperson is a trader. One trades one contribution for another. But this does not mean that the trading must be for one person's profit and another person's loss. There is no inherent connection between trading and making a profit. (I am not of course referring to business practice but to theory and to the implications of language).

The solution is to make the entire wider circle in which all businesses operate an ethical circle. If an individual business or a group business such as the European community operates as a small ethical circle inside a wider unethical circle, it runs the risk of being swallowed up by the wider circle. Emphasizing that one should create value for stakeholders should form another part of Bouckaert's ethical paradox. It cannot represent part of the solution, even on his own terms.

The only solution is for the big circle to become ethical. How is this achieved in practical terms? There is no quick solution. When Karl Marx was writing his works in the British Museum, he was not aware of the revolutions to come in the century after his. Now, those revolutions have failed. Perhaps, one of the reasons for the failure is that there was no genuine motivation for the creation of social value. Adam Smith's model for business, projected in 1775, is still the business model followed today.

The theoretical problem is not a structural one. It does not matter whether businesses are state-owned or privately owned. What matters is that the concept of a business enterprise must be revamped. We do not need to continue to follow Adam Smith's concept of a business enterprise. If we do, we will continue to be affected by the business paradox. The concept of a business grounded on fear (of competitors) and greed (of owners) is not a model for sustainable business. Inequality can lead to many disastrous consequences. Severe inequalities result in poverty, famine and disease due to unhealthy living conditions. The disease can spread to the advantaged countries.

Inequality breeds dissatisfaction, which may eventually generate either wars between countries or attacks by rogue states or terrorist groups. Fears of such eventualities coupled with greed for profits can lead to weapons production. Such weapons production may escalate to the most powerful of all weapons and the dangers may of course become critical dangers.

All of the foregoing eventualities grow from following a model of motivation based on fear and greed. Fear and greed, the bases of our "rational" economic model, are not motivations that can lead to sustainable business in the long term. Our economic textbooks define business enterprise as profit-making from the educational mindset of our future entrepreneurs. One must begin with education. The educators must be educated. Our advanced technology has brought together a global family. We must work hard to overcome the business paradox. Business cannot be perceived along the lines of social Darwinism. We need a cooperative model. The ecology of the universe illustrates how the cosmos operates not in the strife of a Hobbesian all-against-all but in a harmonious community.

If when setting up a business one considers what social value one can create with that business, an ethical motivation will be built into the very nature of the business from the outset. It is possible that such motivations will produce businesses that produce profits for their owners. There is no built-in contradiction between creating social value and creating profit. As long as the creation of social value is the motivation for business, the business paradox can be resolved. Of course, this requires in the end that the big circle is based on social value, not profits. Bouckaert's ethics paradox will also be resolved. For in the new concept of business, the opportunistic roots will not longer exist. Ethical language can be used freely without the danger of its being co-opted. Bouckaert has pointed out that there is a great danger in ethics being made a part of rational management science and consultancy practice. His problem, in my view, stems from a deeper root. The deeper root is that business itself has been misconceived. Commerce is a vital part of human activity. Commerce can be defined as a social value creating enterprise. It is not the idea of sustainable development that is needed today: that is to mistake the effect for the cause. What is needed in today's perilous world is the idea of a sustainable business. It is the paradox of business based on owner's profits that must be resolved. This is not the idyll of an idle intellectual. Great changes in the world have resulted from work cultivated in the stillness of a professor's study. In a world poised on the edge of self-destruction, the need to create a business mentality grounded on value creation and not on fear and greed is not a luxury; it is a necessity.

Luk Bouckaert
Centre for Economics and Ethics
Catholic University of Leuven

When More Ethics Creates Less Ethics: Some Further Clarifications on the Ethics Management Paradox

What a "Socratic" pleasure it is to find colleagues who are willing to invest time and energy to discuss the relevance of the Ethics Management Paradox. Philosophers do love paradoxes as a starting point for deeper reflection, just as scientists have a passion for observations in order to formulate new hypotheses. The comments greatly helped me to clarify some of the analytical, philosophical and practical implications of the paradox.

1. I introduced the idea of an Ethics Management Paradox first of all to solve some puzzles in my observation of business ethics practices. I observed that some companies or organizations launched ethics programs and used ethical language but, once confronted with a deeper financial or other crisis, reacted as if ethics never existed. A case in point is the closing of a plant of Renault in Brussels in the nineties. Renault at that time had developed an ethos of participation and cooperation on the work floor but, once it was confronted with a problem of long-term profitability, completely forgot about its stakeholder philosophy and fired more than two thousand employees without prior communication or negotiation. This is just one example of how "ethics"

on the work floor was instrumental to another logic of long-term profit maximization for shareholders. The point is not that long-term profitability does not matter. It matters a lot, but the fact that the non-communication with other stakeholders was not felt as a moral issue revealed a kind of selective moral blindness. The result of the highly discussed case was a growing distrust of managerial ethical discourse. Other business scandals in the late nineties revealed the same phenomenon of selective moral blindness. How to explain that more business ethics does not always guarantee more ethical behavior?

I tried to understand these phenomena by paying more attention to hidden forms of opportunism and moral disengagement in business. I was intrigued by the growing use of business ethics as a managerial instrument, which I considered (and still consider) progress in terms of making ethics operational and concrete. Instrumental use of ethics relates the introduction of ethics to external goals such as better reputation, fewer transaction costs, less regulation and most of all, more profitability. But there is another side to the coin. One of the mechanisms is that a displacement from intrinsic to instrumental motivations during the process of ethics management can lead to a process of "crowding out" moral commitment (Frey 1997). Transforming ethical problems into strategic problems narrows the "space to discuss ethics" as Ronald Berenbeim emphasizes. It would be very helpful if more empirical research could be done in the field of business ethics to illustrate the mechanism of crowding out genuine moral feelings by instrumental motivations and argument. So far the paradox is an analytical device to understand the phenomena of moral disengagement or selective moral blindness.

2. G.J. Rossouw and to some extent Henk van Luijk reduce the problem behind the ethics management paradox to a conflict between self-interested versus ethical/altruistic behavior. Although instrumental reasoning often refers to self-interested goals and ethical motivation as being at their best when caring for the other, this is not the core meaning of the ethics management paradox. The relevant distinction is the one between intrinsic versus instrumental motivations. This distinction does not always coincide with the altruism versus self-interest conflict. When a manager uses ethical codes as a means to realizing the strategic goals of his organization (instrumental use of ethics), he may be motivated by feelings of loyalty to his organization, which is an altruistic feeling. In this case, instrumental use of ethics is not motivated by self-interest. In a parallel way, intrinsic or inner-directed motivation is not per se altruistic. A lot of intrinsic motivation originates from the personal desire to live in harmony with my "deeper" or "inner" self and is therefore spiritually self-interested. The ethical assumption behind the paradox is that genuine ethical behavior must have its origin in

an inner-directed, non-instrumental inspiration and orientation (be it an altruistic or self-oriented one).

3. The paradox does not imply that ethical behavior must be purely inner directed. That would be an unrealistic and unproductive assumption, "an all too purist view," as Henk van Luijk contends, or an imbalanced view, as G.J. Rossouw explains. The claim is more restrictive: genuine ethical behavior gives intrinsic motivation priority over instrumental motivation. My criticism of the current ethics management practice is that the order is reversed: priority is given to instrumental motivation and argumentation over intrinsic motivation and argumentation. This reversed priority leads to the already mentioned crowding out of moral feelings to selective moral blindness and to the replacement of moral inspiration by an ethics of external regulation. The call for more "spirit in business" or more "spirituality in economics" is a reaction to this reversed order and a trial to restore the balance between inspiration and regulation.

4. How to reactivate genuine ethics in business? My proposition is that we need a more spiritual approach to business ethics. A spiritual approach to business ethics has two objectives: to sustain consistent and inspiring moral commitment in business practice and to radicalize the basic concepts of business life. By radicalization I mean going back to the radix – to the intrinsic ethical and spiritual roots of business ethics. I did it for the notion of entrepreneurship in some of my articles (Bouckaert 2002; 2004). In his comments, Ronald Berenbeim illustrates how intrinsic ethical feelings can sustain moral reasoning. One of the objections (Henk van Luijk) against the emphasis on spirituality is that it concentrates too much on individual, subjective feelings and too little on social and institutional conditions. According to Henk, what we need is a focus on social integrity. We need a set of shared norms and a set of institutional, embedded practices of social accountability. To some extent we have already a very elaborated list of standards and an impressive body of social regulations. But the problem is that we see that all these growing institutions have a natural drive to develop a strong culture of instrumental rationality. They rationalize all (moral) problems into a technocratic and manipulative problem solving format, which always requires more regulation but ends in a loss of moral inspiration and imagination or even worse, in a selective moral and social blindness. The crisis of the European institutions is a good example. The European institutions are driven by a technocratic humanism (as the Green Paper on Corporate Social Responsibility illustrates as well) that fails to mobilize the European citizens and to convince them to go beyond their nationalistic self-interest. The lack of spirituality, which means a lack of a deep inner sense of orientation and linkedness, is in my view not only an individual but most of all a social and institutional problem.

5. My final remark is about the comments of Robert Allinson. His point is that the ethics management paradox is only an echo of a more fundamental contradiction in business. All our ethical efforts will fail if we do not unmask the unethical nature of the concept of business as "activity for profits for the owners." Said in another way: if we want to solve the paradox, we have to replace the capitalist theory of the firm with a radical non-capitalist idea of the firm. The primary goal of the non-capitalist firm is, according to Robert Allinson, the creation of social value. Profit is morally acceptable as a means to realizing the aim of social value creation. Basically I agree with Allinson's position (but not with some of the given arguments). In "Spirituality and economic democracy" (Bouckaert 2004), I defend economic democracy as an alternative to the capitalist shareholder theory of the firm. My main reason is that economic democracy is the full expression of a non-instrumental approach to human cooperation in business. Stakeholders are no longer functionally "integrated" within a cooperation that is finalized to maximize shareholder value. Stakeholder democracy is meant to organize human cooperation in order to create value for all its stakeholders and with all its stakeholders. The final aim is not an external goal but an internalized goal that is defined by all stakeholders and to the benefit of all stakeholders. Undoubtedly, there are problems of efficiency and effective organization that must be solved but not without respect for internal democracy. The radicalization of stakeholder theory into economic democracy is just one example to demonstrate how a spiritual approach to business ethics can have far-reaching consequences.

References

Bouckaert, L., 2002. "Reducing Opportunism through Moral Commitment. The Ethical Paradox of Management." In: H. V. Weltzien Hoivik (ed.), *Moral Leadership in Action*. Edward Elgar, Cheltenham, 2002, 84–97.

Bouckaert, L., 2004. "Humanity in Business." In: J. Verstraten and M. Duffy (eds), *Sustaining Humanity. An Ethics Agenda for European Leaders Today.* European Ethics Network Co-ordination Centre, Leuven, 2004, 99–109.

Bouckaert, L., 2004. "Spirituality and Economic Democracy. A Personalist Approach." In: L. Zsolnai (ed.), *Spirituality and Ethics in Management.* Kluwer Academic Publisher, Dordrecht, Boston, London, 2004, 51–58.

Frey, B.S., 1997. *Not Just for Money. An Economic Theory of Personal Motivation*. Edward Elgar Publishing, Cheltenham.

Contributors to The Ethics Management Paradox Debate

Luk Bouckaert

Luk Bouckaert is professor emeritus of ethics at the Catholic University of Leuven (Belgium). In 1987 he started the Centre for Economics and Ethics in his university's Faculty of Economics. In 1994 he launched a postgraduate, interfaculty program in Applied Ethics. He is founder and director of the SPES Academy and president of the European SPES-forum (SPES being an acronym for SPirituality in Economics and Society).

Luk Bouckaert has written several books in Dutch. His publications in English include:

"Business and Community." In: B. Harvey (ed.), *Business Ethics: A European Approach*. Prentice Hall, London, 1994, 154–189.

"Economics, Politics and Ethics. In Search of a New Balance." *Ethical Perspectives*, 1996 (3), No. 3, 137–148.

"The Ethics of Interest. A Cultural-historical Perspective." In: H. Lange, A. Löhr, and H. Steinmann (eds), *Working across Cultures. Ethical Perspectives for Intercultural Management*. Kluwer Academic Publishers, Dordrecht, Boston, London, 1998, 305–321.

"Business Ethics and the Management of Non-Profit Institutions." *Journal of Business Ethics*, 1998 (17), Nos. 9–10, 1073–1081. (with J.Vandenhove)

"The Project of a Personalistic Economics." *Ethical Perspectives*, 1999 (6), No. 1, 10–20.

"The Ethics of Participation." *Journal of Business Ethics*, 1999 (21), Nos. 2–3. (co-editor with A. Löhr).

"Is Personalism Still Alive in Europe?" *Ethical Perspectives*, 1999 (6), No. 1. (guest editor).

"Reducing Opportunism through Moral Commitment. The Ethical Paradox of Management." World Conference of the International Society of Business,

Economics and Ethics (ISBEE), Sao Paulo, 2000. In: H.V. Weltzien Hoivik (ed.), *Moral Leadership in Action*. Edward Elgar, Cheltenham, 2002, 84–97.

"Spirituality as a Public Affair." *Ethical Perspectives*, 2003 (10), No. 2, 106–118.

"Humanity in Business." In: J. Verstraten and M. Duffy (eds), *Sustaining Humanity. An Ethics Agenda for European Leaders Today.* European Ethics Network Co-ordination Centre, Leuven, 2004, 99–109.

"Spirituality and Economic Democracy. A Personalist Approach." In: L. Zsolnai (ed.), *Spirituality and Ethics in Management*. Kluwer Academic Publisher, Dordrecht, Boston, London, 2004, 51–58.

"Dostoyevsky's Grand Inquisitor as a Mirror for Business Ethics." *Journal of Business Ethics*, 2004 (53), 29–37 (with Rita Ghesquiere).

Henk van Luijk

Henk van Luijk has academic degrees in philosophy, psychology, sociology and theology. He is professor emeritus of business ethics of Nyenrode University, the Netherlands Business School. Outside the Netherlands he has lectured at Bocconi University, Milano; at Bentley College, Waltham MA; at Fletcher School of Law and Diplomacy, Tufts University, Medford MA; at Insead, Fontainebleau; and at Georgetown University, Washington D.C. From 1987–1997 he served as chairman of EBEN, the European Business Ethics Network.

He has published seven books, most of them in Dutch, and 130 chapters and articles in his field. He is a member of a number of supervisory or advisory boards, and occasionally is active as a consultant to companies, public agencies and professional groups.

Ronald E. Berenbeim

Ronald E. Berenbeim is researcher and director of The Conference Board's Working Group on Global Business Ethics Principles. Formed in 1997, the Working Group seeks to facilitate an exchange of views between different sectors of society regarding business principles and to promote a better understanding of the practical issues involved in formulating and implementing global business conduct principles. The Working Group's members include major corporate and non-corporate organizations and leading academics from North and South America, Europe, Africa and Asia.

An authority on business ethics and corporate governance issues, Mr. Berenbeim has written 32 Conference Board studies. His 2000 report, "Company Programs for Resisting Corrupt Practices: A Global Study", was funded in part by a research grant from the John D. and Catherine T. MacArthur Foundation. In 2001–2003 he served as a project director for a World Bank study of private sector anti-corruption practices in East Asia, and co-authored, with Jean-François Arvis, "Fighting Corruption in East Asia – Solutions from the Private Sector" (The World Bank 2003). His most recent Conference Board study on "Ethics Programs: The Role of the Board" (2004) was written with Jeffrey M. Kaplan.

His work has also appeared in *Across the Board*, *Business and Society Review*, *Directorship* and *Nieman Reports*. His speeches have been published in *Vital Speeches* and *Executive Speeches*. Mr. Berenbeim wrote the codes of conduct section for the text "Compliance Programs and the Corporate Sentencing Guidelines" (Clark Boardman Callahan 1993).

He is a graduate of Cornell University, Balliol College Oxford (Keasbey Scholarship) and Harvard Law School. Mr. Berenbeim is currently an adjunct professor at the Stern School of Business, New York University, where he teaches Markets, Ethics and Law.

G.J. Rossouw

G.J. Rossouw was born in Vredendal in South Africa in 1958. He studied at the University of Stellenbosch where he obtained five degrees in philosophy and theology. He started teaching philosophy in 1986 at Rand Afrikaans University where he later became professor and head of the Philosophy Department. He also served on the Executive Committee of the Rand Afrikaans University. In 2004 he moved to the University of Pretoria, where he is the current head of the Philosophy Department. He was appointed as a resident scholar at the Institute for Ecumenical and Cultural Research in Minnesota, USA in 1992.

In 2000 he was a Commonwealth senior research fellow at the Institute of Management Studies at Cambridge University.

He was the founding president of the Business Ethics Network of Africa (BEN-Africa) and is the current president of the International Society for Business Economics and Ethics (ISBEE). He also serves on the editorial board of the Journal of Business Ethics and the African Journal of Business Ethics. He was an academic associate of the World Economic Forum (Southern Africa), and visiting professor at the New Castle Business School at the University of Northumbria in the UK. He also served as a member of the Research Team for the Second King Report on Corporate Governance in South Africa.

He has written four books on business ethics, namely *Business Ethics: a Southern African Perspective* (1994), *Business Ethics in Africa* (2002), *Developing Business Ethics as an Academic Field* (2004) and *Business Ethics* (2004).

Robert Allinson

Robert Elliott Allinson is director of humanities and professor of philosophy at Soka University of America and institute fellow of the Asia Pacific Institute of Business at The Chinese University of Hong Kong. He has been visiting professor or fellow at Beijing University, Fudan University, Yale University, Balliol College, St. Antony's College, Templeton College of Oxford University, Copenhagen Business School, Helsinki School of Economics and Business Administration, University of Hawaii's College of Business Administration Pacific Asian Manage-ment Institute and Waseda University in Tokyo.

He is the author or editor of seven books and over 200 academic papers including "Saving Human Lives: Managing with Ethics" in the Kluwer Business Ethics Series and "Understanding the Chinese Mind" with Oxford University Press, now in its 10th impression. He serves as editor or referee for nine editorial boards including *Business Ethics Quarterly, Business Ethics Interdisciplinary Yearbook, Journal of Business Ethics* and *The International Journal of Management and Decision Making.*